Countryside in Trust

Countryside in Trust

Land Management by Conservation, Recreation and Amenity Organisations

Janet Dwyer
Countryside Commission, UK

and

Ian Hodge
University of Cambridge, UK

JOHN WILEY & SONS
Chichester • New York • Brisbane • Toronto • Singapore

Published in 1996 by John Wiley & Sons Ltd,
Baffins Lane, Chichester,
West Sussex PO19 1UD, England

National   01243 779777
International (+44) 1243 779777

Other Wiley Editorial Offices

John Wiley & Sons, Inc., 605 Third Avenue,
New York, NY 10158-0012, USA

Jacaranda Wiley Ltd, 33 Park Road, Milton,
Queensland 4064, Australia

John Wiley & Sons (Canada) Ltd, 22 Worcester Road,
Rexdale, Ontario M9W 1L1, Canada

John Wiley & Sons (SEA) Pte Ltd, 37 Jalan Pemimpin #05-04,
Block B, Union Industrial Building, Singapore 2057

Library of Congress Cataloging-in-Publication Data

Dwyer, Janet.
    Countryside in trust : land management by conservation,
  recreation, and amenity organisations / Janet Dwyer and Ian Hodge.
      p. cm.
    Includes bibliographical references (p.   ) and index.
    ISBN 0-471-94871-3 (hbk : alk. paper)
    1. Nature conservation – Great Britain. 2. Landscape protection –
  Great Britain. 3. Land trusts – Great Britain. 4. Nature
  conservation – Great Britain – Societies, etc. 5. Landscape
  protection – Great Britain – Societies, etc. 6. Citizens'
  associations – Great Britain. I. Hodge, Ian. II. Title.
  QH77.G7D87   1996
  333.7'2'0941–dc20   95-32005
                                                                      CIP

British Library Cataloguing in Publication Data

A catalogue record for this book is available from the British Library

ISBN 0-471-94871-3

Typeset in 11/12pt Palatino by Mayhew Typesetting, Rhayader, Powys
Printed and bound in Great Britain by Bookcraft (Bath) Ltd, Midsomer Norton

This book is printed on acid-free paper responsibly manufactured from
sustainable forestation, for which at least two trees are planted for each one used
for paper production.

Contents

Acknowledgements

All writing incurs debts, but some projects rely more than most on the generosity and support of others. This work, studying a particular type of institution, has relied to a very great extent on contributions from a wide range of sources over a long period of time. We cannot here thank all those to whom thanks are due but will mention just a few.

The book has arisen from a research project generously funded by the Leverhulme Trust and without that support, nothing would have been possible. In carrying through our research we have received unselfish assistance from many people. Perhaps this is some comment on the attitudes that still pervade the voluntary sector. Several individuals have played a particularly critical role in guiding us through the various parts of the conservation trust sector, we would especially thank Charles Couzens (the Wildlife Trusts), Julian Prideaux (the National Trust), James Ruddock (the Land Trusts Association) and Gareth Thomas (RSPB). Beyond these, many have freely given their time to explain and discuss their activities.

In the later stages, many have kindly read and commented on the material that we had written. We are particularly grateful to John Sheail who read and commented on the entire text. We would also thank Alec Baker, Charlton Clark, Isobel Davidson, Nicholas Durston, C. R. A. Flanagan, Phil Gray, Julian Grimshaw, Greer Hart, Julian Prideaux, Trina Paskell, James Ruddock and members of the LTA committee, Graham Stroud, and Gareth Thomas for commenting on sections of the text.

Throughout what has turned out to be a rather protracted process, Iain Stevenson, of Belhaven and now of John Wiley & Sons, has retained interest and good humour. We are thankful to him for his patience.

None of these bears any responsibility for the final product which has emerged. We should also note that the views expressed in this book are entirely those of the authors as individuals and do not necessarily represent the views of the Countryside Commission or the University of Cambridge by whom the authors are employed.

Janet Dwyer and Ian Hodge
October 1995

Introduction

Whether or not there is a revolution under way in the countryside, we are without doubt witnessing a fundamental change in values which, in the long sweep of economic development, may represent a turning-point for rural areas. This change may be as important as the processes of industrialisation or deindustrialisation for the nation as a whole. In the past, the development of rural areas has been largely determined by the exigencies of food production and the choices of a landed minority. Now, the overriding priority for food production has gone. The locational and residential choices of businesses and families have been expanded through motor transport and telecommunications. And, for the first time in history, we have national policies in place that have the primary aim of restoring and re-creating 'natural' habitats and rural landscapes for public enjoyment.

In this book, we examine an emerging element of the new rural scene. We focus on one way in which heightened public concern for the quality and accessibility of the countryside has been articulated and translated directly into practical land management. This is through the work of a growing number and variety of what we term 'Conservation, Amenity and Recreation Trusts' (CARTs). We define CARTs in this book as follows:

> CARTs are largely 'non-profit' or charitable organisations (mainly trusts) that aim to generate wide public benefits through:
>
>   (a) nature conservation and environmental improvement;
>
> and/or (b) the provision of amenity and opportunities for public recreation;
>
> and/or (c) the conservation of landscape heritage;

and that own, lease or have long-term management responsibility for open land (not only buildings) on which these aims are pursued.

CARTs are by nature collective organisations, representing the aims of a wider interest group with a major concern for environmental improvement. Some may have other objectives too, but all include environmental conservation among their key purposes.

This book presents the results of a study which has aimed to document and analyse the work of these organisations in Britain. We examine the extent and the characteristics of CARTs and assess their existing and potential contribution to the quality of the rural environment. The book divides into three sections. In Part 1, we outline the wider context of historic trends and changing policies in the countryside, and suggest some a priori explanations of the role of CARTs in this context.

The premises of European agricultural policy are being undermined by changes in both national and international economies – a process perhaps more obvious in Britain than in other member states as yet, but increasingly important for the whole Union. This process has led to a stream of agricultural policy reforms, but a truly sustainable policy has yet to be found. At the same time, a growing interest in environmental matters and a realisation of the wider consequences of past changes in the countryside have fuelled a reappraisal of the role of rural policy and the principal objectives which underpin it. Furthermore, there has developed a disillusionment both with the capacity of the state to prescribe, and with the potential of the unfettered market to create, solutions to social, economic and environmental problems. The institutions governing the countryside have co-evolved with people's changing priorities and the shifting pattern of influence. Can they develop further to represent wider public concern for the rural environment?

Some basic economic analysis indicates difficulties. There are few opportunities to market countryside goods, so landowners have little financial incentive to direct their efforts towards the countryside's improvement. And even where collective organisations do act, why should we bother to contribute when we can often enjoy the fruits of their efforts without paying? Clearly people's motivations and collective strategies are more complex, because we can see that these organisations receive substantial financial support and are, in many cases, very successful. We explore this complexity by looking more closely at how CARTs may gain control over land.

As part of this study we have undertaken a survey of as many CARTs as were able to trace. Between 1990 and 1992 we used information from environmental handbooks, government agencies, the media and personal contacts to collect information from CARTs. Each potential CART was sent a brief questionnaire which established whether or not the organisation met our definition and the area of land held. Each was also requested to send any available details about their objectives, organisation and activities, and a copy of their accounts. Some of the results of this general survey are summarised in Chapter 5. As a second stage in the study, field visits were undertaken to the major CARTs and to a range of organisations within four parts of the UK: East Anglia, Cumbria, Wales and Scotland. Within each area, contact was made with a number of CARTs and visits were also made to locally based government organis-ations. These case studies form the basis of the discussion in the rest of the book.

In Part 2 we review the range of CARTs, which come in all styles and sizes. The celebration of the National Trust's centenary in 1995 has given publicity to both the historic roots and the potential scale of CART operations; but this is misleading in that the vast majority of CARTs are much smaller, and many are much younger, than this. However, the National Trust alone comprises a large proportion of the total effort and resources in this sector. We look across the range: from the large established trusts with a national role, to small grassroots trusts whose contribution may only be appreciated in a local context; and from those founded in the Victorian era to those set up in the past few years. Their characteristics vary, from trusts in charge of large landholdings which may seem hardly distinguishable from private estates, to others working more sporadically on a variety of sites often in close partnership with, and perhaps very similar to, government agencies.

In Part 3 we develop our analysis, picking out key elements for more detailed consideration. We look at the actions of CARTs for the environment, and the financial means through which they pursue this. Direct influence over land management is at the centre of CARTs' actions, but beyond this they are often active in other ways, for example in the town and country planning process. But whatever their aspirations, these must always be tempered by their ability to resource their actions. The management of land often generates an income, but with priority given to conservation and amenity, the cost of such management frequently exceeds the returns. The deficit may be at least partially met from running other commercial enterprises, from membership subscriptions, from legacies and from private donations. But we have found that these sources are often insufficient and many CARTs commonly depend on government funds to maintain the full range of their activities.

We also look at CART strategies and development. CARTs do not operate in isolation: they need to be responsive to the interests of their actual and potential sponsors and supporters. An ecological analogy is a useful way to approach this issue. Often as small organisations, CARTs depend upon co-operation with other groups for information and support. For many CARTs it is their relationship with government and/or public agencies that is perhaps most critical to their establishment and progress. But this also stimulates an element of competition between different CARTs. Looking more closely at the role of public policy in influencing these organisations, we find that we cannot assume that they will thrive within a 'free market'. They need to develop strategies to capitalise on the available public incentives for environmental land management. In turn, governments may need to consider developing policies to make best use of the energy, innovation and skills that CARTs can supply. At present, policies towards CARTs tend to be somewhat sporadic and *ad hoc*. We make some suggestions for changes which might be able to direct and extend the evolution of CARTs for the long-term benefit of the countryside. Finally, we draw together the threads of this analysis and look ahead to the future role of CARTs in the countryside.

Note: We generally present figures in hectares but in some instances we have kept to imperial units (acres and miles) where these are used by particular organisations. For the purposes of conversion, there are 2.471 acres to a hectare and 0.621 miles to a kilometre.

Abbreviations

AONB	Area of Outstanding Natural Beauty
BBONT	Berks, Bucks and Oxon Naturalists' Trust
BTCV	British Trust for Conservation Volunteers
CAP	Common Agricultural Policy
CART	Conservation, Amenity and Recreation Trust
CC	Countryside Commission
CCS	Countryside Commission for Scotland
CCW	Countryside Council for Wales
CP	Community Programme
CPRE	Council for the Protection of Rural England
CSCT	Central Scotland Countryside Trust
EC	European Community
ECCP	East Cumbria Countryside Project
ESA	Environmentally Sensitive Area
ET	Employment Training
EU	European Union
GATT	General Agreement on Tariffs and Trade
HC	Heritage Conserved
MGT	Merthyr and Cynon Groundwork Trust
MSC	Manpower Services Commission
NC	Nature Conservancy (UK body, later NCC)
NCC	Nature Conservancy Council (now English Nature in England)
NNR	National Nature Reserve
NPC	National Parks Commission
NT	National Trust
NTS	National Trust for Scotland
PDO	Potentially Damaging Operation
RSNC	Royal Society for Nature Conservation
RSPB	Royal Society for the Protection of Birds
SNH	Scottish Natural Heritage
SPNC	Society for the Promotion of Nature Conservation

SPNR	Society for the Promotion of Nature Reserves
SSSI	Site of Special Scientific Interest
STT	Scottish Tree Trust
WT	Woodland Trust
WWET	Welsh Water Elan Trust
WWF	WorldWide Fund for Nature

Part 1:

Setting the scene

Intensive agriculture. Reproduced by permission of Countryside Commission/Ian Carstairs

The changing rural context and the place of collective action

1

Policies in flux

Policies for the rural environment are in a state of flux. The actions of government in Britain over much of the past fifty years have, to a large extent, been prescribed in legislation which was introduced in the first few years following the end of the Second World War. These were based on a strong consensus as to the appropriate role which the state should play in the life of the nation. The welfare state, the national health service and the town and country planning system all have their origins in this period. But the next forty years of more or less steady economic growth brought about substantial changes. In the past decade or so, the post-war consensus has been under challenge: however, a revised consensus has yet to emerge. The present debate is wide-ranging and fundamental, questioning the appropriate role of government in relation to the management of the economy, the globalisation of economic activity, the place of the United Kingdom within Europe and the devolution of powers to regional and local governments. Fundamentally it is a debate about the extent to which the state can intervene in people's lives to improve our quality of life and at what level of government the state's powers should be held.

These uncertainties have had a significant impact on the way in which we view issues of rural land use. The way in which we use rural land is to a very great extent the consequence of particular government policies; town and country planning controlling urban development, agricultural policy shaping the characteristics of agricultural production, and arrangements for taxation influencing the survival of large landholdings, the attractiveness of forestry and the real cost of investing in machinery. Agriculture and rural conservation were key elements of this post-war policy, and changes at both a national and an international level are forcing a fundamental reassessment of their appropriate treatment within the wider political framework.

The agricultural context

Agriculture has been the dominant form of land use in Europe for many centuries and continues to cover a large proportion of the total surface area (about three-quarters, in the UK). However, farmed land has a significance beyond its capacity for agricultural production. The environmental character of the British and European countryside has been largely a consequence of traditional agricultural practices and property institutions, and is influenced by an ancient tradition of 'de facto' access to many parts of the farmed countryside.

The 1947 Agriculture Act set out the principal objectives of agricultural support. Even though when the UK entered the European Community in 1973 responsibility for agricultural policy was largely transferred to the European Community, the aims for agriculture laid out in Article 39 of the Treaty of Rome bore a close resemblance to those prescribed in the 1947 Act. They were:

(a) to increase agricultural productivity by promoting technical progress and by ensuring the rational development of agricultural production and the optimum utilisation of the factors of production, in particular labour;
(b) thus to ensure a fair standard of living for the agricultural community, in particular by increasing the individual earnings of persons engaged in agriculture;
(c) to stabilise markets;
(d) to assure the availability of supplies;
(e) to ensure that supplies reach consumers at reasonable prices.

The next clause of the article also said that in working out the Common Agricultural Policy or CAP, account should be taken of the different structural and natural disparities of agricultural regions, the need to make adjustments by degrees, and the links between agriculture and the wider economy.

The story of this policy, and its effects, is by now a familiar one. In recent decades European agriculture has developed the capacity to produce greater volumes of temperate foodstuffs than are demanded in the domestic economy at ruling prices, but at too high a cost to enable them to be sold profitably in the world market. This situation has been sustained by the Common Agricultural Policy, which has supported prices received by farmers above the levels of world market prices, and which absorbs a large and increasingly politically unacceptable share of the total budget of the European Union (EU). At the same time, the CAP has failed to achieve its objective of maintaining an adequate level and stability of the incomes of EU farmers, particularly small farmers. It has contributed to instability and conflict in world markets and has accelerated environmentally damaging changes in rural land use in Europe.

The environmental impacts of post-war agricultural development in the UK are well known. Areas of marginal land have been 'improved' for agricultural production by draining, clearing, ploughing and reseeding, leading to the loss of large proportions of the nation's semi-natural habitats. Farms have become more specialised and agriculture has become more regionally differentiated as smaller, mixed farms have been replaced by larger ones concentrating on a smaller number of enterprises. The use of inorganic fertilisers and pesticides has grown and there have been problems of leaching of nitrates and other chemicals into watercourses. The substitution of machinery for labour has encouraged the creation of larger fields, removing hedges and increasing the risk of soil erosion. High stocking densities on farms have increased problems of effluent disposal and the incidence of water pollution. The declining farm workforce has contributed to significant social change in rural communities.

There are therefore many pressures to revise the form and direction of agricultural policy. At the European level these pressures have been further focused in the recent GATT agreement which for the first time placed attempts to reduce the level of agricultural protection at the centre of the debate. Due to the nature of political decision-making within the EU, with fifteen differing national interests seeking agreements on change which are acceptable to all, the reform of agricultural policy presents considerable obstacles. The short-term outcome of reforming efforts appears to be an almost permanent crisis in policy development, generating a series of complex and marginal additions to an already arcane system of support.

May 1992 saw agreement on substantial changes to the way in which agricultural support is delivered under the CAP. The reforms now being implemented involve a phased reduction in the general level of support for output prices in return for direct compensation payments based on areas of crops and numbers of animals kept. These are accompanied by quotas on livestock numbers and requirements for setting aside arable land. While the form of support for farming has changed, the bulk of it remains linked to production activity, if not to the actual volume of production itself. It is as yet too early to know exactly what impact these reforms will have upon UK land use and rural change. It was recognised at the time of their implementation that they would not lead to any significant reduction to the exchequer cost of the CAP in the short run, and this is proving to be the case. Whether or not they will do so in the longer term remains to be seen: there must be some doubt about this. Set-aside policy appears to be having a relatively modest impact on the total volume of production. Experience with set-aside in the United States is not encouraging. The set-aside requirement could be raised in order to constrain production further, but there may be political limits upon the total proportion of land which can be taken out of production in this way, both because of its impact on farmers and its acceptability to the general public. Furthermore, the introduction of direct payments to farmers makes the level of CAP spending more transparent and hence more susceptible to public criticism. Thus the 1992 CAP reforms appear unlikely to have established a form of agricultural policy which can be sustained for long.

In the mid-1980s, it was conceived that the surplus in agricultural production could be seen as representing a 'surplus' of agricultural land. Within the European Community there is more land used for agricultural production than is currently required, given the present intensity of land use, in order to meet domestic demand for food at the prevailing prices. And it seems unlikely that all of the 'extra' land could be used to produce for export. Reforms of agricultural and other land-use policies therefore imply either some agricultural land being diverted into other uses, or land being used less intensively for agriculture. Both these processes offer opportunities for the transfer of land for purposes other than purely agricultural production. Thus what has generally been seen as a problem by production economists also represents a significant opportunity for the diversion of rural land management towards alternative objectives. Environmental groups see an opportunity for protecting remaining areas of semi-natural habitat and making good some of the damage which has been done to the environment, and providing for new uses in the countryside (see Potter *et al.*, 1991, for a further discussion of these issues). In an apparent partial recognition of such opportunity, the 1992 CAP reforms also introduced the agri-environment package, offering EU re-imbursement for various environmental schemes designed to meet the environmental needs of each member state.

Thus the opportunities arising from current and likely future changes in agricultural policy include opportunities to place more emphasis upon environmental values. This could stimulate the enhanced provision of public goods and the adoption of less polluting forms of land-based production which will reduce its external costs.

The conservation context

The history of environmental concerns and the conservation movement in Britain has been largely one of public and voluntary sector partnership. Throughout, voluntary and collective organisations played an important role in evolving conservation policy; channelling and influencing public opinion and political action. We identify four key phases of policy development.

1. Origins: single issues, specific campaigns

Conservation as a political issue began in the voluntary sector in the later 19th century, promoted by a relatively small number of educated and well connected individuals. The first groups were formed to pursue specific policy change (e.g. the Royal Society for the Protection of Birds – RSPB – to stop the exploitation of rare bird species for plumage) or to protect directly the public's enjoyment of certain areas of countryside threatened by urban, industrial or agricultural development (e.g. The National Trust and the Selborne Society). Each of these new groups drew support from the numerous societies of middle-class Victorian Britain – natural history societies with a particular interest in biology, and amenity societies promoting the wider enjoyment of the countryside. Many leaders of these societies were also interested in social reform and sought to improve the lives of the urban poor by promoting the value of fresh air and recreation.

In the first half of the 20th century the concerns of these early groups began to be reflected in limited legislation, as governments passed a series of wildlife and species protection acts and the National Trust Act (detailed in Sheail, 1982). It was essentially a reactive period for conservation policy: bills originated from the voluntary sector and were supported through parliament by influential political figures.

2. Institutionalisation: conservation within the welfare state

The post-war period was an era of government planning in many areas of public welfare, and conservation was no exception to this pattern. Landholding interest groups who were involved in wartime planning with government had a significant influence over the new land-use policies of this period. But at the same time there was a steady growth in small county trusts and a period of consolidation among many of the older groups such as the National Trust and RSPB, which also shaped the emerging policy structures.

The 1947 Town and Country Planning Act was the first major piece of rural conservation legislation. It followed the recommendations of the 1942 Report of the Committee on Land Utilisation in Rural Areas (Scott Committee, 1942). Government acknowledged the Committee's view that 'farmers and foresters are unconsciously the nation's landscape gardeners, a privilege which they share with the landowners'. In the 1947 Act, conservation of the countryside in general was to be achieved by preventing uncontrolled urban development. The Act laid down the framework for the planning systems which today remain the principal means to control built development in the open countryside. Farming and forestry change were not seen as the sort of development for which permission would be needed. A fuller description is given by Shoard (1988).

In 1949, in delayed response to a report prepared during the War by John Dower, parliament passed the National Parks and Access to the Countryside Act. This second major Act gave the legal framework for the creation of National Parks in England and Wales; as areas of 'beautiful and relatively wild country in which landscape beauty is strictly preserved; access and facilities for open-air enjoyment are amply provided; wildlife and places of historic interest are suitably protected and established farming use is effectively maintained'. It also defined Areas of Outstanding Natural Beauty (AONBs), and set up the National Parks Commission (NPC) to oversee both designations. These moves mirrored the aims of the early amenity societies. In response to the concerns of the early natural history societies and others, the same Act created the Nature Conservancy (NC) and established the framework for National Nature Reserves (NNRs) and Sites of Special Scientific Interest (SSSIs). The separation of the NPC and NC mirrored the original dichotomy in the voluntary groups.

The position in Scotland was rather different. There it was argued with more vigour that landscape and wildlife protection and the provision of facilities for outdoor recreation should be retained within the ambit of the planning system (Sheail, 1993). As a consequence National Parks were not established. There was also particular anxiety as to the threat posed by the designation of National Nature Reserves to traditional land ownership and use in Scotland.

3. The 1960s and 1970s: the beginning of environmentalism

During the 1960s concern about wider environmental quality began to emerge. Conservation was increasingly viewed as part of this debate, linked to issues of urban and industrial pollution and economic change. Also, many more households acquired cars and began to visit the countryside, and a number of influential writers began to put rural issues in the public eye to a much greater extent than previously.

This paved the way for the Countryside (Scotland) Act of 1967 and the Countryside Act of 1968 (Sheail, 1993). These Acts formally widened state conservation policy: firstly expanding the remit of the NPC to create the Countryside Commission covering the whole of England and Wales (CC), and forming the Countryside Commission for Scotland (CCS); and secondly obliging other state users of natural resources (Ministry of Agriculture, Fisheries and Food, Water Authorities, Forestry Commission) to have regard to nature conservation in carrying out their duties.

4. The 1980s and beyond: 'think globally, act locally'

Within the last few decades, environmental conservation has influenced policy more broadly and more people have become involved in or are directly affected by the conservation movement.

From a modest handful in 1900, membership of voluntary environmental groups was estimated to be at least two million, or 4 per cent of the UK population, by 1980 (Lowe and Goyder, 1983). Several polls conducted in the early 1980s showed general public concern and particular support for landscape and wildlife conservation had become very strong (Worth, 1984; Wibberley, 1987). These trends have led to a proliferation of voluntary groups dealing with a huge range of different conservation issues. Some retain a specific focus (a local area or a particular issue), while a handful of increasingly international groups deal with almost all aspects of rural land-use practice and policy. Some groups espouse a holistic and fairly radical philosophy, such as Greenpeace and Friends of the Earth. Other established groups whose interests may originally have been quite narrow have expanded their horizons, such as the Councils for the Protection of Rural England and Wales (CPRE/W), and the WorldWide Fund for Nature (WWF) and even the RSPB. Many other groups have a much more pragmatic and local focus. The 1980s also saw a growth in trading companies with specific conservation objectives (Traidcraft, Ark, Ecover, The Ecology Building Society). These reflect a broadening public awareness of these issues and their relation to people's lifestyles. While both voluntary and trading sectors suffered during the recent economic recession, they have also found fresh focus in the new 'sustainability' and 'sustainable development' agendas of the 1990s.

UK government response to changing attitudes towards the environment and conservation has perhaps been less dramatic than its actions in the early post-war period. Although heralded as a major attempt to re-think wildlife, habitat and landscape conservation issues comprehensively, the real influence of the 1981 Wildlife and Countryside Act has been disputed, with some conservation groups concluding that it has worked as much against them as for them (CPRE, 1985). However, the proportion of public funds devoted to the countryside and nature conservation agencies increased over the 1980s and has been more or less sustained through the recession. Agricultural policy has begun to incorporate new measures for conservation and amenity, and new European and national legislation has been implemented in recognition of the environmental impact of various kinds of urban, infrastructure and industrial development.

Voluntary agreements have recently assumed much greater importance as a tool for rural conservation. Their first widespread use resulted from the 1981 Act, under which owners of SSSIs had to be notified and be given a list of Potentially Damaging Operations (PDOs): agricultural operations which might threaten the site's value. Owners then had to give the relevant conservation agency (formerly NCC, now English Nature, CCW (Countryside Council for Wales) or SNH (Scottish Natural Heritage)) prior notification of any proposed PDO, and if seeking to prevent any such operation, the agency had to offer a management agreement under which it would pay compensation for the owner's estimated profit forgone. The agreement would be voluntary. The agency held powers to compulsorily purchase the site as a last resort: however, in practice these powers have rarely been used.

Although the UK's approach to setting payment levels has broadly changed since 1981 from negative 'compensation' towards positive 'incentive', the model of a voluntary management contract to generate environmental benefit has now been applied widely. Environmentally Sensitive Areas (ESAs) were introduced in 1987 and today cover 10 per cent of the UK. In ESAs, landholders can enter agreements which place certain restrictions and specify new requirements for management, to produce new or enhanced environmental and amenity benefits. In return the farmer receives standard annual management payments, with the opportunity of capital payments to contribute to some associated capital costs (hedging, walling and so on).

Broadly similar packages of revenue and capital payments are now offered in several other schemes seeking to protect and enhance the rural environment. These include Countryside Stewardship, the Nitrate Sensitive Areas Scheme and four new schemes launched as part of the UK's agri-environment package under the reformed CAP. Indeed the growth in schemes has been such that voluntary groups and government have identified a need for greater integration, and steps are being taken to merge some schemes in future.

The other main phenomenon of the 1990s has been a succession of broad policy documents flowing from the sustainable development and biodiversity agendas established through the UN's 1992 Earth Summit in Rio. And the UK's environmental policy has been considerably influenced and in some aspects determined by judgements in Brussels, notably in directives on water quality, birds and nature conservation. As yet, these international issues have spawned few major legislative changes in UK rural policy, but it is evident that they have set governments rethinking their environmental strategies and calling for more effective means to deal with them. Much of this thinking seems likely to be taken forward by local and sectoral policies, rather than all-embracing national policies.

We have arguably now reached a stage where the environment, and a concern for 'quality of life', are becoming more integral to the shape of future rural policies. In this process, it seems inevitable that the history of these concerns, and their British origins in collective action and voluntary involvement, should have a central influence upon the new policy agenda.

The political context

In the last fifteen years, the state in Britain and elsewhere has tended to move away from direct participation in economic activity and politicians have questioned the need for centralised control of production and exchange. They recognise that centralised institutions are rarely well-enough informed to plan these processes effectively, involving as they do so many individual, localised decisions about what is wanted and how best to provide it. It is also widely acknowledged that the tendency of a large, centralised bureaucracy is to de-motivate those who work in it, or with it.

At the same time, accumulating empirical evidence undermines the claims of the more radical 'free-market' politicians by demonstrating that the market frequently fails to deliver both efficient and fair outcomes in resource allocation. Sometimes there are simply no available mechanisms to generate the desired 'market' incentives within particular areas of economic activity. These failings remind us that often government action was taken in the first place precisely because the market was unable to operate. And even when market mechanisms can be found, people may reject the distributional implications of using market forces to determine output levels and to allocate access to what is produced: as the debates about the reform of the health service, education and transport now demonstrate.

The consequence of the relative demise of both centrally planned and entirely free-market political agendas has been a reappraisal of the centre ground in public policy. This suggests that there might be a broadened role for local democratic structures in policy development but equally, if not more importantly in the current political climate, there may be an increasing need for the state to act as 'enabler' of new development: with initiative offered by the private sector but supported by the state. This type of development has been discussed by Marquand (1988), who argues that:

> a flourishing political community will be a mosaic of smaller collectives, which act as nurseries for the feelings of mutual loyalty and trust which hold the wider community together, and where the skills of

self-government may be learned and practised. Some of these will be public, for example parish councils, regional assemblies or the governing bodies of schools and hospitals. Others – trade unions, employers' associations, producer co-operatives – will be private.

He believes that these groups should have to argue their cases in public and thus share public responsibility for ultimate policy decisions, making them behave in a more encompassing way than if they did not. It implies power-sharing in partnerships between the state and private groups within society.

The place of collective action

Environmental improvement has long been pursued through a mixture of 'public' domain policy and private activity. For example, legislation provides the organisational framework and sets the operational controls upon areas within which improvement initiatives are established or fail, and government spending both direct (through conservation schemes and subsidies) and indirect (through employment schemes, special tax regimes for charities, provision of infrastructure) influences the development of initiatives. But land management for conservation still relies heavily upon private input. It is an area of policy where the distinction between private and public responsibilities rapidly gets blurred.

National agri-environment schemes have made important environmental gains, but they have suffered from a number of limitations. Firstly, most of them have largely been designed by bodies acting at a strategic, national level. Thus prescriptions may be relatively standardised and it has perhaps been easier to design schemes for the protection of established and well-documented features than schemes which can introduce new features in ways appropriate to local circumstance. Secondly, the controls over the way in which land is managed have to be written into enforceable contracts. Thus agreements have tended to detail the actions which should or should not be taken, rather than the environmental outputs which are sought. As a result, land managers have perhaps been unable to identify these outputs clearly, and to use their skills and make their own judgements as to the best means of achieving them.

Furthermore, most scheme agreements are, in environmental terms, relatively short term. The majority last for ten years, whereas valuable achievements may depend upon longer periods of consistent management. And landowners need to have an eye on what they may do with the land once an agreement ends, or in response to a sudden change in external circumstances, thus they may be reluctant to commit themselves to actions which restrict their long-term options. Finally, these agreements depend upon regular and highly visible payments from state to farmer. These may be hard to justify under conditions of particular pressure on public expenditure, and alongside growing public criticism of the high levels of subsidies paid to farmers.

None of these weaknesses is insurmountable, and agri-environmental schemes look certain to remain an important feature in countryside policy. However, they suggest that we might also seek other means to achieve a more positive and flexible approach to future environmental enhancement. Local character and variety in the rural environment might most effectively be achieved through 'environmental entrepreneurship', in which private bodies develop plans and accumulate resources to pursue different kinds of environmental benefit in different local areas. But such development entails these people taking risks for little or no financial return, and it seems unlikely that private interests alone will be willing or able to meet the apparent public demand for varied environmental benefits.

There is thus perhaps an important case for collective decision-making: for groups owning and managing land with a wider purpose than that normally seen in individual ownership. In economic terminology, this kind of development represents a collective provision of public goods and a means towards the recognition of the wider values which arise from land use by those who have responsibility for its management.

If the public's conservation objective is also held by the owner and/or holder of the land, there will be an incentive for that owner to identify those conservation targets which best match specific local circumstances and to seek out new innovations in the pursuit of these. Also, conservation land management is likely to be planned and implemented over a long period and thus, in theory at least, it need not be wholly dependent upon regular payments from government. Although this concept of environmentally benign landownership clearly extends more widely, voluntary collective groups set up to pursue environmental and amenity objectives are one kind of owner that may fulfil this role.

As indicated in our description of the conservation context, collective groups can and increasingly do take this sort of action in favour of the rural environment. Campaigning work has long been coupled to direct actions to gain control over the management of areas of the countryside. Focusing in particular on this phenomenon, we have termed these collective organisations 'Conservation, Amenity and Recreation Trusts' (CARTs). They are non-profit organisations which have as a major objective the ownership and long-term management of open land for environmental or amenity benefit. They are a significant and growing form of institutional landownership and management in the British Isles.

In the next chapter we look historically at the changing influences upon rural landownership and management and consider how this relates to the growing phenomenon of CART action.

Telford urban fringe. Reproduced by permission of Countryside Commission/David Woodfall

2 Changing interests in rural land

Farming and landownership

The great majority of the rural land area is used for farming and so the actions of farmers ultimately determine the character of the countryside. We tend to think of farming as an industry dominated by relatively small-scale farmers who own and manage their land independently. While there is in practice considerable variety, this is not a bad picture of the current position. Individual farmers do have considerable freedom to choose for themselves how they want to operate their businesses, the main limitations being centrally determined by government. But this has not always been the case. In past centuries the land has been owned and managed in a variety of ways, responding to different priorities for the products which can be provided, to different techniques available for production and to different powers of different groups within society.

Historically, land has always represented a source of power and influence. Landownership has been sought because of the status which it brings to the owner. It is only since the later stages of the industrial revolution that the position has altered. The growth of non-agricultural wealth and the democratisation of the political process have reduced the extent of the influence which landowners wield. But now the significance of holding land is widening for another reason: the contribution which it makes to the quality of the environment.

In this book we are interested in the way in which a collective interest can be exercised over the management of land, reflecting concerns which go beyond those of a narrow group of occupiers. As we shall see in this chapter, there are several examples where this has been a pre-dominant factor in land tenure in Britain in the past. A second theme of the book concerns the growth of interest in conservation and in this chapter we also consider the underlying values of the conservation movement and how this will affect future policy options for shifting the balance of land-use priorities in the countryside.

The open field system

One of the earliest well-documented systems of rural land tenure was the manorial system. This was found widely across Europe and also in parts of Asia (Orwin, 1949, p. 23). Under this, the village played a central role in the organisation of agricultural production. Cropping and livestock were organised along quite different lines. Each individual in the village had a right to grow crops on separate strips of land in the open fields. However, cultivating these strips was often undertaken co-operatively; for instance, ploughing was done by a team with each member making a contribution, maybe of an ox, or of the plough itself. Livestock were grazed on common pastures. Villagers would each have carefully defined rights specifying how many stock they were entitled to graze on the common. The arable fields would often be available for communal grazing at certain times of the year. The whole system was administered by a local court composed of members of the village. It would set planting and harvest dates, enforce the arrangements for the use of the common and oversee any changes in occupation of the strips (Dahlman, 1980).

The reasons for the evolution and long-term survival of this sort of management remain a subject for debate. It had once been supposed that this represented an inefficient form of management, enforced by an inflexible control from outside of the system. In particular the common use of grazing land has been seen as a wasteful use of resources. But more recent analyses (particularly Dahlman, 1980) have suggested that it was in fact an efficient arrangement which reflected the priorities and opportunities of the time. Ostrom (1990, p. 224) comments that the manorial institutions were broadly similar to a number of other successful commons institutions in having a clear-cut definition of who is to use common resources, definite limits on per-mitted uses, low-cost enforcement mechanisms, and local rule-making which permitted change in institutions over time, in response to economic and environmental change.

A mediaeval system of land management may seem a long way from our immediate interest in present-day trusts. But it illustrates a way in which collective and co-operative management can be to the general advantage.

Enclosures

Over a period of centuries, the open fields were steadily replaced by a system of individual holdings more akin to the present-day pattern. This change took different paths in different European countries. In England, there was a widespread process of enclosure which began in the 15th century and continued at differing rates up to the 19th century. In Denmark, there was enclosure in the late 18th century. However, in much of continental Western Europe, individuals retained the use of their holdings, which were divided and subdivided until peasants could be farming dozens of tiny plots. These different processes reflect a variety of differences in circumstance, such as inheritance laws, economic conditions and government policy towards agriculture.

In Britain, enclosure heralded the development and dominance of the great estates, which occupied a substantial area during the 19th century. The process initially led to the establishment of numerous small farms, but these were then often absorbed into larger holdings, especially during the 16th and early 17th centuries (Butlin, 1982).

The great estates

The great estates achieved a peak in landownership in the second half of the 19th century. A complete survey of land tenure often referred to as the New Domesday Survey was undertaken in 1873. This showed (Orwin and Whetham, 1964) that in England and Wales, estates over 1000 acres (owned by 'Peers', 'Great Landowners' and 'Squires'; some 4200 owners) covered over half the land area. Those over 300 acres (less than 14 000 owners) covered two-thirds of the area. Ownership of land was even more concentrated in Scotland, where it was claimed that nearly one-quarter of the land was owned by 12 owners. As a consequence, the majority of the land was farmed by tenants. Over the period 1850–1914, owner-occupation for subsistence or commercial farming represented little more than 10 per cent of the land area (Northfield, 1979, p. 28).

These estates were managed with broad objectives. Thompson (1963) comments that the great object of estate management was 'a life of leisure with freedom to pursue occupations that were not dictated by the compulsions of economic necessity'. Key functions of the estate were to provide countryside benefits to a very narrow segment of the population in the form of leisure activities and landscape amenity. But beyond this, 'land was chiefly valued for the social and political consequence which it conferred, and the facilities for founding a family which it presented'. As a result, 'the profit motive could hardly be the uppermost consideration in its management'. Estates were commonly a drain on family fortunes and there was often a need to make regular injections of capital from other sources, such as by marriage.

The key value of an estate depended upon its being kept intact. Its total value was greater than the sum of its component parts. Ownership could give rights to nominate members of parliament and to appoint church officials, although these might be sold separately. More critically, the owner was at the centre of a sphere of influence which governed many aspects of local life (Thompson, 1963).

Estates in trust

The majority of estates were tied up in legal arrangements aimed at safeguarding family interests, known as marriage settlements. In this, the present occupier was a life-tenant on the estate and his or her powers over it were limited. The settlement limited the ability of the present occupier to sell or to borrow against the value of the estate. It was estimated that in the middle of the 19th century, two-thirds of the country was was held under marriage settlements making the present 'owner' a tenant for life (Thompson, 1963).

The landlord and tenant

On a landed estate, the landlord could control the whole range of outputs. The maintenance of a social position required certain activities, some of which involved particular constraints on the agricultural use of the land. Tenanted land would be farmed according to the broader requirements of the estate. This would sometimes bring tenant and landlord into conflict, but there can be little doubt as to who held the balance of power. Tenancy agreements were generally based on customary practice (Orwin and Whetham, 1964), and most could be terminated by six months' notice by either side. In practice, many families retained tenancies for generations.

The shooting of game could be a source of conflict between landlord and tenant. The sport was very popular amongst landowners and estate management was often directed towards both the preservation and nurturing of game birds. This required the maintenance of cover and food supplies for the birds. In practice, some food would be the tenants' crops; however, tenants were generally not allowed to take game, particularly during the shooting season. Indeed in law, the right to shoot anything was restricted to owners of land worth at least £100 a year, until 1831 (Thompson, 1963). It was not until 1881 that the law authorised tenants to destroy rabbits and hares on their farms without seeking the landlord's permission. In some cases where damage by game was excessive, landlords paid compensation to tenants. But in general priority was accorded to the interests of leisure.

Agricultural holdings legislation more generally introduced from 1875 gave statutory backing to the tenants' position, although the early legislation tended to be ineffectual as it gave landlords an option to opt out (Orwin and Whetham, 1964). Over time, tenants gained a formal basis for compensation for their improvements and for disturbance; opportunities for arbitration; and increased security. In return they were expected to farm according to new 'rules of good husbandry'.

The break-up of estates

A variety of factors led to the decline of the landed estates; underlying these was the relative decline of agriculture with economic and industrial development. This was reflected in the declining political influence of landowners, as a result of the introduction of democratic principles in the Reform Acts. The position of the landed interest was particularly weakened by the repeal of the Corn Laws and the agricultural depression between 1873 and 1896, which caused a decline in the financial position of the estates and a deterioration in their fixed equipment. But the greatest transfers of property did not take place until the demand for land had revived, and substantial areas of land were sold between 1911 and 1914.

After the First World War came the biggest changes. Thompson (1963) estimates that between 1918 and 1921 between six and eight million acres changed hands in England, approaching one-quarter of the total area. In 1914, 11 per cent of the agricultural land in England and Wales was occupied by its owners. This rose to 36 per cent in 1927 (Sturmey, 1955). Thompson comments that these transfers 'marked a social revolution in the countryside, nothing less than the dissolution of a large part of the great estate system and the formation of a new race of yeomen'. But this new breed was almost immediately thrown into a new period of agricultural depression through the 1920s and 1930s, without the support of a landlord and often with debts associated with the land purchase. It was suggested that in the 1930s the banks owned half of Norfolk, and substantial areas of land were abandonded. These changes forced a breakdown in the social system which had generated the more varied pattern of country-side that most people would regard as typically British.

Modern food production

The 20th century has seen landowners and institutions focus almost exclusively on food production, perhaps in a way that has not been seen before. The Second World War dramatically raised the priority for the domestic produc-tion of food and raw materials. This was institutionalised through agricultural legislation which both favoured agricultural products against other countryside benefits and which favoured the emergence of an 'efficient' farming structure. In defining this 'efficiency', outputs were construed wholly in agricultural terms. The agricultural products which have been favoured have simple market characteristics: they are easy to define, homogeneous and transportable. They are clearly suited to provision through a (near-perfect) market. Hence policies have been largely based on farmers responding to a single variable: guaranteed output prices.

Alongside growing production support came the gradual individualisation of decision-making in rural land management. Legislation advanced the rights of the remaining tenants against the interests of the landlords; at one stage, tenants were granted security of tenure for three generations. This has been a factor in the continued decline of the tenanted sector. As noted above, in England and Wales in 1927, 36 per cent of the land was owner-occupied. By 1989 the apparent position had been reversed with 36 per cent of the land tenanted and 64 per cent owner-occupied (although the latter figure understates the true shift, due to the increased practice of land being owned and tenanted within the same family primarily for tax reasons, hence it underestimates the extent of effective owner-occupancy). Unlike many of its European partners, post-war Britain has also seen little growth in collective land management between farmers, such as in co-operatives. Individual farmers have instead become more subject to the corporate influence of large suppliers and buyers.

Since this context has become established, an inertia has developed in policy, associated with the corporatism which has evolved and the political strength of those sections of society determined to protect their asset values and policy entitlements (Bromley and Hodge, 1990). Changes have come slowly, and often only after repeated budgetary crises in policy caused by over-production – a pattern which began in the late 1950s in the dairy sector, and has been repeated in most major farming sectors since the UK's accession to the European Community in 1973. In fact debate has tended to invent new justifications for an existing policy structure (import substitution, agriculture's contribution to the national economy, the advantage to the UK in extracting payments from EC support mechanisms) rather than to contemplate any fundamental change to the structure itself. This has been despite the emerging evidence of the failure of the policy to deliver many of the gains which had been anticipated.

So, in the 20th century and especially since 1945, Britain has evolved a system of countryside management which is unusual, in the extent to which resources have been allocated through mainly individualistic decisions. The policy framework has been very successful in meeting the production goals which were set for it; but not without cost. As described in Chapter 1, the policy incentives combined with continuing technological change have had severe impacts upon the countryside. Today, that post-war consensus which focused policy upon agricultural output has been broken; although largely due to the costs of the support policies and international trade pressures, rather than through a more fundamental shift in policy objectives for the countryside.

Institutions for a new countryside

Over perhaps particularly the past twenty years, the pattern of public demand for the products of the country-side has shifted. Land is now valued not only for its productivity in farming and forestry and its natural resources of water and minerals, but also because it can generate other public and private benefits. Amongst these non-agricultural benefits, some are marketable, including recreational facilities such as golf courses, water-sports centres, theme parks and adventure holiday centres. But the non-marketable benefits are arguably more numerous, including other recreational and amenity facilities such as opportunities to take informal walks, have picnics and see scenic landscape as well as a range of landscape, wildlife, cultural and historic benefits: values which may equally be felt by people who do not visit or live in the countryside at all. These will only partially be reflected in any conven-tional markets, such as the markets for property and rural tourism. There has been increasing public concern for the protection and increase of the non-market benefits of rural land. People value these qualities now and, perhaps more importantly, they wish see them passed on to future generations.

Because there are no markets in which these other benefits from land are directly priced and traded, there is little financial incentive for individual landowners to produce them to meet public demand. Simultaneously, in the marketplace there are no financial penalties imposed upon landowners who impose costs on other people through pollution. The first of these failings is known by economists as the problem of providing public goods, the second as the problem of controlling external costs.

The demand for food is income inelastic in contrast with the demand for environmental goods. Increasing leisure time and mobility, and the relocation of the population towards rural areas, have all tended to increase the marginal value of countryside benefits – the values derived from landscape, wildlife, history and public access – as compared to the marginal value of food. The tendency has been exaggerated by an agricultural policy which has encouraged a reduced production of countryside goods and an accelerated rate of environmental damage.

In terms of the relative priorities attached to alternative countryside benefits, the owners of the landed estates may have reflected more closely these current and likely future patterns of public demand. We should note however that they pursued their own particular type of 'conservation', whereby gamekeepers curtailed the populations of wild, predatory mammals in order to boost the population of game species. However, the resulting land-use priorities appear to have been more balanced than those of the present generation of agricultural occupiers, under the institutional structure of landownership and product markets which has emerged in the past fifty years. But there can be no return to the landed estates: few individuals today would be in a position to assemble the necessary resources. And in any case, the social system which stood at the heart of the great estates has gone for good and there is little wish to return to it. While incomes are on average much higher than they were a century ago, they are also less unevenly distributed (Rubinstein, 1986). But perhaps more significantly, ownership of an estate does not confer the status which it once did. And it is uncertain that the modern town and country planning system would permit the changes which new owners might wish to impose on their newly acquired countryside.

The demand for countryside benefits is widely, if not evenly spread through the population. Many of those who demand these benefits have no association with landownership and few rights to the benefits which can flow from land use (although public rights of way are an important exception). Without a ready-made market in which they could acquire such benefits directly, their only option would be to buy rural land itself, and this is of course not feasible for the great majority. The best alternative action for many has been to buy a house in a rural area or on the outskirts of a town, and/or to lobby directly for the state to intervene or contribute towards new collective action for the environment.

Recasting value in the countryside

Under estate ownership, demand for the rural environment and control of resources were located together. As priorities narrowed to the production of food, so the control of land resources was shifted largely towards those closest to food production. In view of the more recent changes in priorities, how then can the provision of other countryside benefits be secured for the wider public, in a modern context?

To understand the strengths and weaknesses of different policy options, it is useful to delve a little into the nature of these non-market values. Underlying notions of landscape, wildlife and historic and cultural value, there are perhaps three main arguments for environmental conservation in the modern context.

1. An undervalued and vital resource for the future economy

This argument focuses upon future use-values, and asserts that the rural environment as a whole, and its genetic resources, will be of direct and increasing use to society if conserved. Today's economy relies upon many non-renewable resources, and our farming and forestry are mainly dependent on a small number of non-native species. Furthermore, production under today's large-scale monoculture conditions increases crop vulnerability to disease and stress, so costly efforts must be made to stabilise and regulate local growing conditions. All these things could be seen as 'high-risk' strategies for production, in the longer term. By contrast, native species were once common sources of fuel, food, medicine, household goods and construction materials. They are renewable, and better adapted to the changing British environment. Conserving their biodiversity thus gives society the option to make renewed use of them in future.

More broadly, wildlife, habitats and the physical components of rural landscapes play an important role in determining local climate, hydrology and other environmental conditions. The juxtaposition of different elements within a landscape can thereby affect the sustainability of the agricultural and forest production systems it supports. As we understand more about the consequences of environmental degradation and seek new ways to preserve those essential resources which sustain human life (water, air, soils, etc.) rural landscapes and their components will be one important focus of attention.

2. A resource for history and education

It is now widely accepted that the countryside is part of 'our natural heritage'; a record of the past and a source from which to learn. Rackham (1986) argues that the landscape is a record of our roots and the growth of civilisation, that each individual historic wood or heath is uniquely different from every other, and each has something to tell us. To conserve the countryside's historical record means conserving sites and patterns in the landscape which are either natural (formed without conscious design by people) or traditional (part of our cultural heritage), or which are the living record of important past events (historic markers or milestones). In this way we can trace our cultural links with the land over many centuries.

3. Other cultural meaning – beauty, local character, distinctiveness and emotional attachment

This is perhaps the argument most readily recognised by the overwhelming majority of people who support conservation in one way or another. While some continue to assert that 'beauty is in the eye of the beholder', there are undoubtedly common themes identified in all these

appeals for conservation and enhancement of the countryside. In the main, the old is preferred to the new, the more
diverse or intimately interconnected to the simple and
fragmented, the more uniquely adapted, rare or locally
particular to the more widespread and common, the less
obviously man-made and industrially managed to the
clearly artificial and anonymous, and the less visually and
structurally uniform to the more so. Where an individual
or community has become attached to a particular site or
landscape, its value may simply be its familiarity – from
particular fond memories which it holds for the people
who live or work nearby.

One uniting theme among these three different arguments is variety. Local and regional variety in land use and
management is central to the wider environmental and
amenity value of the countryside. Another important point
is that people's ability to enjoy the benefits of these kinds
of landscapes directly, by seeing them, living within them
or visiting them, is also bound up with at least two of these
arguments. So, policies which are seeking to re-balance
land use and tip that balance more in favour of these
values must allow for a variety of local solutions; and they
must give the wider public more direct ability to enjoy
such local variety.

The available policy options

Social control or 'collective pressure'

Much of the control exercised by the owners of landed
estates arose from customs based on social relationships
rather than on statutory control. But the break-up of the
estates and the individualisation of decision-making on the
one hand, and the sheer variety of countryside benefits and
costs on the other, will limit the scope for this type of
coercive, less formal influence by those who seek more
benefits upon those who are able to produce them. Some
pressure may be exerted by peer groups – for instance
farmers themselves recognising that it is wrong to engage
in 'excessive' environmental damage – but this will
probably fall far short of the kinds of benefit which other
groups within society would like to see in the countryside.

State control

Regulation, or perhaps more fashionably these days, cross-compliance (where conditions are imposed upon the receipt of farm support), could seek a broader range of countryside benefits by somehow requiring farmers to retain features of interest and to take specific actions to enhance or increase the range of benefits generated on their land. One difficulty with these methods is that the requirements needed to deliver the appropriate benefits will be complex and specific to particular places – thus it would be hard to define all cases through some generalised rule or criterion for applying sanctions. As the achievements of the Common Agricultural Policy or CAP amply demonstrate, applying centralised public policy structures to land management can all too easily encourage standardised and relatively uniform outcomes, which in this case have combined with market forces to generate greater homogeneity and a reduced range of benefits in the countryside.

Also, where maintenance or enhancement requires concerted management effort, a regulatory method is unlikely to encourage a positive response by land managers to this obligation – the incentive will always be to do the minimum necessary to comply. Nevertheless, some environmental objectives are currently pursued through regulation and, where there is widespread acceptance of the standards which they set, they can be a useful option (examples include straw burning, point-source water pollution, and certain elements of planning law).

Private market transactions

It might be possible to achieve the desired balance of values in land through developing the operation of market forces between those owning land and those seeking other benefits from it – a direct 'commoditisation' of these benefits. For instance, some landowners sell licences to riders giving them access to networks of bridleways. Broader environmental contracts could be established between users and individual owners which specified requirements for land management. This leaves the pattern of property rights in place. It is, perhaps not surprisingly, an approach advocated in the UK by the Country

Landowners' Association (1989). The major difficulty in terms of its operation lies on the demand side. How are the diffuse demands for countryside benefits to be reflected by single parties capable of entering into such a contract? There are clearly risks of high transaction costs and 'free-riding' by those who avoid having to pay but still receive the benefits.

The most simple way for a single party to represent a broad range of interests in countryside benefit is for that party to be government. Public agencies or government can create new markets for other countryside benefits by offering voluntary incentives for action. As described in Chapter 1, this is the approach which has been most widely adopted in rural environmental policy in recent years. Again as explained in Chapter 1, these approaches have certain limitations, particularly in the long term.

But also, voluntary conservation bodies, representing a collective interest in conservation or amenity and acting directly in the market, can and indeed do organise the provision of countryside benefits. Anderson and Leal (1991) place considerable emphasis on this type of organis-ation quite generally in environmental management, in harnessing the demand for 'near-public' goods. They advocate its role, for instance, in competing for public resources and for the protection and enhancement of instream flows in watercourses. They claim that voluntary bodies make decisions based upon a 'realistic' assessment of the opportunity costs, taking development opportunities where they are consistent with their wider goals. Like individuals these groups may face difficulties with respect to free-rider problems, although Anderson and Leal (p. 95) comment that 'there is a lot of evidence that people make significant contributions to environmental groups, even when they could free ride'.

The phenomenon of Conservation, Amenity and Rec-reation Trusts obtaining control over land in the UK has indeed been an ever-present and growing feature of the environmental sector. In the next chapter we look at the conceptual issues surrounding the development of this type of collective organisation.

Farm visit, Sacrewell Farm and Country Centre. Reproduced
by permission of The William Scott Abbott Trust

Collective action and the public interest

3

As we discussed in the previous chapters, although there is now a broadly-based concern for the condition of the rural environment, it is not so clear how this concern can be translated into direct control over land and action for environmental improvement. The issue is a common one, not just associated with environmental concerns. It is an issue at the very centre of political life. Many of the common qualities and benefits which most people seek from society have characteristics which mean that they are not likely to be produced by individuals pursuing their own direct interests.

The problems of collective provision

It is usual to think of economic activities being undertaken by individuals or by firms. In agriculture, farms, as with other small businesses, are often operated by a single person. But it is not uncommon for more than one person to be involved; a farmer might share responsibility with one or more members of his or her family. In such cases, the farm business may be operated as a partnership or occasionally as a company.

But as we have seen, the collective management of rural land is also a longstanding tradition in Britain. It can involve collective management to generate products, or it may be to provide something for the enjoyment of all those involved. For instance, with common grazings, a number of farmers have the right to graze their stock on a single area of land. This arrangement is still often found in the uplands where farmers may have some privately managed land in the valleys and also hold rights to graze a defined number of stock, alongside others, on the open hill. Another 'productive' example is the current popularity of machinery rings, where farmers share expensive capital equipment. Examples of collective action for personal enjoyment would be fishing or golf clubs, where members jointly organise the provision of a desired service. They may collectively own the assets of the club, or they may simply have the right to engage in the particular activity, as when a fishing club does not own the lake or reservoir in which its members fish.

This type of organisation often makes sense because of the total cost of providing the service. A golf club needs to lay out a course and construct a club house. The course needs constant management, maintaining the greens and fairways. The cost of providing this service for one person is not very different from the cost of providing it for many. The only difficulty is that if too many people want to use it, they will get in each other's way and spoil their enjoyment. Hence most players make do with shared facilities in a club, but the problem of crowding is minimised by restricting the number of members who are allowed to join the club.

With all these forms of collective management, those who participate in the group can exclude non-members from the benefits generated. Thus the goods which are produced in these ways are essentially private goods. Commoners produce wool and sheepmeat, which are sold in a market and the farmers can be sure of being paid. The use of the common for grazing is reserved solely for the commoners. Likewise with golf and fishing clubs, members use the facilities and can exclude non-members from them. The members pay for maintenance and improvement and they get the benefit of this.

In the case of the provision of countryside goods like wildlife, landscape or amenity, the problem of collective provision is that the good being produced cannot be restricted to the members of a 'club'. In the jargon, these kinds of countryside good have 'public good' characteristics: they are undepletable and non-excludable. Undepletable means that the consumption of a good by one person does not reduce the consumption available to anyone else (to a large extent), and indeed the use of the term 'consumption' in the context of something like, for instance, enjoyment of a beautiful view, may seem inappropriate. Non-excludability means that once the good has been provided for one consumer, it is not possible to prevent other people from consuming it. As a consequence of these two characteristics, theory suggests that private producers will not be keen to invest in the production of public goods, because their ability to profit (in money or in advantage) from such investment will be reduced.

In practice there are few, if any, *pure* public goods. The critical question is whether it is possible to exclude people from benefiting from something once it has been provided. But even with landscape, exclusion is sometimes possible. Special areas of landscape may lie within a park or a single estate and it may be possible to keep people out. In principle it would be possible to construct a high fence around the area. The problem is often that exclusion is costly and perhaps impractical, rather than being impossible.

To illustrate the problem arising from non-excludability, imagine that there is a public car park near a picnic site where a charge is levied on an honesty basis. The local conservation trust has ageed to maintain the area, provided that the revenue is sufficient to cover its costs. If it fails, the car park will be closed and there will be no access to the picnic site. But from my personal point of view, why should I bother to pay? The site is being paid for anyway and I might reasonably feel that my contribution is unlikely to influence things. This problem is described in the textbooks as the problem of the Free-Rider.

The difficulty is sometimes described in the form of a game called the 'Prisoner's Dilemma'. At its most simple this involves two prisoners. Both prisoners are known to be guilty of a minor crime. But, while they are suspected of a more serious one, the evidence against them for this is not sufficient to produce a conviction. Each one is offered the choice of confessing to the police, giving evidence against the other prisoner. If he does, he will be given a light sentence but it will guarantee the conviction of the other. The question facing the prisoners is to decide whether they should co-operate and hold out against the police or whether they should confess. The two are held separately and so are unable to discuss their position. Table 3.1 shows the length of sentences (in years) which will be given under the possible circumstances.

Table 3.1 The prisoner's dilemma

| | | Prisoner 2 | |
		Confess	Not confess
Prisoner 1	Confess	10, 10	1, 20
	Not confess	20, 1	2, 2

If prisoner 1 decides to confess and 2 does not, the first will get one year's imprisonment and the second twenty years. If both confess, they both get ten years. If neither confesses, they both get two years for the minor crime. It will be seen that individually, each does best by confessing, irrespective of what the other does. However, collectively they would do best not to confess. In this case together they would get four years while the best they can achieve by any other strategy is twenty years. Clearly the pursuit of self-interest leads to an unfortunate solution for the pair of them, collectively. (See Bromley, 1989, for further discussion.)

The game can be extended to describe the relationship between an individual and a collective which has the potential to produce a public good (Hardin, 1982, pp. 25–26). This considers the choices faced by an individual in deciding whether or not to contribute to the provision of a public good.

Assume that there are ten people who have the opportunity to co-operate to provide a public good, and nine of them act together as a collective. The other acts independently. If the good is provided, all will benefit and the value of the benefit will be equal to twice the cost. Every person is asked to make a contribution of £2 towards the cost. The decision of whether to contribute is taken without the knowledge of the decision to be made by the other party. Table 3.2 shows the value of the outcomes in net terms for the person alone first and then for an individual in the collective.

If both parties choose to pay, each person pays £2 and so the total paid in equals £20. This gives a total benefit of £40, and so each person benefits by £4. Thus the net gain to each is £2. If neither pays, the good is not provided and so there are no costs or benefits. If the collective pays and the individual does not, total payment equals £18, and the benefit to each person is £3.60. Each member of the

Table 3.2 Individual and the collective

		Collective	
		Pay	Don't pay
Individual	Pay	£2, £2	−£1.6, £0.4
	Don't pay	£3.6, £1.6	£0, £0

collective pays £2 and so the net gain is £1.60. The individual has no cost but still gets the benefit of £3.60. On the other hand, if the individual pays and the collective does not, total payment equals £2, giving a benefit of £0.40 each, while the individual bears a net cost of £1.60. From the point of view of the individual, the preferred strategy is always not to pay.

The model suggests that people are unlikely to co-operate to produce benefits which will be widely available to others. The rational, self-interested strategy is not to contribute. If others do so, then individuals can take advantage of their efforts for nothing. This is a disappointing result for those interested in the collective provision of public goods. However, the analysis has been extended in various ways which lead towards slightly more optimistic conclusions.

Repeated games and assurance

The analysis so far has only considered a single decision. What happens if the players know that they may have to repeat the game at some future date? Under these circumstances, each player is likely to take account of the possible future behaviour of the other. The question is whether these circumstances will encourage co-operative behaviour. Co-operative action would be in the group's common interest and it may emerge if decision-makers expect that other players will act co-operatively, and if the decision-maker fears that a failure to act co-operatively on his part will lead to retaliatory action by the other players. Thus, once there is a general expectation that players will act co-operatively, this can become the dominant mode of behaviour. However, there must be some way of detecting whether individuals are co-operating or not. It is only possible to take action against defectors if their defection can be identified. Co-operation is thus more likely in small groups where each person's action can be observed by other members of the group.

Imagine a group of farmers each wanting to graze their cattle on an area of common land. They might meet each month to decide how much grass is available and to allocate grazing rights amongst themselves. Each will know what the other is doing and a failure to keep within the agreed limits is likely to lead to being excluded from the group. On the contrary, consider a conservation trust making a collection to pay for the maintenance of an area of land for public access. It would be too expensive to erect a fence around it and to pay someone to collect an entry fee and so anyone can enter the area free. The number of visitors is large and the chance of being recognised as not having paid is minimal. The incentive to co-operate is clearly much less.

Additional motives

People may respond to a request to contribute to an organisation because they value its activities in some less immediate way. They may perhaps not expect to gain any benefit in the short term, but may see some possibility of one in the more distant future. For instance, a person may contribute to a collection for the protection of a scenic area which he or she has never visited, but it may be that he or she has a faint hope of visiting it at some time in the future. Other kinds of future and indirect environmental and amenity value were explored in Chapter 2. In some respects contributions made for these reasons would be self-interested, but in a much less obvious way than is usually evident in spending decisions.

An alternative motivation could be based on some by-product which comes with a donation to an organisation. People may join organisations which provide a public good of some sort in order to obtain a private good which is also offered to members. For instance, trade unions provide a public good in the form of wage bargaining and negotiations with employers for better working conditions.

These are public goods in that they are available to all employees and not just the trade union members. But the union may also sell insurance to its members or entitle its members to receive discounts for particular purchases.

In relation to environmental organisations, it is common for them to offer some private benefits such as a magazine, an educational service, certain unique kinds of consumer products, or preferential access to their properties. It may be this private benefit which motivates members to join, as much as, if not more so, than the wider public benefits pursued by the organisation. Such incentives to join are probably more relevant for the largest national environmental groups such as the National Trust and Royal Society for the Protection of Birds than they are for small organisations who may have few resources with which to produce these kinds of attractive 'services' for members.

A second private incentive may be to do with participation. A contribution to an organisation may make the contributor feel closer to the aims and activities of the organisation. It is a way of·participating in the work of that organisation. Some people participate particularly closely by giving their time and expertise to an organisation. Clearly both environmental and political organisations depend to a large extent on voluntary labour in order to keep them going. Of course, in this as in other things, motivations are likely to be complex. Undertaking voluntary work may be a way of expressing support for a venture which you want to succeed. But it may also be a way of making and meeting friends or it may simply be an enjoyable activity.

There are a number of explanations of why some people choose to contribute, even when it may appear not to be to their own advantage (Hardin, 1982, p. 103). One reason may be for 'moral motivations'. Some people simply adopt the view that certain things are good in a general sense, and that they should therefore be supported. There is a self-interest in this to the extent that their donations may do a little to create the sort of society in which they wish to live, but they expect no immediate return for their contribution. This sort of public-spiritedness is probably an important element in the contributions made to all sorts of charitable causes, including environmental ones.

These kinds of motivation may also reflect some optimism, or conversely some ignorance or misunderstanding on the part of those who contribute. They may believe that the organisation which they support can make a greater contribution to their own quality of life than it in fact does. They may also overestimate the impact which their own personal contribution may have on the overall behaviour and impact of these organisations.

A variety of organisations

The basic theory of collective action suggests many reasons why private organisations are unlikely to provide public goods. As the more restrictive assumptions of the theory are relaxed, then some rationale for private contributions toward public goods provision becomes apparent. In this respect, different organisations are in differing positions. We can think of a range of possible types of organisation which represent collective interest. At the two extremes are the private club and the public charity, and most environmental organisations probably fall somewhere between these two poles.

Some, for instance a local organisation set up to provide access to the local community, will be quite similar to golf clubs in the way in which they operate. But the access which is provided may be available to anyone who wishes to take advantage of it. Other organisations seek to promote the environment in ways which are quite unlikely to be of direct benefit to those who contribute; such as organisations which aim to protect rare species in remote parts of the globe, but contributors may still have some expectation of gaining personally from the organisation's activities. But overall, the most relevant model is of the charity; where, generally speaking, those contributing to a charity do not expect to benefit directly from its actions.

In some cases, members gain directly from the activities of the organisation. In others, members do little more than contribute funds to pay for the organisation. In most cases, members probably feel that they do get some advantage from CART activities, but that the organisation's main objective is to provide a benefit which is enjoyed by the public at large, both now and in the distant future.

Conclusions

Clearly charitable donations and private non-profit organisations have a significant and growing role in modern society. They make an important contribution to the quality of life in a variety of ways. But while it may be difficult to prove, the argument that even these private organisations will fail to provide as much of a public good as it is in the public interest to provide seems clear. This is the theoretical basis for goverment intervention, both in terms of the direct provision of public goods and in state support for those private and voluntary organisations which do so.

In this book we are concerned with one particular kind of private-sector collective provision; CARTs generating environmental benefits through the ownership and management of rural land. We consider the options available to them for the control of land in the next chapter.

Walking dogs along the coast, Start Bay, Devon.
Reproduced by permission of The NT Photo Library

4   The control of rural land

The control of land

To influence land use, governments can introduce regulations or can offer financial incentives to encourage private landowners to take action in the public interest. But private groups who wish to pursue environmental goals need to gain some degree of direct control over land-use. In this chapter we review the range of options which are available and consider the factors which influence the approaches taken by CARTs in practice.

Ownership of land by CARTs

The most common and direct control comes through landownership. Ownership of land involves the ownership of a large number of specific property rights. These include the right to enjoy the benefits of land use, the ability to exclude others from many of these benefits, to protect the land from damage by others, to rent rights out and to sell rights. Owners' rights are never complete: the state generally reserves certain rights, such as the power to compulsorily acquire land in the national interest (e.g. to obtain the land required to build a road). Similarly, rights to develop land are generally held by the state, so that if I want to build a house on my land, I need first to apply to the local authority for planning permission to do so. Rights may also be held by other private individuals, separately from the 'owner', such as the right to shoot game or to prospect for minerals.

The owner's use of land is also constrained by a duty not to inflict undue costs on others. For instance, if I want to undertake a land use which causes excessive noise or noxious fumes, I could be subject to legal action by my neighbours. However, because of the non-market values of land discussed in Chapter 2, in practice landowners regularly take actions which interfere in some way with the value which others gain from their land or which affect other people's quality of life. This is at the centre of the problem of managing the environment and is frequently discussed – see for example Hodge (1995) or Pearce and Turner (1990).

Chapter 1 outlined how the users of agricultural land have introduced changes which have reduced the quality of the environment as experienced by many people. However, the legal system has so far failed to bring the great majority of private landowners to take the costs of these environmental losses fully into account. This has been a major factor leading CARTs to become landowners in order to undertake environmental conservation and enhancement.

Within the limitations outlined above, a CART as an owner of land can choose how its land is to be occupied and managed. By definition, CARTs place particular value on conservation benefits and will give priority to creating them when deciding how to manage their land, even though this may generate little monetary return. As they have to pay the cost of management, they will generally have an incentive to seek out least-cost ways of generating and protecting the conservation values under their particular control. They may need to trade off management costs against conservation gains. This suggests that they will seek out new methods of achieving conservation goals more efficiently and will respond quickly to changes in relative prices and technology.

If trusts are to acquire land on the open market, they usually have to outbid others who place a greater emphasis on maximising profit. The land use which is planned by a CART to promote conservation benefits will rarely generate sufficient financial income to show a positive return on the investment in land acquisition, so it will not generally be able to borrow the necessary funds on a commercial basis. There will be a need for finance from some other source, both to buy the land and to support its subsequent management. Purchasing costs are often raised through an appeal, and/or given by a government agency or other major donor which may in turn lower the effective purchasing price (see Chapter 13). It is also quite common for trusts to acquire land as a gift.

Ownership and tenancy

The owner of land need not also be the occupier. A CART can let out the land to a tenant who takes the day-to-day responsibility for management. This may often be appropriate for a CART which does not have the time or perhaps the expertise to take full responsibility for all aspects of land management. However, as an owner the CART can still exert influence over the tenant's actions. On letting the land, owner and tenant have to make an agreement which can define precisely what each party may and may not do (rights), and what each must and must not do (obligations).

Tenancy agreements on agricultural land usually take a standard form, which has evolved over the years. It is only relatively recently that there have been moves to introduce more flexibility into the choice of agreement between landlord and tenant. Today, where the landlord has particular concerns for the management of the land, as most CARTs will do, it is usually possible for these to be written into a tenancy agreement. Since 1984, legal provision has been made for requirements for conservation on the land to be prescribed in the form of conservation clauses. As we shall see in Chapter 6, the National Trust has been active in introducing such clauses into its tenancy agreements. As we write this book, legislation has been introduced which significantly frees up choices over the form of agreement between landlord and tenant, and some CARTs see considerable potential to use the new business tenancies in their future land management.

A landlord will have less complete control than an owner who manages land in-hand. This may not matter where the CART's desired land use can be predicted with reasonable certainty, and the management requirements written into an agreement. The use of land may need to be fundamentally restricted by the landlord, perhaps only allowing light grazing. In these circumstances it is most likely that land will be let under licence, giving annual grazing rights only. Wherever the use of land let through a tenancy or through a short-term licence is restricted, there may have to be an equivalent reduction in the level of rent or fee paid. Where all commercial uses are effectively prevented by management restrictions, clearly no ordinary tenant would be willing to pay a rent. In fact it might even be necessary for the landlord to pay the tenant to manage the land. The National Trust has suggested that this arrangement may prove necessary in order to keep the uplands in agricultural use, in the future. Indeed there is a sense in which government is already directly paying for a form of land management through headage-payment support to farmers in Less Favoured Areas; since in some instances the value of this subsidy exceeds the level of income made by the farmer. We do not normally think of private landlords as having to pay tenants, but this could well be the case when non-profit-making conservation management is the aim of the landlord (e.g. where the landlord is a CART).

As an option for managing land owned by a CART, a conventional tenancy agreement may be inappropriate wherever the site may need frequent or radical changes of management which could impose substantial costs on the tenant. In such circumstances, the land is more likely to be managed in-hand. Nature reserves, where the conservation interest takes priority and management often needs to be fine-tuned to meet the needs of vulnerable species, are often managed directly by CARTS as owners.

Control without ownership

Direct control of land management does not always depend upon ownership. It is possible for a non-owner to contract with an owner to manage the land in a particular way. Thus, for instance, a CART could make an agreement with a farmer for him or her to maintain parts of the farm for conservation or for public access. In this case, the CART might have to pay the farmer for lost production opportunities or any extra work which might be caused, or, as is more common, the CART may actually organise and resource such land management itself and little money will change hands between owner and CART (see later).

As mentioned in Chapters 1 and 2, the use of management agreements between private organisations is relatively rare, though the approach is widely adopted by national and local government and its agencies. The main hindrance to CARTs making this sort of agreement must be the difficulty of securing regular finance for them – after all, the environmental benefits of management will be public goods which cannot be sold to generate income.

In practice, CARTs are more often at the other end of a management agreement, receiving public money to manage land according to a public agency's environmental guidelines. However, in these cases there is clearly a commonality of objectives, thus both parties may gain from the arrangement.

Covenants on land

One option may offer further prospects for the future. This involves the use of covenants. Strictly, a covenant is any promise contained in a deed, but there are particular forms of covenant which relate to land. Covenants can involve a legally binding agreement to manage an area of land in almost any desired way, and in some circumstances they can continue to affect land even if ownership of that land changes; in lawyers' jargon, such covenants 'run with the land'.

Covenants may be permanent or they can be for a specific, limited time. But any covenant can be varied or discharged by agreement between both parties (who might not be the original parties to the agreement, but who are currently affected by it), even if the covenant was originally intended to be permanent. More detail about covenants in a conservation context is given by Hodge *et al.* (1993)

There are however limitations on the way in which covenants can be made if they are to run with the land. CARTs which already own land can make agreements with the owners of adjacent land in the form of restrictive covenants (i.e. those which limit potential land uses), over the future use of that land. Such covenants can be of value in protecting the value of the CART's land, for instance, by restricting the use of chemicals or land drainage which could affect the CART's land, or in protecting the land-scape setting of an area by preventing development.

CARTs could also create covenants over other areas by buying land and then re-selling some of it but imposing a restrictive covenant upon it as they did so. They would have to retain ownership of some land in order to have the ability to 'take the benefit' of the covenant. Some CARTs regularly use covenants in this way: for example, the Oxford Preservation Trust holds restrictive covenants preventing development on open land around Oxford, where it also owns land.

A few organisations have been given special powers in legislation to enter into and take the benefit of covenants over land which 'run with the land'. Mostly, these are public bodies – including local authorities, English Nature and the Forestry Commission. But, as discussed in Chapter 6, the National Trust is probably the only private organis-ation which has special powers to make restrictive covenants without having to own neighbouring property.

Taking other roles in land management

CARTs frequently take other roles in order to influence land management. A CART can itself be a tenant, it can be directly employed as a manager or, as already mentioned, it can have an agreement with another landholder which allows it to take the responsibility for land management. In these cases, it will have to operate subject to the interests of the landowner. A common reason why CARTs may adopt these kinds of 'subservient' roles is where the owners of the land wish to promote conservation objectives, but for some reason feel that they cannot do this alone. Perhaps the CART may have management expertise which is not available to the owner – this is often the case with privately owned, vulnerable nature reserves. Sometimes owners may not feel they have sufficient local resources and skills, and so may prefer to enlist the local manage-ment skills of an appropriate CART. Such an owner may itself be a national CART, contracting management from another, local CART: the Woodland Trust takes this approach for some of its woodlands. Another common instance where a CART may manage land on contract or lease is where land is neglected by the owner and held only as a capital asset. In such a case, a CART might take on a management role with the consent of the owner, for perhaps a minimal peppercorn rent, if at all.

Long-term manangement: sustainability or dead hand?

There is one further issue about CARTs' control of land which we need to consider here. There is a potential conflict between, on the one hand, a desire to create insitutions to preserve land of high conservation value in its present state by means of legal constraints on management, and, on the other, allowing sufficient flexibility to enable responses to changed circumstances. The control which is established by a CART over land needs to represent an acceptable compromise between the desire for protection, and the need to have the opportunity to introduce appropriate new management when conditions change.

One of the key concepts of sustainability is that the stock of natural capital, our environmental resources, should not be depleted. In the countryside this means resisting further loss of wildlife habitats which have developed over centuries and which we may be unable to re-create. The rationale of a preservationist approach is clear. In order to do as much as they can to guarantee the long-term survival of the countryside, CARTs can be set up and can make binding agreements which prevent undesirable actions from being taken in the future. It is necessary that these arrangements should be strong and difficult to undo so that they have as good a chance as possible of preventing environmental loss. This would certainly seem to be the stuff of sustainability.

But there is another side to this. Lawyers in particular express concern as to the dangers arising from the 'dead hand'. Is it appropriate that those who happen to have considerable wealth at one particular time should have the power to control the uses of that wealth for all time? Wealthy individuals can make bequests and set up trusts specifically so that money should be used for a particular purpose in perpetuity. For instance, a legacy may be used to establish a fund to pay to help the poor in a particular parish or for the care of retired pit ponies. When the legacy is established, it may seem that there will be a permanent need for such a fund. But, of course, the purposes of such a fund can become outdated and so it may be appropriate to redirect the uses of the income from the fund in a way in which the original donor would have been totally unaware.

The same types of concern apply to the protection of the environment. It may seem quite right that we should make lasting arrangements to restrict the way in which particular pieces of land should be used so as to preserve their value. We might, for instance, establish a CART to prevent an area of wetland from being drained and restrict uses to those which are regarded as being sustainable, such as certain sorts of fishing or the production of willow rods for basket making. It would seem quite appropriate and indeed desirable that such a trust should be established to run in perpetuity. Anything less may mean that the protection of the site is incomplete and it may discourage donors from contributing towards the work of the trust.

However, the environment is dynamic, and problems can arise when circumstances change. It might be that changes in economic conditions mean that the only allowable uses are no longer profitable. Thus, using the example given previously, there may be no demand for willow baskets and no interest in fishing in the area, so that the trust no longer has a source of income to maintain the water channels and pumps which are needed to preserve the wetland. If the terms of the trust prevent all other uses, there will be no income available to the trust. And without this income, the wetland could fall into disrepair and its conservation value would be destroyed. There may be an alternative use which could generate an income for the maintenance of the wetland in the future, but a use which was not anticipated when the trust was established. Clearly, it would seem sensible to have drawn up the initial trust deeds to permit the managers to allow alternative uses, but only those which would not under-mine the conservation value of the site.

More fundamentally, it may be that the basic value of the land is damaged in future for reasons beyond the control of the trust – perhaps some chemical contamination or a significant change in climate. In these circumstances, the trust would be left either with its basic function impaired or even without any basic function at all. There needs to be some provision for amending the conditions of a trust in order to respond to new circumstances. But some might argue that to include such conditions when a trust is originally established could imply to others that such changes are acceptable and hence make them more likely.

In sum, these issues remind us that the protection of the environment cannot be achieved simply by prescribing fixed rules which will operate in perpetuity. Environmental management is an active process requiring judgement. Circumstances change, often in ways which cannot be anticipated by the present generation. These things may be critical considerations for those who set up trusts to pursue conservation and amenity, simply because trusts have no fixed lifespan and their obligations are difficult to change. At the end of the day, we must give future generations freedom to respond where changes become necessary, and we can only hope that such changes will be made responsibly.

In this chapter we have considered the ways in which CARTs choose to gain control of land – in our terms, one of their defining characteristics. In the next chapter we outline the extent and range of the CART movement in Britain in practice.

The Punch Bowl, Abergavenny. Reproduced by permission of The Woodland Trust

5 CARTs today

Introduction

Collectively, CARTs have a combined membership of nearly four million (although this double-counts individuals who are members of more than one trust), a staff of some 4500, and a financial turnover (calculated from 1990 accounts) of over £110 million per year. They therefore constitute a significant sector within the UK economy, and particularly within the field of public goods provision. Their total turnover, for instance, was 50 per cent higher than the total expenditures of the Nature Conservancy Council and the Countryside Commissions for England and Wales and Scotland combined, in 1990. The landholdings of CARTs by 1990 were over 1.3 million acres, or around 2.7 per cent of the land area of the UK.

The National Trust dominates these figures, accounting for about half of the total turnover. Its properties cover about 600 000 acres, making it one of the largest landowners in the country, and it has a membership of 2.2 million (the separate National Trust for Scotland controls about 100 000 acres). Also of a significant size is the Royal Society for the Protection of Birds, holding about 230 000 acres. A third major player, operating at both national and local levels, is the Wildlife Trusts Partnership, which brings together the network of local Wildlife Trusts under the umbrella of the Royal Society for Nature Conservation (RSNC). Together the Wildlife Trusts own or manage over 135 000 acres. Altogether, these four large CARTs control the management of over 80 per cent of the land held by CARTs in the UK.

In addition, there is a significant and growing number of local and national organisations which operate as CARTs.

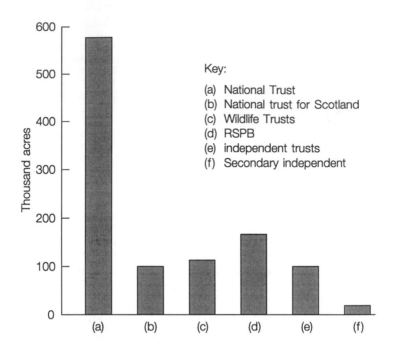

Figure 5.1 Land ownership by CARTs, 1991

In this book, we refer to these as 'independent CARTs'. We have identified some 122 such CARTs which together own or have assumed long-term management responsibility for over 125 000 acres of open land in the British Isles and we summarise their characteristics in the remainder of this chapter. The pattern of land ownership is shown in Figure 5.1.

Although RSPB, National Trust and RSNC date from the late 19th century, by far the majority of the smaller and largely unfederated CARTs are young organisations – they appear very much a phenomenon of the 1970s to 1990s. The age distribution of the independent trusts is illustrated in Figure 5.2 as at 1991. The mean age is 16 years and even this is a little misleading in that the age distribution is heavily skewed, so that most trusts are younger. The median age is 9 years and modal age only 2.5 years.

The recent growth in the influence of CARTs as land-holders is further indicated by the growth in their combined landholding. The land held by independent CARTs has more than doubled since 1985 – in 1991 alone,

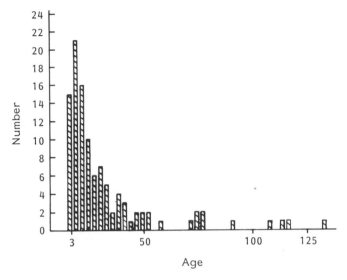

Figure 5.2   Age distribution of independent CARTs

several thousand acres of land in the British Isles newly came into the ownership and management of these trusts. The rapid growth in the land held by the independent trusts is illustrated in Figure 5.3. The landholdings of the National Trust, RSPB and Wildlife Trusts have also continued to grow steadily in recent years.

Aims and objectives

Whilst all of these organisations meet the definition of a CART which we outlined in the Introduction to this book, there are marked differences in their individual strategies. These give an indication of the wide range of their pursuits and throw light upon the reasons why such organisations have come into being. On the basis of these differences, several more or less distinct types of CART can be described. Table 5.1 sets out a brief characterisation of CARTs according to their principal objectives, illustrating how some of the independent trusts may be grouped and related to the larger national CARTs.

Firstly, there are those trusts whose very existence is for the pursuit of environmental conservation, amenity and

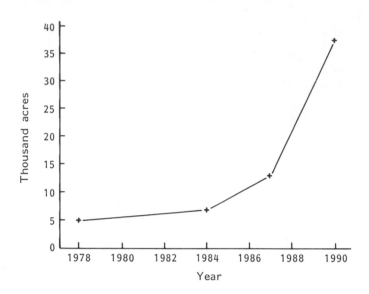

Figure 5.3 Growth of independent CARTs' landholdings

heritage, and for whom land management is either a central means to these ends, or a by-product of them. There are at least 124 such 'primary trusts' currently operating in the UK, and it is these that are the central focus of our study. They can be roughly grouped according to which of the three objectives dominates their management strategy (as indicated in the table): conservation, amenity or heritage.

Primary conservation trusts are those with particular interest in the conservation of Britain's native flora and fauna. The 47 Wildlife Trusts, and the RSPB, are typical of this category, but there are a significant number of others, including Butterfly Conservation, the British Herpetological Society (frogs and related species), Elmley Conservation Trust (preserving a wetland area in Kent, a Ramsar site), the Wildfowl and Wetlands Trust, the Meadows and Pasturelands Trust (preserving grasslands in one area of Dorset) and the John Muir Trust (mainly preserving upland habitats).

The landholdings of primary conservation CARTs are mainly remnants of the semi-natural habitats which once covered large areas of the UK: ancient woodlands, marshes

Table 5.1 Types of CART

Primary conservation CARTs – those for whom nature conservation is their main role, who buy or manage land as nature reserves

e.g. *Wildlife Trusts, RSPB, Elmley Conservation Trust, Otter Trust, Butterfly Conservation, British Herpetological Society*

Primary amenity and recreation CARTs – groups for whom the ability to provide public recreation and amenity sites is the main reason for acquisition or management

e.g. *Buchan Countryside Group, Bryson House Better Belfast Project, Magog Trust, Groundwork Trusts, Shetland Amenity Trust, Shenley Park Trust*

Primary heritage CARTs – those for whom the heritage value of land and landscapes are the main reason for acquiring and managing sites

e.g. *National Trust, Landmark Trust, Painshill Park Trust, Welsh Water Elan Trust, Oxford Preservation Trust*

Secondary CARTs – largely non-commercial groups whose objectives are mainly elsewhere but whose management of open land follows the same principles as CARTs

e.g. *Educational trusts with environmental emphases (Commonwork, Bridge Trust, Camphill Trusts, Findhorn)*

Recreation groups with 'reserves' or conservation areas (mountaineering groups, wildfowling societies, railway/canal trusts)

and fens, lowland meadows and grassland, upland heaths and bogs. Their main objective in holding land is to preserve these areas intact, as viable ecological systems. Acquisition of land by the trust is therefore often achieved when there arises an immediate threat to a valued habitat, for example from building or infrastructure development, quarrying, agricultural improvement or inappropriate changes in management. Some primary conservation trusts are also involved in re-creating traditional habitats on former agricultural or industrial land. The Countryside Restoration Trust, for example, has been set up to rehabilitate over-intensified farmland. Its aim is to show that profitable farming, attractive countryside and abundant wildlife can co-exist. This is to be demonstrated by purchasing

intensively farmed land and rehabilitating it for wildlife. In
Scotland, the Will Trust aims to re-create Caledonian pine
forest on its land by reducing deer numbers to promote
natural regeneration and by planting suitable species where
regeneration is not possible. For the species-orientated conservation trusts such as Butterfly Conservation, habitat recreation may go hand-in-hand with the reintroduction of
species into areas where they have become extinct.

Primary amenity and recreation trusts, the second type,
are mainly groups with a central interest in preserving or
improving public access to open spaces in their area.
Although less nature-conservation-based than primary
conservation trusts, they often acquire semi-natural habitats and landscapes and manage them in traditional ways
which will improve and maintain these characteristics.
However, many of their site management practices involve
making particular provision for aesthetic or recreation-
durable management; for instance creating public paths,
lawns and picnic areas. Examples of this type of trust
would include those Groundwork Trusts who hold open
land (some Groundwork Trusts do not yet hold land), the
Buchan Countryside Group, Oxford Preservation Trust,
Shetland Amenity Trust, and Shenley Park Trust.

Primary heritage trusts are those whose primary emphasis
is upon tradition above all else – preserving what are seen
as the 'best' elements in past landscapes and the heritage of
the British countryside. Such an objective brings together
historians, archaeologists and private estate-owners, all of
whom value particular elements in the countryside which
are the outcome of former human institutions. Their
interest may lie mainly in non-living 'monuments' – landscape features (e.g. Cambridge Preservation Society,
Selborne Society, Landmark Trust) – or it may equally be
in preserving social and community relations; for example,
a village community's working relationship with a historic
estate (e.g. the Guiting Manor and Wadenhoe Trusts). The
National Trust, in its post-war period of development at
least, could be considered the largest primary heritage trust
in the UK, although within its estates it now pursues all
three of the broad objectives (conservation, amenity and

heritage). Similar, though at a smaller scale, are the private land trusts which are often established to maintain existing estates and communities intact.

None of these types of CART are mutually exclusive: many individual groups embody aspects of more than one type and there are examples of all possible permutations and combinations of these three types. But the classification forms a useful reference point for examining the development and current behaviour of primary CARTs.

Secondary trusts. As well as the trusts which are clearly CARTs 'by design', there are a number of related organisations managing land with similar non-commercial objectives and in very similar ways. These kinds of group can be termed secondary CARTs, divided along similar lines to the divisions drawn for the primary CARTs. Prominent among these organisations are:

(a) 'environmentally minded' railway and canal preservation societies or trusts, and a range of voluntary amenity societies with small parkland areas which are secondary to their wider management responsibilities;
(b) educational establishments for whom environmentally sensitive land management is an integral part of their philosophy and operations;
(c) public and private partnerships where private landowners or local authorities offer areas of their land for conservation, amenity and/or recreation to the general public, in partnership with voluntary or charitable organisations.

Railway and canal trusts often own areas of open land (towpaths, track margins, station and lock surroundings) which they have chosen to manage for general public benefit and environmental improvement, creating wildlife areas and maintaining and improving footpaths. Their transport activities may be operated on a commercial or a charitable basis, but they do not manage their open land for income generation.

Other voluntary organisations originally formed for broader recreational or charitable purposes now manage some land for wildlife or amenity, simply as a sideline. Examples would include a number of City Farms, the

Cairngorm Club and British Mountaineering Council, and several Wildfowlers Clubs. For these, their main purpose is the provision of educational or recreational benefits for user groups, while the provision of public environmental benefit through landholding is a secondary consideration.

Educational institutions' teaching and philosophy may involve pursuing CART-style land management objectives. A number of communities for the mentally or physically handicapped use organic farming and/or wildlife gardening on their land as part of their overall programme of activities. These kinds of land management are seen as beneficial to the environment of the community and also of direct use to them because of the occupational training thus afforded. Examples are the Peter Selwood Trust (Minstead Project) and Camphill villages. Other educational organisations' reason for existence is specifically to teach and promote aspects of conservation or environmental awareness. For these, the management of land serves as both model and teaching area for the environmental techniques and interests they promote. However, because their main purpose is to promote these things elsewhere, landholding is a secondary issue. These groups are very diverse, with examples including Commonwork, Dartington and the Findhorn Foundation (alternative lifestyles), Parnham and Middlewood Trusts (traditional woodland industry), Edward James Foundation (rural arts and crafts) and the Field Studies Council (environmental studies).

Public–private environmental partnerships include some made between private estates and local countryside charities, and others between industrial companies with open land, local authorities and/or local environmental charities. In all cases, landowners agree to allow CART-style management of their land by others, either because income generation from it is unimportant to them, or because this is seen as compatible with their wider use of the land. Examples of such partnerships include the Countryside Education Trust and the Beaulieu Estate, the Penwith Peninsula Project, Greenspace, and Taf and Cleddau Rural Initiative.

The numbers of independent CARTs which we have identified in our survey in the various categories are set out in Table 5.2. There are without doubt many that we

Table 5.2 Categories of independent CART traced in survey

	Primary CARTs		Secondary CARTs	
	No.	%	No.	%
Conservation	21	17	10	8
Amenity/recreation	38	31	20	16
Heritage	12	10	1	1
Education			20	17
Totals	71	58	51	42

have failed to discover during the period of study, as well as a steady stream of new CARTs being established. However, none of those trusts with whom we were in contact in 1995 had ceased to operate.

Origins, organisation and operation

Founding interests and development of CARTs

CARTs represent a diverse range of organisations. A major influence upon these differences is the means of each organisation's formation, whether it has been from local or from 'outside' bodies and whether from traditionally landowning or traditionally landless interests. Many of the older CARTs were formed by private landowners or small groups of philanthropic individuals with a particular interest in providing public goods. The Selborne Society, Oxford Preservation Trust and Cambridge Preservation Society would be examples of this kind of trust.

A 'public-spirited' individual landowner may decide to use some or all of his or her own land to establish a CART. That landowner may be a large or powerful landlord but this is not exclusively the case: there are several examples of people with only a few acres of land putting it into an individual CART. Such landowners may, of course, choose to donate their land to an existing organisation, particularly the National Trust. But for various reasons some choose to establish an independent arrangement. CARTs formed by private landowners may seek to protect and enhance environments valued by relatively powerless local

interests, or to represent the long-term interest of a relatively powerful local individual or family, or even to serve
as a collective structure representing both interests simultaneously.

CART formation by otherwise landless groups of people
appears to be less common than the formation of CARTs
by public-sector bodies 'in the interest' of such groups, but
we have traced a number of examples of the first type. In
these cases, the CART often comes into being because local
people who value a particular privately-owned site see that
value threatened by encroaching development and they
come together to raise the funds and the skills to acquire
management control of the site in order to preserve its
current status. They may value the site for nature conservation, amenity or heritage, but starting from scratch
like this without significant capital assets, the group's
arguments must be sufficiently convincing to attract
funding and support from a variety of sources. The Buchan
Countryside Group would be a representative example of
this kind of CART.

A particular feature of the growth of CARTs in the last
ten to fifteen years has been CART formation through
public-sector bodies – local government or government
quango. The Groundwork initiative is an obvious example
of this kind of CART formation. Groundwork was
originally set up through the initiative of the Countryside
Commission. The Commission provided funding and a
central support body for the establishment of local
environmental improvement and amenity trusts around
the country, developed in close financial partnership with
local authorities. Today, a central Groundwork Foundation acts as 'enabler' to bring local trusts into being,
resourcing staff appointments and encouraging them to
develop their operations in partnership with local government and local industry. It is intended that the local trusts
gradually integrate sufficiently into local communities and
local economies to become self-supporting within a few
years. However, the initial underpinning by Countryside
Commission and local authorities, and the continued
support of Groundwork HQ by the Department of the
Environment, have been crucial factors in the development of the Groundwork Trust network across England
and Wales.

Another kind of public formation of CARTs occurs when

a public authority provides land and other assets to set up a fully-independent conservation or amenity trust to look after the land involved. New Town Development Corporations (Milton Keynes and Telford), Water Authorities and District Councils have all been involved in forming CARTs in this way around Britain.

Internal organisation and the public interest

All the primary CARTs traced in our survey were explicitly established to serve the public interest in some way. However it is evident that they have taken widely differing views as to how the public interest can best be met through their management structures and decision-making procedures. At one end of the spectrum some CARTs operate democratic systems for decision-making and control, in which to play a part any individual merely has to join the club and exercise their right to vote. This is often the case for grassroots trusts which are established in response to an environmental threat.

At the other end some CARTs adopt a more philanthropic position, such that the public interest is intended to be represented through a number of nominating bodies or individuals who together form a board of management. Often the individuals or organisations which were instrumental in the establishiment of a CART retain a say in its development by being able to appoint a trustee to the board. Typically, this applies to CARTs formed through the public sector, or to private land trusts which are created from a family estate where the family retains some influence.

CARTs may be run by directly-elected or privately-appointed individuals, and be with or without professional staff. Many, but by no means all, have a board of non-salaried trustees who make all salaried staff appointments. An estimated 25 of the 71 primary independent CARTs traced in this survey elect their trustees or council of management democratically from a subscribing membership (one-member, one-vote). Of the other 46, 38 have no subscribing membership, and all have trustees and/or management councils appointed, elected or otherwise chosen by bodies named in the original Trust Charter. This variability exists among all three types of primary CART and across the range from public-origin to private-origin CARTs.

Although the existence of specific representatives (members or board) in the management of a trust may be the most obvious way in which the public interest is maintained within CART activity, it is not the only option. Some of the CARTs with wholly nominated trustees stress the importance of grassroots community links in shaping their activities. For these CARTs it is not their members who influence decision-making, but the members of the parishes, villages and towns where sites are located that do this, through jointly planned and executed management operations. The Woodland Trust's Community Woodlands initiative was based upon this approach to serving the public interest, and several other examples have been traced.

CART activity is influenced, often quite strongly, through grant-aid and other assistance from government Departments and agencies representing the public interest. This is a further way in which the public interest can shape CART activities.

Operation

The main elements of CART action involve raising funds, managing land and sharing the benefits. We will consider the details of the finance of CARTs in later chapters, but here we should outline the different types of source which are common. The available options depend in part upon the way in which a CART is constituted. Some are established with sufficient assets, some sort of endowment, to generate income for the management of property, although few can cover all costs in this way. Those trusts which have a membership usually charge a membership fee, although this is often relatively modest in comparison with membership fees charged by private clubs for golf or squash. This reflects the limited benefits which members get from direct use of the CARTs assets. Clearly many CARTs also depend upon donations from both private individuals and from private firms and corporations. As we will see, the government is also an important source of funds both for the purchase of assets and to cover day-to-day management costs. This includes both grants provided directly and tax relief, which is in effect an indirect contribution from taxpayers. Finally, many organisations develop commercial activities to raise funds. They may operate shops or do paid work for others, often applying the skills they have developed in the management of their own land.

Land management and other CART operations are undertaken by a variety of labour sources. Labour may be voluntary, or professional, or a mixture of both. Collectively, the primary independent trusts employed an estimated 450–600 salaried staff in 1991, but the staff complement of individual trusts ranged from at least nine trusts with no paid employees to a small number with over 15 staff each. Almost all fulltime staff posts will be either professional or administrative – people who work from the trust's offices – although some of the largest trusts also employ fulltime professional reserves staff working directly on land management. The remainder of trusts use labour which is not 'in-house' for most of their site management tasks.

Generally speaking, it is those CARTs that have a large and enthusiastic subscribing membership and/or a small professional staff which are most likely to use voluntary labour for site management, although in some areas, non-membership trusts also get help in this way from local Conservation Volunteers. Other CARTs will tend to employ professional contractors for major site work, and occasionally these contractors work for less than their usual commercial rates (sometimes work is donated free).

But concentrating upon practical land management would tend to understate the value of voluntary input to CARTs' management overall. Open land areas often need to be biologically monitored, surveyed, conveyanced, or just 'kept an eye on'. And most trusts must publish a full set of accounts each year. In these functions many CARTs rely heavily upon people who are willing to give their time and professional expertise voluntarily. These are often the most active members and/or financial supporters of CARTs. And many elected and appointed council members of CARTs are highly qualified people with skills which they place freely at the disposal of the trust.

The management of land and the other activities of CARTs give rise to a range of benefits. While they aim to meet public demand, it is not the case that all benefits are always shared evenly. Where there is a trust membership, members usually enjoy some sorts of privilege, such as free access to sites where non-members must pay. This is one important attraction of National Trust membership. However, in other cases access to sites is equally available to everybody. Other advantages of membership may include receipt of a newsletter, information on tours and events and the opportunity to participate in these or in voluntary work, or discounts on a wide range of items sold at trust shops, or through mail-order facilities.

In the next part of the book we focus our attention on particular types of CART. Firstly we examine the largest organisations: the National Trusts, the Royal Society for the Protection of Birds and the Wildlife Trusts. We then deal with independent CARTs, grouped in relation to their origins. Some trusts have been set up in order to manage an established area of land with conservation interest. Some of these were previously private estates, others control land which had been in the possession of the public sector. Some groups have been formed in response to an environmental threat, often at a local scale, others have come together to enhance degraded areas and create new environmental value. We cover all these aspects.

Part 2:
Trusts in action

View of Temple of Neptune, Sheringham Park. Reproduced by permission of The NT Photo Library

Conserving tradition: the National Trusts

Introduction

The National Trust for England, Wales and Northern Ireland holds a central position in the nation's efforts to protect its heritage. It operates at a vast scale, with a membership of over two million. Amongst all charities in the UK, it typically has the greatest voluntary and total income, and it is the second largest landowner after the Crown. It owns many of the nation's special places and buildings. It is also held to have close connections with the centres of power and influence; with some justification, many people are unclear as to whether the Trust should be regarded as a private organisation or a government agency. It is in reality a wholly independent, private charity. And yet its origins can be attributed to the initiative of a small group of individuals who had vision, and the persistence and the ability to translate this into reality.

The beginnings of the National Trust

As described in Chapter 1, a number of organisations were established in the mid-19th century to resist some of the consequences of unplanned and insensitive development. Notable amongst these were the Commons Preservation Society (1865), the first preservation organisation, and the Society for the Protection of Ancient Buildings (1877). The spread of the railways, a boom in housing and, until 1870, a highly profitable agriculture raised the value of land for development and hence the pressures for the enclosure of the remaining commons. This led to a series of encounters, primarily in the area around London, between the Lords of the Manor who claimed rights to enclose common and forest land and the Commons Preservation Society which was established to resist them.

Three people are generally thought of as the founders of the National Trust: Octavia Hill, Robert Hunter and Hardwicke Rawnsley. The conflict over the development of Hampstead Heath in 1884 brought two of the future founders together, particularly through the activities of the Commons Preservation Society: Robert Hunter, a solicitor who had taken the prime role in legal actions to protect the commons, and Octavia Hill, who had been active in promoting the improvement of housing conditions and the provision of small areas of open space. They were both members of a committee which was established to buy land to increase the area of the Heath.

The third of the founders of the Trust, Canon Hardwicke Rawnsley, was actively opposing developments in the Lake District. He was instrumental in founding the Lake District Defence Society in 1883. It was a conflict in the Lake District in 1885 which brought the three together. Landowners closed a footpath, in response to which Rawnsley organised a mass action, uprooting the barriers which had prevented access. When the owners issued writs for trespass, Rawnsley sought the support of the Commons Preservation Society in defending the action.

Gaze (1988) argues strongly for the inclusion of a fourth founder, the Duke of Westminster. He was also a member of the committee established to buy land on Hampstead Heath and his influence with a variety of charitable activities was important in the early establishment of the National Trust. He was its first president.

The proposed sale of Lodore Falls, south of Keswick, threatening its future protection, provided the stimulus for a more direct form of action. Octavia Hill proposed a public trust and Robert Hunter put forward a proposed framework based on that used by the Trustees of Public Reservations in Massachusetts. Octavia Hill had suggested that it should be called 'The Commons and Gardens Trust for accepting, holding and purchasing open spaces for the people in town and country' (Legg, 1990–91). Robert Hunter's suggestion for 'The National Trust' was the one chosen.

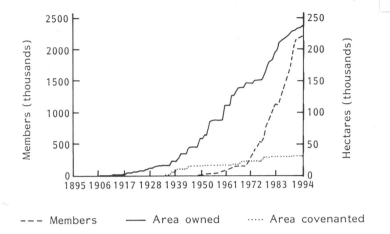

Figure 6.1 Membership and land owned and covenanted by the National Trust

The first public meeting was held in July 1894 and the National Trust for Places of Historic Interest or Natural Beauty was formally registered on 12 January 1895. The latter date has been chosen to mark its beginning, the centenary of which has been celebrated in 1995. This has seen a variety of coverage of the Trust's history and operations, including books by Jenkins and James (1994), describing the Trust's history and its wider context, and Weideger (1994) offering a more critical treatment of the Trust's style and activities.

The growth in membership and land ownership over the hundred-year period is shown in Figure 6.1. The area owned grew relatively slowly initially; after twenty years the Trust owned only 6000 acres. The rate of growth increased during the Second World War and has been maintained since then. The growth in membership began even more slowly. Membership reached 725 in 1914 but fell back during the First World War, only overtaking this figure in 1921. Membership also took off after the Second World War. However, over the whole period, the *rate* of increase in growth has been remarkably constant; it has been exponential with troughs between 1915 and 1925, 1939 and 1945 and briefly in the late 1960s. The data for the past couple of years may suggest another trough in the mid-1990s.

Table 6.1 National Trust sites

	% by area
Hill farming	19
Lowland farming	23
Woodland	6
Parks and gardens	3
Commons	20
Coast	17
Other	12

The estate of the National Trust

Over the years, the Trust has assembled a vast estate. In 1994, it owned 591 000 acres and held a further 79 000 acres under covenant. This comprised a variety of types and included property throughout the country. A break-down of sites by land use in 1988 is given in Table 6.1.

The table shows that the types of land which may be most familiar to visitors, the gardens and coastline, are not wholly representative of the overall holdings of the Trust. A substantial component of these is agricultural land. Some of this land, especially in the uplands, was acquired in order to protect particular landscape values but some, too, represents 'ordinary' farmland, which has importance more as a financial investment to generate a return than as a holding of environmental or historical significance to be preserved. However, even here land acquired historically as part of an endowment to generate maintenance funds for a historic house has subsequently acquired significance for its environmental quality in its own right. And the National Trust is under pressure to maintain all of its properties to high environmental standards.

The Trust owns considerable areas of land of high nature conservation value: 26 National Nature Reserves, 51 nature reserves leased to County Wildlife Trusts, all or part of 466 Sites of Special Scientific Interest in England and Wales (28 per cent of National Trust land), and five Areas of Special Scientific Interest in Northern Ireland. On the landscape side, there are 355 properties that lie within

Areas of Outstanding Natural Beauty. Historic value is also important – there are some 40 000 archaeological sites in the Trust's care. The natural assets held by the Trust are discussed further by Hearn (1994).

The powers of the Trust

The special legal position of the Trust has been established by a number of Acts of Parliament. The first of these in 1907 specified its public interest responsibilities in the objective of promoting 'the permanent preservation for the benefit of the nation of lands and tenements (including buildings) of beauty or historic interest and as regards lands for the preservation (so far as practicable) of their natural aspect features and animal and plant life'. In pursuit of this the Trust was given special powers to hold land inalienably. Under the Act, property declared inalienable may not be disposed of by the Trust and may only be acquired compulsorily by government by consent of Parliament under a Special Parliamentary Procedure which requires the approval of both Houses. The Trust applies this power to that part of an estate which is both of the highest landscape and historic quality, and which is essential to the preservation of the core of the property and its surroundings (National Trust, 1983). This places the Trust in an advantageous position with respect to potential donors who seek reassurance that property given will be preserved in perpetuity.

The Trust also has unique powers, under the 1937 National Trust Act, to enter into binding covenants with the owners of land to restrict the use of that land, without it having to own adjacent land (as would be a requirement for all other private landowners). As described in Chapter 4, this gives it a special ability to control the way in which land is used and developed. However, covenanted land has less protection than land declared inalienable in that it remains potentially subject to compulsory purchase by normal methods.

The Trust currently holds about 400 separate and binding covenants over approximately 80 000 acres of open land, scattered in many locations. The clauses of these covenants generally restrict major land-use changes on a

site such as development, woodland clearance, the ploughing of permanent pastures, draining of wetlands or uplands, improvement of moorland, filling in of ponds or
watercourses or the removal of hedgebanks or walls. The
vast majority of these covenants (an estimated 70 per cent
by number) have been given to the Trust by the landowner
during his or her lifetime.

Site acquisition

The first acquisition of open space by the National Trust
was in the form of a donation of a small area of rocky cliff
overlooking Cardigan Bay. The first building, the Old
Clergy House in Alfriston, Sussex, was purchased by the
Trust for £10 in 1896. This immediately posed what probably remains the major problem faced by the Trust, that of
raising funds for the repair and maintenance of property.
   These acquisitions were followed by a variety of others
across the country, leading the founders to set up a committee structure to administer the organisation and the
management of its holdings. The Trust has extremely
broad objectives; the permanent preservation of lands and
buildings, with no prescription as to what sorts should be
targeted. And the initial acquisitions of the Trust reflect
this. By 1907, the time of the National Trust Act, properties
consisted of some areas of coast, several areas of open hill
land and common land, a few relatively modest houses, a
number of monuments and two areas of fenland, and only
one substantial house.
   The Trust has continued to acquire properties of all sorts
across the country. The early involvement in the Lake
District has continued and now the Trust owns more than
one-quarter of the area of the Lake District National Park.
The management of land in the Lake District is considered
later in the chapter. There are also large holdings in other
upland areas, for instance the Trust also owns over 12 per
cent of the Peak District National Park. However, over the
years two types of acquisition have become of particular
importance. They have been acquired through more
focused schemes run by the Trust: the Country Houses
Scheme and Enterprise Neptune, purchasing land along the
coast. We examine these acquisitions in more detail below.

The Country Houses Scheme

Despite its early focus on open space and small buildings, the Trust has come to be particularly associated with the ownership and protection of country houses. This aspect developed in the 1930s. The forces which were leading to the decline of the great estates meant that it was becoming increasingly difficult for private owners to generate the funds needed for the upkeep of the large country house and its contents, which formed the hub of an estate. The increasing level of death duties was an important factor, rising from 8 per cent in 1904 to 15 per cent in 1914 and then gradually to 50 per cent by 1930 (Gaze, 1988). There were also pressures from depressed agricultural rents and rising prices (Drury, 1987).

An early achievement was the exemption in the 1931 Finance Act from death duty for property given to the Trust to be held inalienably. Building on this, the Trust established the Country Houses Scheme. This enabled an owner of a house to donate it, together with an endowment in the form of land or investments, to the Trust. In return, the Trust would typically permit the donor and heirs to continue in occupation rent-free for two generations, and thereafter at a market rent. The detailed arrangements have varied from case to case, being laid down in a Memorandum of Wishes. The house would be declared inalienable and so could not be sold or mortgaged. It would also thus not be liable for death duty. These arrangements were permitted through further legislation. The National Trust Act 1937 extended the general purposes of the Trust to include the preservation of buildings and their contents and allowed the National Trust to hold land or buildings as an investment to generate funds for the support of property held for preservation. A futher complication was addressed in the National Trust Act 1939, arising from the complex legal settlements which had been used in order to protect such estates from dismemberment. These settlements in effect placed the estate in trust and made the present occupant a lifetime tenant of the estate. The 1939 Act gave powers to vest settled lands in the Trust.

These arrangements have in succeeding decades brought over 110 country houses into the ownership of the Trust, so that they now represent perhaps the major type of asset.

The highest rate of acquisition was in the 1940s and 1950s, when 64 houses were acquired. Since then the rate has slowed, and now averages a little over one house per year. However, in some respects these houses also represent the Trust's major liability; 44 per cent of the Trust's direct expenditure is spent on large houses (Hearn, 1994). Some would argue that this commitment has unduly limited the capacity of the Trust to participate in other forms of conservation.

The emphasis in acquiring estates has been, and still remains, to maintain the house and contents complete, and retain a working estate and not allow it to become a museum. Lees-Milne (1992), who was responsible for the Scheme in its early years, comments that the Trust saw itself as 'assuming the mantle, in so far as an institution could do such a thing, of the squire . . . it soldiered ahead in its amateur way whilst striving to preserve the status quo and displaying the fruits thereof as often as it thought fit to an appreciative public'. Today the approach depends much more upon professionals dealing with the complex issues of conserving houses and contents and managing the associated estates. But the continued occupation of the house by an established family remains an important objective. There is in this arrangement a need to find a balance between the interests of the donors and those of the Trust and its membership. It has been a source of criticism over the years that the Trust has tended to treat its donors rather generously and paid insufficient attention to its membership, particularly in terms of limits placed on the opening hours of many houses.

Trust ownership of country houses invariably implies some changes. Provision has to be made for the public, and associated with this there is often a shop, café or other facilities. There are a few properties where public access is not allowed, where the change is clearly less dramatic. But even so, traditional uses for the estates have often become increasingly costly to maintain, and the Trust faces the difficult issue as to what extent new uses should be allowed, when this means changing the character of the property. But of course the estates never were static: some changes may even represent moves back to an earlier use, for instance it may be possible to reintroduce a deer park or other historic feature as a visitor attraction. Again, conservation involves judgement. It will generally not be appropriate, or even possible, to preserve estates in the form which they happened to take at one particular historic period. It is necessary to allow estates to evolve in response to a changing social and financial environment, as they would no doubt have changed under the continued management of their previous family ownership.

Not all Trust properties are large country houses, however – cottages and small but interesting examples of townhouses have also been acquired over the years. In 1993 the Trust opened its first semi-detached house in Worksop, Nottinghamshire. Built in 1905, the contents have hardly changed since the 1930s.

Enterprise Neptune

The second major element of Trust action referred to above has been to protect the coastline. This was also a relatively early aim; indeed, as noted above, the first open space acquired by the Trust was on the Welsh coast. Between the wars, there was concern about damage to coastal areas arising from speculative development and a lack of planning control. Today, despite planning laws, threats continue: from housing, from new roads, from development associated with the use of mineral and energy resources, both on-shore and off-shore, from caravan sites and marinas, from fish farming and from general congestion due to tourism.

In the 1930s, proposals were made, stimulated by George Trevelyan, to acquire stretches of coastline and other property which were thought to be at risk from development, but in advance of any specific development proposal (Gaze, 1988). Until this time appeals had tended to be responsive. Early acquisition required a more flexible form of funding and an element of forward planning, which was undertaken in 1931, in anticipation of a fund being established by the Pilgrim Trust which was to be used for the purchase of land in advance of the threat of development. Amongst areas to be targeted were the Pembrokeshire coast, the Dover cliffs and Seven Sisters in Sussex. While in the event the funding did not materialise as had been hoped, the exercise did establish the principle of a 'forward policy'.

In 1965, an appeal 'Enterprise Neptune' was launched

for the protection of the coast. This was based on three aims (Gaze, 1988):

(a) to focus public attention on the problem of coastal preservation;
(b) to acquire control over coastal land deemed most worthy of preservation either by gift or purchase of the freehold, or of restrictive covenants;
(c) to improve and maintain the Trust's existing coastal properties and any later acquired.

In preparing for the campaign, the Trust set up local committees, including local landowners and planning officials, in order to maintain contacts between the Trust and local landowners and to review priorities and pro-posals. In the early stages of the campaign, the government announced that it would make £250 000 available to be used for specific acquisitions. The first purchase was Whitford Burrows, a 670-acre peninsula in Glamorgan, and other acquisitions quickly followed in many parts of the country.

Enterprise Neptune was launched with the objective of securing for the Trust 1000 miles of coastline of out-standing beauty. This represents the only area where the Trust actively campaigns to acquire property. The half-way mark was reached in 1988 in the purchase from British Coal of beach at Easington in Durham for the sum of £1. While not obviously an area of 'outstanding beauty', as would be accepted for the Golden Cap estate in Dorset or the Seven Sisters in Sussex, it includes some important habitats and indicates the wider criteria applied in site acquisition. By 1994 the Trust had acquired 550 miles of coastline, covering 120 000 acres of coastal land and rep-resenting nearly 18 per cent of the total length of coastline in England, Wales and Northern Ireland.

While stretches of the coast are the subject of a variety of designations, such as Heritage Coasts or Sites of Special Scientific Interest, ownership by the Trust gives far greater control. Notably, it is possible to regulate developments which would generally be permitted under planning regulations, such as short-term campsites and the levels of access which are permitted to sensitive areas. However, threats remain which are beyond the Trust's control, such as pollution of the sea or changes in the sea level. Such

factors depend upon national and often internationa
operation for environmental control.

Acquisition and management objectives

The Trust exercises strict control over the properties which
it is prepared to acquire. They need to reflect the objectives
which the Trust is given by statute and to avoid individual
properties becoming an undue burden on Trust finances.
The criteria have been summarised in the 1992 Annual
Report.

1. The property must be of national importance because
    of its natural beauty, historic interest or nature
    conservation value, or of local importance because of
    the protection it would afford to a property already
    held for preservation.
2. The property must provide benefit for the nation,
    which will usually include public access.
3. The property must be in danger of deterioration if it is
    not acquired by the Trust, or of inappropriate alter-
    ation or of development that would harm its character
    or environment.
4. The property must be, and be expected to remain,
    financially self-supporting.
    And, additionally,
5. The Trust should be the appropriate owner.

The criteria for acquiring covenants are similar to those
relating to property more generally. Alienable land may be
sold subject to covenants where there is landscape or
architectural importance which the Trust wishes to see
protected in order to protect a view from inalienable
property, or to protect the value of land or buildings.

The Trust is the landlord of some 1200 farms leased to
tenants, with and without buildings. A financial return is
an important objective for the management of this land.
However, in the late 1970s the Trust faced criticism from
other conservation groups that it did not take its conservation duties seriously enough on its agricultural
estates. Many estates had suffered from the agricultural
improvement which had been encouraged by pressures to

increase production during and after the last war. In response to this, the Trust initiated biological surveys of its properties (undertaken by the Biological Survey Team) and virtually all properties had been surveyed by 1988. The Trust is making efforts to improve conservation management of all the land in its ownership. On its large area of tenanted farmland, much of which is part of country house estates, the Trust has gradually introduced conservation clauses into its tenancy agreements. And there have been other interesting developments: for example, the park at Hardwick Hall in Derbyshire which had been damaged by dairy farming, is now stocked with Longhorn cattle, Whiteface Woodland sheep and Tamworth pigs, all of which have local historical associations with the area (Gaze, 1988). The collection of rare breeds at Wimpole Hall Home Farm in Cambridgeshire is an entirely new enterprise which nonetheless has conservation objectives.

Surveys were also conducted of landscape and of archaeological sites. The information collected allowed the Trust to be much more precise about the conservation goals for managing its agricultural land. As we mentioned in Chapter 4, the strategy of writing conservation clauses into tenancy agreements was introduced in 1984 for all new tenancies and, wherever the sitting tenant is willing to comply, for renewals of tenancies. The 1984 Agricultural Holdings Act was important in supporting this approach. Prior to this, the introduction of conservation clauses had depended upon the goodwill of the tenant. The 1984 Act made provision for such clauses to be enforced by the landlord. A wide variety of clauses are used which may detail stocking, grazing and cutting conditions on some areas, list all the hedges and other landscape features which are to be maintained, and may specify the tenant's obligations to provide for safe effluent disposal. These different clauses are often specific to particular fields on the holding, and are very detailed. Monitoring and enforcement are the responsibility of the landlord, exercised on the ground primarily by National Trust Regional Land Agents.

By 1992, specific conservation clauses had been included in 290 tenancy agreements. Hearn (1992) estimates an average reduction in rent equal to £5.90 per hectare as a result of these clauses. However, there is considerable variation between holdings, with about half involving no reduction in rent. The number of clauses has been increased in the past few years, including many positive obligations as well as negative ones. In some cases, for example if stock numbers are reduced, this can also be in a tenant's immediate interest, in that there is less need for major investment in new livestock housing or effluent disposal facilities.

Most recently the emphasis has shifted towards payments being made to tenants for positive conservation work and a variety of habitat restoration projects are under way, including the restoration of grassland and heathland on arable land, heather moor and salt-marsh. Water-meadows are being restored on the Sherborne estate in Gloucestershire. The Trust is also adopting a broader approach to the environment, examining each environmental resource and taking preventative measures so that resources are not damaged or wasted. This includes the adoption of very high water quality standards and may for instance imply changing farming systems completely (Hearn, 1994).

Semi-public organisation and decentralised control

The National Trust, with a long tradition of involvement by ordinary members and a close relationship with government over the years, also has a long record of membership debate and influence over its decision-making and administration. In marked contrast to the UK's other largest CART, the Royal Society for the Protection of Birds (discussed in Chapter 8), the Trust has undergone a series of major reorganisations and internal 'enquiries' in the last twenty-five years, in an attempt to address the concerns and demands of its membership.

As a private organisation, the Trust is not directly subject to political control in the way in which a government agency would be answerable to a minister. But neither is it entirely controlled by its members. A recent Trust-instigated but otherwise independent report on its constitution by Lord Oliver (Oliver, 1993) concludes that the Trust is not directly subject to the control of its members: they are not members of a club, but rather subscribers to a charitable work. The Trust is for the nation as a whole, including generations yet to come, and powers and duties of the governance and administration of the Trust are committed to the Council by statute. In Oliver's words, the Council is 'the ultimate repository of the entire responsibility for the management of the affairs of the Trust'. Council is comprised of 52 members, 26 of whom are appointed by outside bodies and 26 elected by the members of the Trust. The direct management of the Trust is undertaken by an Executive Committee, under which there are a number of Regional Committees.

Notwithstanding this judgement, conflicts inevitably arise over some of the Trust's specific policies and the Trust's Annual General Meeting is often the main means by which parties can have their concerns discussed. One of the most recent has been the issue of stag hunting on Exmoor. A resolution was narrowly passed at the 1990 Annual General Meeting calling for a ban on stag hunting on Trust land in Exmoor and the Quantocks. In response, the Trust's Council set up a working party to examine the conservation and management of red deer, which reported in 1993. It found that the deer population was larger than had been believed and still rising, so that culling would be necessary if a healthy population was to be maintained. It also argued that deer hunting pays a key role in promoting co-operation between landowners and farmers and that a ban on hunting would have a significant impact on the local community, making it much harder for the Trust to undertake its duties of preservation and conservation. On the basis of this, the Council decided against a ban and is seeking to establish an effective deer management scheme in the area. This is not regarded as sufficient by those who campaigned vigorously for the ban.

Other earlier membership debates led to the setting-up of the Benson enquiry, which reported in 1968, and the Arkell enquiry (1983), both looking at aspects of the Trust's organisation and control. The outcome of these reports has been a strengthening of the regional and local links between members and administrators, giving the Trust a quite decentralised approach to site management and development issues, by comparison with other national CARTs.

However, to some extent whatever the approach adopted it will not please everybody. For instance, Legg (1990–91) has drawn attention to the early emphasis of the founders of the National Trust on the vigorous protection of commons and open spaces and on campaigning for public access for all to the countryside. Against this, he argues that the Trust has become 'the major safety net for preventing the decline and fall of the English stately home . . . becoming an elitist club for art connoisseurs, and defensive in the protection of a collection of prize dinosaurs'. He called on the Trust to allow its 400 square miles of farmland to revert to primaeval, semi-wooded landscape, where people and wildlife could once again share a place. And Strong (1988) comments on the staff of the Trust propagating 'an arcadian vision of a vanished aristocratic England'.

The changing financial position of the Trust

Table 6.2 indicates the major sources of income received by the National Trust in 1982 and 1992, the percentage from each of these sources in each of the years, and the percentage change over the period. It excludes extraordinary receipts from gifts and legacies. Total income from these sources rose by 337 per cent in nominal terms, which is about double in real terms, over the period.

The growth in membership is reflected in the 407 per cent increase in membership income, with this source rising from just over 30 per cent to nearly 40 per cent of the total. Income from investments also rose and, while a relatively small proportion of the total, the surplus generated by National Trust Enterprises, representing commercial activities such as trading and catering, rose by over 700 per cent.

As membership gives free admission to properties, it is perhaps not surprising that the proportion of income arising from admissions has fallen while membership has increased. Similarly, the rents, about half of which are from agriculture, also represent a smaller proportion of income in 1992, partly reflecting the relatively poor performance of agricultural incomes, the introduction of conservation clauses, and the recession in other areas of property. In 1990 it was estimated that conservation clauses in tenancy agreements resulted in a loss of income to the Trust of £250 000. Since then, the number of agreements has continued to rise, suggesting an increasing loss. The annual

Table 6.2 Major sources of National Trust income, 1982 and 1992

	1982		1992		% change 1982–1992
	(£000)	%	(£000)	%	
Membership	9195	32	37382	39	307
Direct property	8772	31	20304	21	131
Admission	2776	10	6620	7	138
Rents	5386	19	12886	13	139
Produce sales	610	2	798	1	31
Investment income	4544	16	17669	18	289
Enterprises	975	3	7029	7	621
Grants and contributions	5091	18	13911	14	173
Total	28577	100	96295	100	237

Sources: National Trust Accounts 1982 and 1992.

level of receipts from legacies also rose considerably, from a range of £5–8 million in the early 1980s to £20 million by 1992.

In 1992, the Trust spent a higher proportion of total expenditure on properties than it had done in 1982; the proportion was 84 per cent as compared with 72 per cent in 1982. Total expenditure rose by a greater extent than did income, by 389 per cent over the period. The estimated cost of work outstanding on the maintenance of property at the end of 1992 was £165 million.

Something not reflected in the accounts is the work contributed by volunteers. In 1993 over 28 000 volunteers put in 1.6 million hours of work. This includes room stewards, professionals offering various services and young people on projects.

The National Trust in a regional context

Because of its particularly decentralised structure, it is not possible to describe the day-to-day management operations of the National Trust as landowner and manager without recourse to a particular local situation. In the preparation for this book the authors visited Trust offices in three different regions of England and Wales, to look at this issue. In each case, the picture of management was quite different and reflected some of the main characteristics of each locality. Thus to illustrate this aspect of the Trust's work, we here include the example of its Cumbria office – working in one of the 'heartlands' of the National Trust's historic and current activity.

The Trust has has a longstanding involvement in the protection of the Lake District following on from Hardwicke Rawnsley's work before the Trust was established. A few farms were acquired in the 1920s, and then after the war Beatrix Potter was a notable benefactor to the Trust in the Lake District. She and her husband left about 4000 acres and a substantial sum with which to buy more land. By the 1950s the Trust was a large enough local landowner to seriously affect the lives of a large number of local people – for example, it owned 220 cottages. It now owns 140 000 acres in Cumbria, owning or leasing all of the central fell area, most of the valley heads and six of the main lakes.

In Cumbria there is no strong tradition of large estates with benevolent landlords; it is an area of traditionally dispersed settlement and small farms together with some relatively small estates. The Cumbrian farming people have always been relatively independent, and their land was never valuable by comparison with areas such as Yorkshire, Northumberland and Lancashire which had either agricultural or sporting value. Therefore there have been no major landowners in the lakes since monastic times. So here, unlike other areas, the National Trust had no obvious role to inherit as a large estate manager. Because of this, some staff feel that there tends to be a paradoxical attitude towards the Trust: on one hand, there is an instinctive resentment of any organisation being able to wield so much influence over the land and the people, but, on the other, there is an appreciation of the stability which National Trust ownership has brought. It has reduced the threat to farmers' existence in a marginal agricultural area.

When the National Trust bought land in Cumbria, its main aim was to continue the traditional management practice, as a means to achieve landscape conservation. Thus the best type of farming was felt to be family farming: 'one man and his dog'. The Trust's agents felt that farm amalgamation was not good because it stretched the labour resource too much; so it was in the National Trust's interests to keep farms small, to retain labour on farms and thus encourage careful management of their conservation value. In 1991 the Trust had 89 farms in the Lake District which it sought to retain as 89 viable units. The wider benefits of this should be in keeping the local communities viable. The Trust therefore has an interest in both agriculture and in the rural communities within which it functions. However, there are continuing pressures for farm amalgamation in order to maintain farm incomes and to hold down the landlord's costs, including costs of pollution control. There are also arguments that in some contexts larger farms are better placed to maintain the conservation value of the countryside.

The Trust is now actively seeking forms of diversification for its tenant farmers. Tourism is one obvious option, but it is also pursuing marketing developments. The Trust has built a link with a carpet company willing to take all the traditional Herdwick wool produced by its tenants' sheep, through the Wool Marketing Board, and it has also sought to do something similar with meat from traditional breeds.

The Trust employs estate teams to do practical work on and off farmland, including work which would traditionally have been part of the tenants' responsibilities. The team, roughly two men for every valley, does walling, fencing and tree management, and it can step in to manage a farm temporarily if the tenant falls ill. Teams are also responsible for low-level work for amenity benefits: small planting, hedging or small footpaths. An effort is currently being made to put more resources into the management of high-level footpaths. The Trust began improving paths in the mid 1980s, working on the sections on the valley floors, then moving to sections between that and 1000 ft (300 m), and so on. The Trust now employs four teams of four men to repair footpaths at a cost of over £250 000 per annum. The teams work on all the major tourist paths, using the technique of old traditional packhorse route construction – 'pitching'. Work has been completed on over 40 projects and is now proceeding on projects over 2000 feet (600 m). Volunteers are also involved, to collect the stones, while skilled gangs do the construction work, at which they are experienced.

The Trust in Cumbria also has about 22 wardens, not counting those involved in the estate teams and a woodlands team of about 25 people, who work on all the Trust's large woodlands; there are about 9000 acres of woodland in-hand. The Trust employs 28 builders to undertake the maintenance of the 700–800 buildings which are owned, and contracts some jobs out to some local contractors who tend to work for the National Trust most of the time.

To look after the volunteer input, there is a Regional Volunteer Co-ordinator, who probably spends about 60 per cent of his time on managing the open space volunteers, and 40 per cent on the indoor volunteers (there are many volunteer guides and room stewards at the Trust's properties in Cumbria; all of the room stewards are now volunteers). The Trust has successfully built up a core of long-term volunteers who tend to work for six-month stretches at a time – often for work experience. The Trust houses them in a small network of bothys around the Lakes, occasionally also using properties that are temporarily vacant. It can then mix the long-term volunteers with short-term ones, such as school groups, colleges or the army. Work is also done for the Trust by BTCV (the British Trust for Conservation Volunteers), and by the National NT Acorn Camps, who have a base near Windermere.

Overall, the most effective use of voluntary help is always to mix them with regular work teams. But the Trust has some highly skilled volunteers, for example, in landscape survey work. On the whole the Trust in Cumbria tends to attract young and often transitory people to voluntary work, by comparison with other National Trust areas where the volunteers are often people who are retired and settled in the area.

In the past, the Trust has made extensive use of the various local employment training schemes. Task Force North used to provide trainee labour, and the Trust used around 150 people under the Community Programme. Many of the current staff on the estate teams and footpath teams started off as Community Programme trainees. With Employment Training, the Trust had some trainees through the Cumbria Training Services agency, getting them to work mainly in the land management or buildings maintenance teams. Again, a large number of these people either came onto the permanent staff afterwards, or, in time, they became freelance contractors to the Trust. However, changes in training schemes have limited the opportunities available. Until recently up to 50 people were employed on Community Action and Training for Work projects, but currently (in 1995) there are fewer than 20 people in Community Action programmes.

Trust property in the area is comprised more of open areas than of country houses, which means a very large number of relatively small jobs to be done. For example, in the management plan for 1991 there were 2700 jobs, costing £1500–5000 each. This makes management much harder to control and to organise than that for a few major jobs. The Trust's use of small contractors and personal contacts to get things done also makes the planning and co-ordinating process more difficult.

The need to protect the landscape limits the options available for land use to such an extent that it tends to represent a financial liability in Cumbria, rather than an asset to generate funds for the maintenance of footpaths and buildings. Farm rents fail to cover the expenditure on farms and open land, let alone on buildings. In total, the Trust spends about £5.2 million annually in the Lake District, as compared to an income from farm rents of about £930 000. So there is a need to find alternative sources of income. Some of this comes from boating and fishing rights, and some from Trust shops and information centres. However, income is still much less than expenditure, and so the Trust has been running the Lake District Appeal for the past decade, to raise funds to make up the deficit. In the meantime, any remaining deficit is funded from central sources.

The Trust would like to be able to raise more resources from the estimated 20 million tourists who come to the Lakes each year. An estimated third of them walk on Trust land while they are in the area, but their contribution to the Trust is minimal. The problem is always to find ways of harnessing this potential source of funds without damaging the land. At popular tourist sites, there are recruiting teams, which are successful in recruiting new members, but there are generally no direct payments.

In the view of the Trust's previous regional manager, the future of upland agriculture is the major concern to the Trust in Cumbria – there is visible landscape degradation at present, but it is not clear how maintenance will be paid for. The designation of the area as an Environmentally Sensitive Area has made a considerable impact and this and similar schemes will be important in maintaining the landscape. If it falls into neglect, the whole of the Lakeland landscape will change. Farming has been in a serious medium-term decline: farm incomes have fallen substantially through the past decade or so. Farmers' wives who run their own bed and breakfast businesses used to do it for a bit of extra money, but today it is often the main income-earner on the farm. This leads to readjustment both in the social relations within the farm family – the wife becomes the main breadwinner – and to the nature of the rural economy. If incomes continue to fall, the implication is that the Trust would have to offer negative rents in order to maintain local farming systems.

Bound up with this personal view of future dangers to the Trust's estate is a perceived threat to local communities. Long-distance commuting is developing in the area. As a substantial owner of property, the Trust can have an important influence on the type of people who live in the area. Thus, most of its small cottages are only let to people who were born and have lived and worked locally. As the cottages are very popular with local people, the Trust can afford to be selective, seeking those who fit in with the local environment in each case. But this can be difficult. With the farm tenancies also, the Trust tends to pick local people as tenants. Farming practice here is still relatively co-operative, so this policy makes sense – in the Trust's view, it is more reliable to pick tenants who are already familiar with local custom in this respect.

Beyond agriculture, there is a threat to the Lake District from commercial pressures. There have been some questionable developments, for instance a large timeshare development in Langdale, and there has been a public inquiry into waterskiing on Lake Windermere. This sort of development changes the kinds of visitor – they may help the local economy, but they are not people drawn to the Lakes for traditional forms of recreation, so they can be less appreciative of its particular environmental character. The progress of the Environment Bill, being debated in Parliament in 1995, will be influential in respect of the development of noisy sports in National Parks.

In 1991 the Trust was consolidating its holdings in the area and would not buy or even accept new land if it was a long way away from existing holdings. It would however purchase small areas around present holdings, especially if the purchase would help to ensure the survival of the whole farming community, for example by avoiding farm splits, keeping some farms intact and viable. But the Trust must maintain good management on all its existing properties as its first priority. The Trust's acquisition policy is being reviewed in 1995.

The Trust is seeking to be more open and to consult more widely in the planning and development of its role in the area. It would particularly like to get more help from and better relations with Parish Councils and local groups. On the land management side, it is seeking to demonstrate good environmental management, notably through pollution-control work with farmers and in the maintenance of the upland footpath network.

The National Trust for Scotland

This chapter has focused upon the National Trust for England, Wales and Northern Ireland because this organisation is clearly the dominant landowner among all UK CARTs. But the discussion would not be complete without mention of the separate National Trust for Scotland (NTS), which dates from 1931 and is certainly a large CART in a UK context. It is similar to the National Trust for England, Wales and Northern Ireland in many respects. It is established under separate legislation 'for the purposes of promoting the permament preservation for the benefit of the nation of lands and buildings in Scotland of historic or national interest or natural beauty . . .'. This is pursued by means of purchasing property and by entering into conservation agreements, which are similar to the National Trust covenants.

The NTS owns a total area of around 100 000 acres and holds conservation agreements over a further significant area. However, unlike its sister organisation south of the border, the Trust's landholdings are predominantly of open land and there are relatively few large country houses. One consequence of this difference is in the financial status of the NTS, where its ability to raise funds from paying visitors is severely limited. Unlike the situation in

England, for example, where some regions are self-sufficient in management funds because a few major famous houses and gardens generate the income to support all other properties, in Scotland the holdings of the NTS operate at a loss both locally and nationally. Subsidising management from membership fees, legacies and fundraising is thus particularly important, as is the contribution to NTS funds from the Scottish Office.

However, the NTS has continued to grow and to enjoy a good level of membership support – the numbers of overseas members are particularly high, by comparison with other CARTs. It has worked closely with the National Trust on some of the major appeals, and has a good reputation in Scotland among local communities and other local conservation groups for its low-key but reliable approach to site management.

Preserving the nation's heritage

As organisations, the National Trusts appear to be widely respected. By almost any criterion they have achieved enormous success; as reflected in the scale of their estates, the size and continuing growth in their membership, and the extent to which they continue to receive donations of property and money. These bodies are widely trusted as the keepers of the nation's heritage. While they tend not to campaign for general changes in government policy (Strong, 1988), they also appear to be effective behind the scenes in promoting their interests.

Murdoch and Marsden (1994) have examined in detail an application to extract sand and gravel in Buckinghamshire. It appeared that the application may have been successful, in spite of local objections, until it was suggested that the proposed development could affect the hydrology of the area and could have an impact on the ornamental lakes in gardens at Stowe School designed by Capability Brown, which are leased by the National Trust. The introduction of the National Trust and the Stowe School 'old boy' network into the debate appeared to overwhelm the developers' arguments and led them to withdraw the application. The implication is that the National Trust was able to exert its influence quietly behind the scenes in order to prevent the development, and this would seem to be the Trust's general approach.

However, the threats to the Trust's properties from the government's roads programme were not so easily disposed of. In 1994 it was reported that over 40 road schemes had the potential to affect Trust properties (Wilson, 1994) and the issue has prompted the Trust to make more general criticisms of the government's roads strategy. The same year also saw the Trust arguing against the privatisation of the Forestry Commission in order to preserve opportunities for access and to protect the value of the Commission's woodlands for wildlife (Stirling, 1994). This is still some way from the campaigning approach that some feel could be taken by the Trust in defence of its properties and in favour of conservation issues more generally (Weideger, 1994) and it must be recognised that the protection of the Trust's assets depends upon many aspects of wider government policy-making, such as environmental protection, agricultural policy or town and country planning. There is a difficult balance to be struck between maintaining a positive and co-operative relationship with decision-makers in government on the one hand and using the force of numbers of its membership in overt campaigning for conservation and access on the other.

As has been noted, management involves making decisions about the ways in which properties should evolve. Central to this, in the absence of unlimited finance, is the extent to which the emphasis should be on a more positive and vigorous conservation which accepts the need to adopt commercial enterprises as a basis for generating the finance to facilitate the positive conservation. An alternative might be to adopt a less interventionist approach which might allow more 'genteel decay'; perhaps avoiding irreversible structural loss but accepting over-growth of gardens and the creation of 'wilderness' areas.

In its operations, the Trust for England, Wales and Northern Ireland adopts a consistent approach. This involves a high level of management and maintenance. Landscapes are kept in 'good repair'. Houses tend to be developed to a standard format in terms of presentation of information, shops, cafés and car parks. This approach suits many Trust members and visitors, as reflected in the scale of the membership. But it tends to exclude other, probably minority, interests. In practice, some groups are bound to find Trust properties less attractive and accessible. For instance, by their nature, many properties tend to be located in relatively remote locations and are therefore not easily accessible by public transport.

The National Trusts have special powers and privileges not available to any other private organisation. These have enabled the two organisations to assume a predominant position in national life, at least partly because these privileges represent barriers to entry, preventing effective competition by alternative organisations which might choose to offer a somewhat different approach. This monopolistic position thus precludes the possibility of the public being offered a choice of preferred visions of the past or approaches to the future.

The point here is not so much to criticise or commend any particular approach towards the conservation of the natural and historic environment. It seems unlikely, for instance, that Legg's vision of 400 square miles of primaeval semi-wooded landscape would be attractive to a large proportion of the population, especially at the cost in terms of lost agricultural livelihoods. Rather the point is to note the extent to which the judgements made by the National Trust dominate the options available to the nation as a whole, across a broad range of conservation issues.

Strumpshaw Fen. Reproduced by permission of Countryside Commission/Richard Denyer

From grassroots to federation: the Wildlife
7 Trusts

The Wildlife Trusts, comprising all the former County
Wildlife Trusts, newer urban trusts and the umbrella
national body, the Royal Society for Nature Conservation,
has a combined membership of nearly 250 000, equivalent
to 0.4 per cent of the population, and is responsible for
over 55 000 ha or 0.26 per cent of the land area, of the UK,
Guernsey and the Isle of Man combined. Total operating
income in 1994 amounted to over £7 million. On these
criteria the Wildlife Trusts Partnership currently constitutes
the third largest landholding conservation organisation in
the UK, after the National Trust and the Royal Society for
the Protection of Birds (RSPB). Among the Wildlife Trusts
are some of the oldest conservation groups as well as some
of the fastest-growing new ones: their combined wealth of
experience and expertise in conservation management is
considerable.

History: the Society for the Promotion of
Nature Reserves

The origins of the Wildlife Trusts movement are intimately
linked with the development of the Society for the Promotion of Nature Reserves (SPNR), subsequently becoming
the Royal Society for Nature Conservation (RSNC). The
SPNR was established in 1912 in order to assist the
National Trust and local bodies in obtaining sites for
nature reserves (Sheail, 1976).

The National Trust did have a concern to promote
nature conservation; as mentioned in the previous chapter
the 1907 Act specified the establishment of the Trust
'for the general purposes of promoting the permanent

preservation for the benefit of the nation of land and tenements . . . and as regards lands for the preservation (so far as is practicable) of their natural aspect features and animal and plant life'. Wicken Fen in Cambridgeshire was the first reserve to be acquired in 1895 and by 1910 the National Trust had acquired thirteen sites of nature conservation value. But there was concern amongst naturalists at the slow rate of progress and the almost random way in which potential nature reserves were acquired (Sheail, 1976). As a result, a group of individuals decided to form a new body which would stimulate the National Trust and other bodies to create nature reserves. It was not the intention that the new body should itself own or manage land. Its purposes would be pursued by identifying areas containing rare species liable to extinction on a systematic basis, and then seeking support for their acquisition and management by other bodies, including the National Trust.

However, in practice relatively little progress was made for the first thirty years of its existence and there was relatively little contact between the National Trust and the SPNR. There was no evidence that the National Trust followed SPNR advice on the acquisition of reserves, and it refused custody of some potential reserves. There was also concern over the standard of management of Trust reserves. For instance, in 1924, the Royal Society for the Protection of Birds discussed the poor state of Trust reserves (Sheail, 1976). Generally, the National Trust placed a higher priority on historic and amenity conservation than on the conservation of nature.

A new and more significant role for the SPNR emerged during the period of planning for post-war reconstruction during the early 1940s. Following a conference on the preservation of wildlife after the war, a Nature Reserves Investigation Committee was appointed in 1942 under the auspices of the SPNR. The modest cost of this exercise was funded by a grant from the Pilgrim Trust (Sheail, 1976). The aim of the committee was to identify those plants and animals which were in danger of becoming extinct and then recommend where national nature reserves should be established and how they should be managed. The procedure adopted was to undertake the work through 24 regional subcommittees, sometimes based on existing local organisations, such as the Yorkshire Naturalists' Union.

Views were also sought from other bodies (Sheail, 1976). A final list of 55 sites was published in December 1945.

The origins of the Wildlife Trusts

It had been hoped that the regional subcommittees would continue in existence and play an active role in nature conservation at the local level and a few, such as Berkshire and Oxfordshire, did recruit new members. But the committees had no official status. A review by the SPNR in 1954 found that only three of the original 24 were still active and decided to disband all of them, hoping that those more active committees could be resurrected under a different name (Sheail, 1976). A.E. Smith (1990), who had advocated at the time that the committees should be kept, comments that this 'threw away ten precious years of opportunity'. Nevertheless, in some counties the momentum was maintained. In Lincolnshire, for instance, this momentum led to the establishment of a county trust in 1948 and Smith initiated a drive for a national network of trusts (Lowe and Goyder, 1983).

Two trusts had been established before the Second World War. The first was the Norfolk Naturalists' Trust in 1926. Early in the century, two nature reserves had been acquired in Norfolk and handed over to the National Trust; Blakeney Point and Scolt Head Island. However, after a successful appeal to raise funds for the purchase of Cley marshes, the National Trust refused to accept the land. As a result, the Norfolk Naturalists' Trust was created to own this and future reserves. The West Wales Naturalists' Trust was begun in 1937, but a third trust was not established until 1946 in Yorkshire. The early growth in county Trusts and membership is shown in Figure 7.1.

The vast majority of trusts were founded in the period 1955–70, when nature conservation became an established national and international issue, and a smaller number – Cleveland, Montgomery, London, Bristol, Bath and Avon, Sheffield and Ulster – have been formed in the 'greening' years since the late 1970s.

Forty-five of the Wildlife Trusts operate within the UK and two cover the Isle of Man and Guernsey. The names and locations of the individual trusts are illustrated in

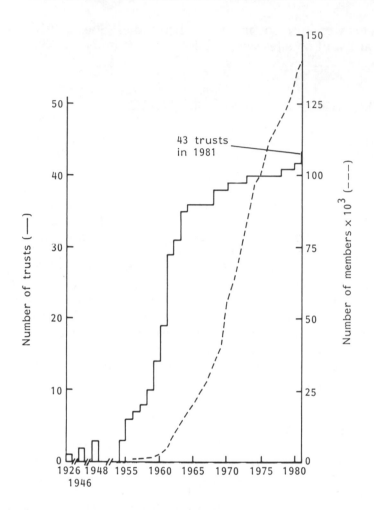

Figure 7.1 Growth in the number and combined membership of county trusts for nature conservation
Source: Lowe and Goyder (1983). Reproduced by permission of P.D. Lowe

Figure 7.2. Thirty-nine trusts represent pre-1974 and post-1974 county areas of England and Wales, and there are also trusts in Birmingham; Bristol, Bath and Avon; London; and Sheffield, and single trusts represent all Scotland and Ulster. In several cases a trust covers more than one county area; as with Berkshire, Buckinghamshire and Oxfordshire (BBONT); Hertfordshire and Middlesex; and Bedfordshire, Cambridgeshire, Northamptonshire and Peterborough. There has also been some change over time: Hereford

47 Wildlife Trusts

1	Bristol, Bath & Avon	16	Glamorgan	32	Nottinghamshire
2	Beds, Cambs, Northants & Peterborough	17	Gloucestershire	33	Radnorshire
		18	Gwent	34	Scotland
3	Berks, Bucks & Oxon	19	Hampshire & Isle of Wight	35	Shropshire
4	Birmingham & Black Country	20	Herefordshire	36	Sheffield
5	Brecknock	21	Hertfordshire & Middlesex	37	Somerset
6	Cheshire	22	Kent	38	Staffordshire
7	Cleveland	23	Lancashire	39	Suffolk
8	Cornwall	24	Leicestershire	40	Surrey
9	Cumbria	25	Lincolnshire	41	Sussex
10	Derbyshire	26	London	42	Ulster
11	Devon	27	Manx	43	Warwickshire
12	Dorset	28	Montgomeryshire	44	Wiltshire
13	Durham	29	Norfolk	45	Worcestershire
14	Dyfed	30	Northumberland	46	Yorkshire
15	Essex	31	North Wales	47	Guernsey

Figure 7.2 Wildlife Trusts in 1995
Source: The Wildlife Trusts

and Radnor formed jointly in 1963 but separated in 1987 and the Northumberland and Durham trusts did likewise in 1971; Montgomeryshire split from the North Wales Trust in 1982 and the new urban trusts have been formed only recently. Some minor boundary changes have also occurred between neighbouring trusts, in order to improve the effectiveness of their operations following local government reorganisation.

Towards a federation of trusts

The relatively young age of the majority of Wildlife Trusts by comparison with the National Trust and RSPB (both founded in the 1890s) belies the movement's roots in the initiative embodied by the founding of the SPNR in 1912. The Guernsey trust 'La Société Guernesiaise' is somewhat unusual in having retained its status as a Learned Society since its foundation in 1882 and never formally becoming a Trust, despite its responsibility for a number of nature reserves held jointly by trustees.

The emergence of the Wildlife Trusts had rather left the SPNR without a clear purpose. It made some grants to county trusts and played a limited role in the acquisition of reserves (Sheail, 1976). However, its activities were limited by its inability under its charter to raise a subscription and the relatively poor prospects for bequests. In consequence, the activities of the SPNR were directed towards supporting the work of the county trusts, by offering advice on scientific management and land agency, by giving publicity to the work being undertaken by the trusts and, at the suggestion of the county trusts themselves, co-ordinating the trusts' activities. In fact, the Council for Nature was established in 1958 but this was ineffective as a 'federal centre' for the trusts and so a new committee was established within the SPNR with this purpose. By 1965 all trusts had nominees on the Council of the SPNR, effectively making it their national association (Smith, 1990). The changes were formally recognised in a Royal Charter in 1976 which established a federation with the trusts as corporate members of the Society. The name was changed to the Royal Society for Nature Conservation in 1981.

Table 7.1 Trust objectives

To achieve a better future for wildlife by:

(a) protecting and enhancing wildlife and wildlife habitats both common and rare, as an investment for the future;
(b) creating a greater appreciation and understanding of wildlife and wildlife habitats and a greater awareness of the need for their conservation;
(c) encouraging active participation by people of all ages;
(d) providing more opportunities for all to enjoy wildlife and wild places in towns and countryside;
(e) infusing the philosophy and practice of nature conservation into all uses of the environment and natural resources.

Source: RSNC Corporate Strategy 1989–1992

The Wildlife Trusts Partnership

Through the Wildlife Trusts Partnership, all trusts affirm a set of primary objectives (Table 7.1) and all share a basic commitment to the establishment and ongoing management of wildlife sites as nature reserves. Following a Nature Conservancy Council-sponsored study of the operation of County Trusts in 1978 (Society for the Promotion of Nature Conservation (SPNC), 1978), the RSNC encouraged trusts to exchange information on their performance and to work with formalised management strategies, preparing development plans and monitoring their achievements.

Affiliation to the Wildlife Trusts Partnership means that each trust pays a capitation fee to the national organisation (in proportion to its membership numbers) and in return it receives national campaigning and co-ordination services, and triannual national journals for distribution to its members and junior members. Over the last decade the RSNC has put a renewed emphasis upon developing its central co-ordinating and campaigning role. For example, it has helped to supply many trusts with cars by obtaining national sponsorship from Fiat and Volvo. It has a credit card scheme to benefit trusts and it encouraged the launch of UK-wide 'County Wildlife Appeals', to raise core funds for the trusts, in the mid-1980s.

The activities of the trusts

All the Wildlife Trusts are involved in the ownership and ongoing management of nature reserves, although the urban trusts may not have anything more secure than project-based control of management. The group as a whole therefore qualifies as a CART with a primary emphasis upon nature conservation.

In 1990, for the purposes of this study, data were collected both from the RSNC and from a survey of the individual Wildlife Trusts. The RSNC provided trusts' reserves' hectarage data from its own records, collected from the trusts during the late 1980s. It supplied copies of the Corporate Strategy, Annual Review 1988/89 and details of a number of current national projects in which the Partnership is involved. It also supplied a copy of the NCC/SPNC study of the nature reserves' policies of the trusts (SPNC, 1978).

Accounts and annual reports (for 1988/89) were obtained for 46 trusts, along with a varying amount of other information from each trust, almost always including a reserves' list and the latest newsletter. The Manx Trust could not supply an annual report and accounts because their first issue of these was not yet produced. Apart from this one exception, the data on trusts' reserves' area, membership and structure is therefore complete for January 1990, while the financial figures are complete for 1988/89.

Almost all the UK trusts are Registered Charities (though Scottish charities need not register with the Charity Commission) and non-profit-making Companies limited by guarantee (with no share capital), and all exhibit a similar pattern of management growth and structural development. With the exception of the newest trusts, most began life as groups of committed amateur naturalists who sought to pursue their conservation objectives through the establishment of reserves of particular wildlife interest, to be protected by them for the benefit of future generations, and through local campaigning and/or educational work. The newer and more urban trusts have tended to adopt a more overtly campaigning, less site-based approach.

Each trust is presided over by an honorary council of trustees elected by members at the AGM (on the principle of one-member, one-vote). Ultimate decision-making power rests with this body but practical day-to-day management is usually devolved to a number of executive committees formed by members and professional staff. Each trust operates a range of activities and services for individual, family and corporate members, junior members (particularly through 'WATCH' nature-study and activity groups) and the public at large. These include organising social events, open-days, shops, talks, walks, lobbying campaigns, producing educational materials and so on. Most of the trusts also have 'local groups' organised and attended by members on a voluntary basis, which are variously involved in fundraising, education and/or land management.

Figures 7.3–7.5 illustrate the recent growth of the county trusts. Since 1977, the trusts' combined membership has more than doubled (from 115 000) and their reserves' area has increased by 80 per cent (from 30 000 ha). In 1977 their combined income was only half a million pounds, so this increased by over 500 per cent in real terms in the eleven years up to 1988. In 1977 only five trusts had an annual income above £20 000, but by 1988 the equivalent income (adjusted upwards for inflation) was raised by 36 trusts. As one might expect, the rapidly expanding financial turnover of the Wildlife Trust movement has brought many changes to the management and activities of its constituent members.

As the trusts' management responsibilities, membership numbers and resources have grown they have appointed a growing number of professional staff to managerial and administrative posts. Staff are selected by the council of trustees and paid for by a combination of fundraising efforts, membership subscriptions and grants from state and private organisations. In particular, the trusts have traditionally worked very closely with their counterparts in the former Nature Conservancy Council (as described by Lowe and Goyder, 1983) and the NCC committed substantial amounts of funding towards the creation and maintenance of these staff posts over the past decade or so. Today, English Nature (NCC's successor) runs a special 'Reserves Enhancement Scheme' to help support the English trusts' management of particularly valuable reserves (SSSIs and National Nature Reserves). Other sources of grant-aid for trust staff have been the Countryside Commission and

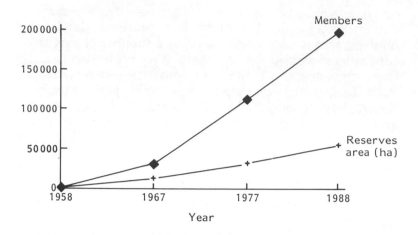

Figure 7.3 Growth of county trusts 1958–1988

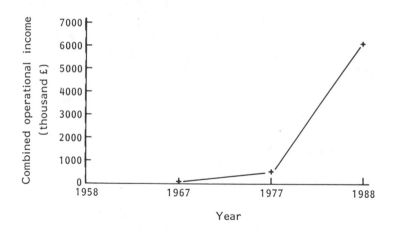

Figure 7.4 Growth in income of county trusts 1967–1988

the countryside agencies in Scotland and Wales, the WorldWide Fund for Nature, UK2000 and many local authorities as well as the RSNC itself.

In terms of their range of activities and responsibilities, the 47 Wildlife Trusts are a very heterogeneous group which could be likened to a stand of mixed-age, mixed-species trees in a wood. Some are old and well-established and others much newer, some large and others much

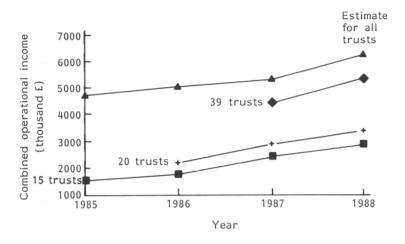

Figure 7.5 Combined income of county trusts 1985–1988

smaller. Groups have apparently developed at very different rates; some pioneering and growing quickly, others expanding more slowly and some remaining for many years at a plateau. Like commercial firms, all express aspirations for growth and development and yet these aspirations have run concurrent with the national aim, embodied in their partnership with the RSNC, to establish separate trusts for local areas – to cover the country with local nature conservation trusts. In this way they differ from the famous 'trees in a forest' description of commercial firms used by Alfred Marshall, where each firm seeks to grow and develop in a competitive sense, capturing market share from other firms. The Wildlife Trusts, rather, seek to exploit geographically different market 'niches' so that the entire movement maximises its market through local specialisation ('geographical diversification') and no trust explicitly *sets out* to take members from or to take over neighbouring trusts (even when these things have occurred in practice).

A similar attitude of 'peaceful co-existence' towards other conservation organisations operating within their areas (such as the National Trust, RSPB, Woodland Trust and various local amenity groups) is expressed in trusts' literature. This is perhaps unsurprising because evidence from a number of studies (e.g. Bull, 1986; Micklewright,

1986) suggests that many trust members simultaneously belong to these other organisations. Also, several trusts have a track record of working in partnership with such groups, particularly the RSPB, to manage local nature reserves jointly.

A typology of Wildlife Trusts

In seeking to describe the variety of these trusts three general 'types' have been identified, each type representing a stage in a more or less common path of growth and development, albeit a path which is pursued at different rates and to different degrees by individual trusts. It does not follow Lowe's suggested typology for environmental organisations (Lowe, 1983) which is based upon their age, because many trusts exhibit a mixture of his separate 'aesthetic, scientific and political' emphases in their activities. Also, many have changed their emphasis a great deal since their foundation, such that a trust founded during what Lowe described as the 'scientific' period in the development of the conservation movement may have begun with this sort of outlook but have since developed a very political stance. Other authors (e.g. Micklewright, 1986) have suggested a classification into newer 'urban-style' and older 'rural-style' trusts, but the problem with this is that many trusts now operate both urban and rural programmes, and their overall character draws from both these sources.

Instead, we group the trusts loosely in terms of their annual income and number of professional staff (as gathered in 1990), in order to describe their general form and activities. As the trusts themselves state and as the data appear to suggest, these are the 'limiting factors' which most crucially determine their ability to take on different responsibilities and activities. Beyond this, each trust will have its own particular characteristics; for example in the balance which it strikes between conservation through direct land-use control and conservation through broader campaigning influence; a balance which apparently bears no obvious relationship to other trust characteristics.

Type one. The small group

These trusts generally had a membership below 3000 and were responsible for the management of a modest number of nature reserves in 1990 (less than 40 each). Beyond this, they had a WATCH group (as described earlier), a members' newsletter and an annual programme of social and fundraising events – these constitute the baseline range of activities undertaken by all the trusts. Most had a trading outlet for RSNC and local goods whose profits accrued to the trust.

However, their resources were generally too limited to take on more ambitious projects: for example, some have done a small amount of contract work for other organisations and some employ one or two people through employment training schemes, but most have been unable to organise their own trainee reserves' management teams since the demise of the Community Programme (CP) in 1988/89. In 1990 they had fewer than five paid staff (full and part-time): usually a Conservation Officer, an Administration Officer or Membership Secretary, and an Education Officer to run the WATCH group, perhaps with one or two part-time office or sales staff. Revenue income, including that from grants and appeals, was in the range £10–60 000.
Examples: Brecknock, Radnor, Manx, Staffs, Durham (10–13 trusts in 1990).

Type two. The developing and campaigning group

These trusts had amassed sufficient resources (manpower, capital investments and/or land) to begin to develop comprehensive strategies for the conservation and improvement of the local environment, by 1990. Many were involved in routine scrutiny of planning applications to County and/or District Councils. Some had environmental consultancies bringing in a significant share of trust income, many organised extensive work programmes with local Conservation Volunteers and community groups, both on and off their own reserves. Most had experience of fighting environmentally damaging development proposals through the planning system. Most had undertaken a management review in recent years and set out plans for

expansion in the coming decade. However they are mainly known only within their own local area, using local rather than national media for their publicity. In 1990 they employed between five and twelve staff including a Development Officer, Administrative Officer, one or two Conservation Officers and/or a Reserves Manager, an Educational Officer and office and sales staff. Their income was in the range £61–200 000.
Examples: Warwicks, Cumbria, Derby, Surrey (about 23 trusts in 1990).

Type three. The nationally influential group

These trusts have grown to the extent that their resource base is reasonably secure and they are able to consolidate activities and campaign at the level of national awareness, often drawing members and substantial support from outside their local area and being known throughout the UK. Their reserves' area may still be relatively modest (London WT only managed 234 ha in 1990) but their influence over both local and national land use is greater than this because of the extent of their work with national and local authorities and private landowners, and the tangible effects of their often extensive campaigns. They may have helped to plan and implement wider public and private land management schemes, or successfully fought damaging development proposals through presenting evidence to public inquiries, producing research reports and making representations to parliament. Some prefer to work through long-established contacts 'in the corridors of power' while others opt for more media-orientated means of influence. Within their local areas many have elicited firm environmental policy commitments from local industries and public bodies in relation to these organisations' landholdings. Most make a significant contribution to the local economy through their various activities and many have the ability to generate substantial revenue either from their own assets or from their high-profile projects. These trusts employed at least 15 staff and had an income of £201–700 000 in 1990.
Examples: Kent, Norfolk, London, Scottish, Suffolk, BBONT (10 trusts in 1990).

Issues

The Wildlife Trusts' *Corporate Strategy 1989–1992* laid out the following key targets:

1. Stronger corporate image; two major campaigns on wildlife conservation issues a year by 1990; 10 per cent growth in community-based environmental events and projects and 10 per cent growth in membership of trusts annually.
2. Locally a 15 per cent increase in funds raised through voluntary supporters; a 25 per cent increase in private and public-sector support, locally and nationally; both to be reviewed annually.
3. A new structure agreed by June 1990; viability for all corporate members (the county trusts, to be achieved through RSNC financial and practical support) by 1992.

It further stated that:

> In addition to the key targets, which measure **progress on its priorities** the Society will also measure the **achievement of its aim**. Quantitative and qualitative measures will be devised, relating to conservation activity, people involved, financial performance, relationships with other organsations and capacity for change. The mechanisms will aim to impose the minimum of administration on corporate members [the local trusts] based primarily around an annual return to the RSNC Office, regional meetings and regular RSNC Office staff visits.

The following section examines some issues of progress and achievement among the Wildlife Trusts, since then.

Membership

From their literature it appears that county trusts have adopted a policy of aiming for a minimum membership of 1 per cent of the population of their area. By 1990, this target level had been attained by six of the trusts: Brecknock, Radnor, Somerset, Lincolnshire, Norfolk, and Guernsey (1990 membership, 1988 population estimates). However, there does not appear to be a strong relationship between the trusts' proportionate membership and the extent of their local activity as described in newsletters and annual reports (events, projects, responsibilities, etc.). The 1 per cent level has been attained by some small trusts operating in areas with very low population density, such as mid-Wales (Brecknock has a 2.3 per cent membership, Radnor 2.4 per cent), and not attained by large and active trusts operating in densely populated areas such as London and Lancashire (each with approximately 0.05 per cent membership). This suggests that the 1 per cent membership threshold is a less significant indicator of a trust's 'success' than is implied by the trusts themselves in their literature.

Rather, all trusts may have a certain minimum absolute viable size – say, of between 500 and 1000 members – which is required, independent of population density, for the trust to fulfil its basic range of functions as described for Type one trusts. Finding these first members would be the necessary condition for the establishment of an independent and fully-fledged trust. For some trusts this membership size would already be over 1 per cent of their local population. Beyond this level, it may then be that local population size influences the trust's ability to *increase* membership, so that a trust could measure its success in attracting members over and above this figure in relation to local population size.

Furthermore, for trusts operating in rural areas with a lot of recreation and tourism, many members may be from outside the area itself. For example, Dyfed Wildlife Trust and La Société Guernesiaise both refer to a significant proportion of their membership having joined because they visit the area (often regularly) on holiday. Hence to relate the membership of these trusts to the local population size is misleading: their activities are clearly of direct interest to a wider group of people.

As a measure of trust achievement, growth in membership might appear more useful than membership as a proportion of local population. However, should this be measured in relation to absolute or relative growth, and is a growth of equal absolute or proportionate membership in different trusts an indicator of equal achievement? As Bull points out (1986), members will join a trust for a variety of factors which include those entirely outside the trust's control, such as the degree of local threat to wildlife conservation. For example, although the Kent Trust saw its membership grow in recent years while involved in campaigns about the Channel Tunnel, this growth cannot, arguably, be attributed solely to the Trust's own effectiveness.

Land management

It is difficult to discuss the conservation effectiveness of land management by the county trusts with any quantitative precision because, to do so, one would have to weigh up the relative value of holding different sites with very different management requirements. Probably all the trusts would say that their land management could be improved, given greater resources. However, it is possible to compare the extent of trusts' landholdings, both by hectarage and tenure and by the proportion of the total area of their county held, to compare the level of management responsibility that they carry.

The total landholding per trust in 1990 ranged from 120 ha for the Herefordshire Trust to 17 700 ha for the Scottish Trust, which implies a huge variation in their associated management responsibilities (see Figure 7.6). Even excluding the Scottish Trust, which is somewhat unusual in being a national group with nine regional offices, the variation is very great: the Lincolnshire and the Northumberland Trusts each controlled over 2000 ha.

In relation to the total area within which each trust operates, the proportion of land held by each varied from 0.03 per cent for Ulster to 0.5 per cent for Norfolk, and the mean was 0.24 per cent. There is a weak relationship between the age of a trust and the proportion of county area which it currently controls – older trusts generally look after a greater proportion of the land in their area. But there are exceptions to this pattern – notably Guernsey – and the variation between the large number of trusts in the middle age range (28–35 years old) is very great.

In theory one would not automatically expect a clear

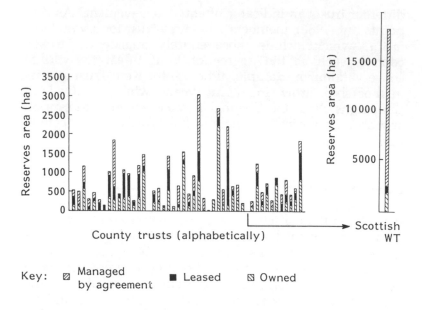

Figure 7.6 County trust reserves owned, leased, managed by agreement

relationship between the age of a trust (i.e. the number of years in which it has been acquiring reserves) and its landholding as a proportion of total county area. Firstly, land of high nature conservation value is not equally distributed or equally affordable throughout the UK: generally speaking, the more urban the area within which a trust operates the smaller its nature reserves will be, for both of these reasons. Secondly, the landownings of other CARTs, particularly those which are older than the Wildlife Trusts (e.g. RSPB and National Trust) are unequally distributed. So in an area where these other CARTs manage a large area of land, the local trust may have fewer opportunities. On the other hand, these may be areas where a strong tradition of nature conservation has been established (e.g. Cumbria), such that the presence of one high-profile CART assists the expansion of others by stimulating a knock-on effect. Finally, the oldest trusts are not always the wealthiest, and younger but wealthy trusts may be able to buy and/or manage more land than old but relatively poor trusts.

Table 7.2 Tenure trends for trust reserves[†] (proportion by area of reserves)

	All trusts including Scottish*		All trusts excluding Scottish	
	1978	1989	1978	1989
Owned	37	30	24	42
Leased	30	19	46	28
Managed by agreement	33	51	30	30

* These total figures are heavily influenced by the large area of land held by the Scottish Wildlife Trust (17 694 ha in total), little of which was owned.
[†] see note 1 at end of chapter.

Tenure trends

The Wildlife Trusts have three basic options for creating a nature reserve. They may own the land (either they buy it or it is donated or bequeathed to them), they may lease it for a given period from the landowner, or they may enter into an agreement with or take out a licence from the landowner to manage the site for a given period, either with associated financial transfers or free of charge. Generally speaking, leaseholds are for a longer time period than agreements or licences, which may even be arranged annually.

As shown in Table 7.2, in eleven years after 1978 there was a general shift away from leasing reserves and towards either owning them or managing them by agreement or under licence. However there was wide variation between individual trusts' tenure of reserves, as shown in Figures 7.6 and 7.7.

Among trusts with a large absolute area of owned land were Norfolk, Kent and Essex, each with over 1000 ha. Cumbria, Scotland and Lincolnshire had large areas of land managed under agreement or licence, and Northumberland had a particularly large area of leased land. If the proportion of each trust's reserves owned, leased or agreed/licenced are compared, 16 trusts owned over 50 per cent of their reserves' area, 8 leased over 50 per cent of their area, and 13 held over 50 per cent under agreement or licence. The trusts with the largest landholdings were not also the largest landowners, in every case.

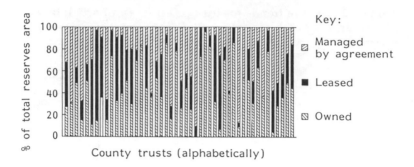

Figure 7.7 Tenure of trust reserves (% owned, leased, managed by agreement)

In theory, one might expect that a richer trust would own a larger proportion of its reserves: mirroring the RSPB view that ownership is the surest way to protect a reserve, long-term, so long as management resources are adequate. But when trust income is compared to percentage of trust area owned (Figure 7.8), the correlation between these two variables is not strong. Some quite wealthy trusts still lease or manage a sizeable proportion of their reserves. Part of the explanation may be that in some cases the landowner of these trust reserves is another CART. For example, 10 per cent of the total area of the Cornwall Trust's reserves is owned by the National Trust. In this case it is reasonable to expect the Cornwall Trust to feel that the reserve's status is adequately guaranteed by its current 'benign' owners.

Another form of the 'benign ownership' idea occurs in a few instances where trusts encourage their members to acquire sites, which they then designate and manage as trust reserves. This arrangement has existed for many years in one or two trusts, and often the landowner bequeathes or donates the reserve to the trust at a later date. However, this phenomenon is insignificant in terms of the total national landholding of the trusts.

There appears to be a correlation between the total area of reserves owned and the income of the trust (Figure 7.9). This would suggest that independent of the total area of reserves held by a trust, its ability to *own* reserves is related to its income. The implied causality here need not be unidirectional. A richer trust is probably able to buy more reserves than a poorer one:

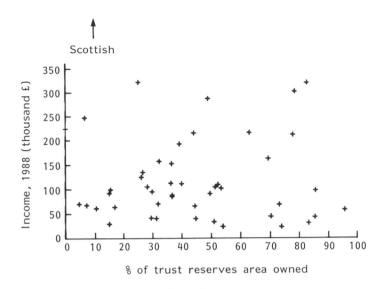

Figure 7.8 County trusts: proportion of total reserves area which is owned in relation to operational income 1988/89

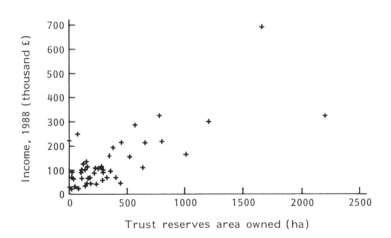

Figure 7.9 County trusts' reserves area owned in relation to operational income 1988/89

area owned $= f$[income] (where f is a functional operator)

but then a trust which for some reason (perhaps by bequest) has acquired large reserves with a high 'earnings' potential – for example from visitors' entrance fees or from produce such as coppiced wood – or reserves with a high profile which may attract many visitors and potential members, may thereby be able to increase its income substantially:

income $= g$[area owned] (where g is a functional operator).

The SPNC study (1978) found that the trusts with largest incomes tended to get a much higher proportion of their income from reserves than did the poorer trusts, which makes the second equation equally as plausible as the first. If both operate simultaneously one gets a 'feed-forward' effect on trust growth. However, we cannot investigate this relationship further because we do not know what proportion of each trust's owned reserves' area is acquired by purchase and what proportion by donation, legacy or capital grant.

Some trusts may have decided to avoid buying sites in favour of establishing reserves in partnership with state and private landowners. Two younger trusts – London and Ulster – have apparently followed this practice since their formation, while the Scottish Wildlife Trust (SWT) appears to have adopted it perhaps only as a temporary strategy. Up to 1989 the area owned by the SWT had remained almost constant since 1978, while the area managed under agreement increased four-fold. Despite having one of the largest incomes of all Wildlife Trusts, the London WT did not own any of its reserves in 1990: the majority were owned by London boroughs and managed by the LWT under licence. This tenure strategy has an interesting parallel in the strategy pursued by other new CARTs, such as the Groundwork Trusts, which explicitly avoid land-ownership. These trusts effectively rely upon local authorities and others as 'benign owners' in a similar way to the Cornwall Trust's relations with the National Trust.

The behaviour of these trusts suggests the hypothesis that the recent tenure trend identified for the trusts as a whole (towards ownership *or* management by agreement) indicates a 'parting of the ways' between two emerging styles of trust operation. In one direction the trust becomes primarily a partner in the planning of nature conservation within the county, pinpointing opportunities for *other landowners* to create reserves or other valuable areas which the trust develops and manages without ownership. In the other direction, the trust seeks to purchase its own reserves wherever possible, in order to ensure that these prime sites have the maximum likelihood of remaining as wildlife habitats in the long term. One could see these tactics as analogous to David Ricardo's theory of economic rent where, in response to increasing demand for land, users either expand the 'extensive margin' (increasing the total area over which they have management responsibility) or expand the 'intensive margin' (pursuing *ownership* to give the highest possible protection to the land which they do control).

It is possible for these two strategies to co-exist within one trust. The Essex Wildlife Trust in 1990 had two categories of site: nature reserves of county or national significance and nature conservation areas (NCAs) of local value. The system was indirectly linked to the trust's priorities for site acquisition, in that it only accepted further NCAs if management responsibility was taken by its own local groups, whilst continuing to 'pursue active acquisition by lease or purchase' of nature reserves (EWT Development Plan, 1990). A number of other trusts' devel opment plans similarly discussed the need to devolve management responsibility to local groups as they expanded, but only the Essex trust made such a clear distinction between local control of locally valued sites and whole-trust control of county, regionally or nationally valued sites.

Reserves' access

Of the 47 trusts who responded to our 1990 survey, comprehensive reserve access details were given by 29 trusts. The following pattern emerges:

   5 trusts (17%) had open access to all reserves for both public and members
17 trusts (59%) had public access to over half their reserves

Table 7.3 Access[†]

	Numbers of reserves	%
Total for which data available	904	(100)
Generally open to public without permit or chaperone	457	50
Generally open access to members only	169	19
Access with permit/by prior arrangement	224.5	25
Reserves closed/severely restricted	53.5	6

[†] see note 3 at end of chapter.

> 5 trusts (17%) offered members-only access to over half their reserves
>
> 2 trusts (7%) had roughly equal numbers of reserves open only to members and reserves open to the public (with a minority of closed reserves)
>
> only 1 trust had over a third of its reserves closed to everyone

If reserve-by-reserve access data from this sample is combined regardless of trust, the results are as shown in Table 7.3.

The majority of trusts stating an access policy in their publications say that they have open access to members wherever possible. Of these, a significant proportion extend this to include the public, but one or two trusts obviously see access as a particular benefit of trust membership. However the figures in Table 7.3 suggest that membership of a local trust is by no means a prerequisite for access to its nature reserves. Trust members are generally much more fully informed about the reserves and their accessibility than the general public but this is a more subtle (albeit conscious) form of exclusion than directly barring access to non-members. It is generally true that a keen non-member could probably visit almost as many reserves as a member, for little or no extra cost. The low profile of many of the Wildlife Trusts' reserves probably ensures that public access to them will not reach levels at which the wildlife is seriously threatened. Where reserves are well known locally and nationally, access is more likely to be controlled by charging entrance fees or by restricting entrance to certain people or limited opening hours. Otherwise, access may be controlled at sites where

Table 7.4 Sources of operational income, 1988/89

	%*
Membership subscriptions**	21.7
Profit on sales of goods	6.3
Contracting and consultancy	3.7
Grants (not including job training schemes)	30.7
Donations	12.8
Investments	9.3
Other (events, produce of reserves)	15.4

* Mean proportions for all trusts.
** Including corporate members and tax reclaimed on covenants.

the flora or fauna are very sensitive to disturbance (e.g. bat holes and small sites harbouring very rare plants), and when the trust has agreed to this as a condition of the management or lease of a reserve from a private land-owner. Again, this is more likely to arise on sites of particular wildlife rarity and/or sensitivity.

Generally speaking, therefore, it appears that access is not viewed as a privilege of membership but more as a by-product with public benefit which results from the trust's aim to manage reserves for longer-term environmental objectives. It would be a misapprehension to think that county trusts are exclusive clubs which accumulate nature reserves purely for their own members' benefit.

Operational income

The combined operational income of the Wildlife Trusts was £6.05 million in 1988. This sum was raised as shown in Table 7.4.

The combined operational income of the Wildlife Trusts has grown substantially since 1978. This rate of growth was also a feature of the previous ten years: since 1968, total trust operational income has multiplied over ten times in real terms. The individual incomes of trusts varied markedly (Figure 7.9).

In 1978, trusts relied to a greater extent upon income generated through membership and much less funding came from grants (an estimated 12 per cent: SPNC, 1978). The increase in grant aid available to the trusts since 1978

Table 7.5 NCC grant aid (operational), 1988/89

	Amount (£)	%
Staff posts	274 237	65.5
Reserves' management work/equipment	90 989	21.7
Computers/cars	16 471	3.9
Publication/education	18 719	4.5
Administrative reviews	3 911	0.9
Storm disaster: work and staff	14 375	3.4

Source: NCC.

Table 7.6 Total WWF grant aid (operational), 1986/87–1989/90

Year	£	Estimated % of trusts' combined income
1986/87	31 428	0.63
1987/88	100 925	1.92
1988/89	94 645	1.53
1989/90	170 227	n.a.

Source: compiled from RSNC records.

– particularly from the NCC and its successor agencies –
has undoubtedly been a major factor influencing their
ability to expand since the 1980s. In 1976/77, the NCC
paid out £15 533 to the trusts through its Section Three
grants for general management (SPNC, 1978). By 1988/89
the NCC paid £418 702 in grants to the county trusts, or
6.9 per cent of their total operational income. The amount
was apportioned as shown in Table 7.5.

The WorldWide Fund for Nature (WWF) has long been a
financial supporter of the county trusts, grant-aiding both
operational and capital expenditure. In the financial years
1986/87–1989/90, the WWF gave grant aid for operational
expenditure as detailed in Table 7.6.

The figures in Table 7.5 illustrate the relative secondary
importance of subsidy provided by the WWF as compared
to that from the NCC over a similar period, although for
individual projects within particular trusts the two sources
may have been equally important. The WWF funded a
similar range of operational expenditure to that of the NCC
(as given in Table 7.5). The Countryside Commission, the
government-sponsored UK2000 Environment Initiative and

local authorities also funded a range of expenditure by local trusts, but figures could not be extracted from trust accounts and were not sought from each donor organisation directly.

Another important change in sources of trusts' operational income, though not yet developed to a great extent, is the commercial contracting of trust services and skills to other landholders. It did not contribute greatly to the trusts' combined operational income in 1988, but its potential to raise funds was indicated by the Cleveland Trust, which in 1990 won a contract for more than £250 000 from the Teesside Development Commission to 'green Teesside'. This grant effectively more than doubled its annual income and the Trust increased its paid staff from 10 to 17 as a result.

Operational expenditure

The operational expenditure of the trusts in 1988 – £6.2 million – was greater than their combined operational income because a number of trusts recorded financial losses in this year. The expenditure figures were difficult to divide into meaningful categories because of wide variation in the management strategies and accounting procedures of the trusts. The classification used in Table 7.7 is therefore somewhat arbitrary and is based upon accounting breakdowns supplied by 33 trusts.

Land management implications

From 1977 SPNC figures, it appears that expenditure on land management at that time accounted for around 19 per cent of total expenditure, which corresponds to just under £3/ha of reserve area. In 1988, total expenditure on management is estimated to have made up a similar proportion (17 per cent) of total expenditure, but this corresponds to approximately £23/ha of the reserves' area now held. Even adjusting the figure for inflation, this means that expenditure on land management per hectare of reserves' area rose over three-fold in the ten-year period. This reflects both an undoubted increase in the financial resources available for land management and an increase

Table 7.7 Trusts' operational expenditure, 1988

Proportional expenditure on:	%
Salaries of all staff (except those on training schemes)	43
Administration expenses (includes travel costs, conferences, promotions, insurance, legal costs)	15
Land management costs (e.g. rents, machinery and materials)	17
Equipment costs (office equipment, cars, buildings rents, repairs and maintenance)	13
Education and publications (newsletters, books, 'WATCH')	7
Other (including RSNC capitation fee)	5

in the land management activities undertaken by the trusts.

The increase in the financial resources available for land management may have been largely fuelled by government-sponsored employment programmes. Many trusts have lamented the demise of the MSC Community Programme (CP) schemes through which they were able to organise a great deal of reserve management work throughout the 1980s. Many hundreds of people were employed by the Wildlife Trusts under these schemes, and major reserve management projects were accomplished by them. Even though trusts' own expenditure on employment under the schemes was minimal (and government expenditure on job creation through the programmes has been excluded from the accounts data presented here), the availability of this pool of labour allowed the trusts to undertake much more substantial management tasks than they would have otherwise been able to contemplate. These tasks frequently involved additional management expenditure on equipment, employee supervision and training materials, which would figure in the accounts presented here.

The Employment Training (ET) schemes which replaced the CP in 1988/89 are more restrictive both in terms of the numbers of people they employ and their ability to be operated by trusts as means to fund reserve management teams. They are intended only as specific career-training opportunities for the long-term unemployed, and less for the benefit of the community at large. Trusts must show that the work they provide is fully training employees in a range of skills over a scheduled time period. Setting up this type of training course is often beyond the means of such relatively small voluntary groups, and the effect has been to greatly reduce the use which they can make of these government-funded schemes. To illustrate the importance of the change: in 1987/88, 25 trusts employed over 800 people under the CP. By 1989/90, ET schemes were supporting fewer than 150 jobs within these same trusts.

The trusts' experience with the CP and ET schemes illustrates two points of current importance. Firstly, the changes made them very aware of the risks involved in relying too heavily upon vulnerable, short-lived resources when planning ahead. It may be safest to retain greater flexibility and 'adaptive opportunism' when it comes to making the most of a resource which becomes available only temporarily. Secondly, the nature of ET as opposed to CP makes working in partnership with other training agencies a much more attractive option than trying to go it alone. For example, many trusts now organise work through other local ET agencies such as NACRO (National Association for the Care and Resettlement of Offenders) rather than managing their own teams. This kind of partnership means that trusts need increasingly to plan their activities in collaboration with other public and private bodies, which suggests being able to adjust their own styles of operation accordingly.

Looking at ways in which land management has changed since 1978, there has clearly been marked expansion in this sector of trust operations. As well as having access to significant amounts of paid labour through CP and ET, several trusts purchased or hired expensive items of machinery for management (in 1988/89 at least seven trusts spent more than £1000 each on this). Some trusts now own grazing livestock and employ stockmen and women, and several others have employed agricultural and other contractors for major management projects. Also, as well as managing 'established' habitats, most trusts are now involved in creating or restoring wildlife habitat in areas of low conservation value. These changes indicate a much greater commitment to active reserve management than existed within the trusts in 1978.

It could be suggested that whereas in their early years trusts were predominantly acquiring sites with an established management history and/or low management costs, today they take on a wider variety of reserve types, notably including 'urban reserves' which may be entirely re-created from small derelict sites around towns and cities. Whereas twenty years ago trusts perhaps acquired many sites which had been traditionally managed in an environmentally benign manner by their previous owners, today such sites will be scarce and the new areas available to trusts may well have much less stable management histories. Abandoned and disused former industrial sites have increasingly become an important concern of local trusts, and the work involved in preparing 'scrapes', lakes, woodland and grassland areas at some of these sites has been considerable. Nowadays also, the semi-natural woodland and open heathland or meadow acquired by trusts is very likely to have been neglected for many years, whereas similar reserves established 20 years ago might still have been managed by previous landholders. Restoring overgrown woods and 'scrub-bashing' on open sites to encourage the reappearance of wildflowers and associated fauna again entail a major input of labour and equipment.

The other important factor must be an increased awareness of the need for active management of sites, which has also grown within the trust movement over the last ten to twenty years. Whereas the acquisition of new reserves may have been the major priority in 1970, it is now equally likely to be the arresting of habitat decline upon those reserves which trusts already hold, within which traditional management may have ceased either before or after acquisition.

It must also be noted that these figures relate to expenditure on *land management* and not purely reserves' management. In particular, those trusts which aim to expand their contracting business may have invested in equipment for the dual purpose of management of their own reserves and for present or future management work done elsewhere, under contract. This would be recorded in the table above as land management expenditure and yet it would not necessarily represent a greater level of investment in *reserves* management. The expanding range of some trusts' land management activities outside their own reserves (e.g. in collaboration with local authority environmental improvement schemes) will have contributed to an apparent increase in management costs per hectare of reserves.

Capital income and expenditure

For those 38 trusts which recorded major growth in capital and appeals funds during 1988, the growth in these funds totalled £3 million and was derived, on average, 23 per cent from public sources and 77 per cent from private donations and voluntary events (see note 4 at end of chapter). A total of 22 trusts had purchased land during the year and, of these, 13 trusts spent in total £899 700, or an average of £69 000 per purchasing trust, for purchases totalling an estimated 927 ha of land. This means an average price of £970/ha was paid for these reserves. If all trusts had spent an equal average amount per hectare on purchases, their combined expenditure would have amounted to approximately 40 per cent of the capital income of the Wildlife Trusts during the year. Overall, therefore, the trusts were apparently accumulating capital funds during 1988.

The size of trusts' capital income in 1988 was heavily influenced by the various county and regional Wildlife Appeals, mostly launched in the mid-1980s to run for a limited period (usually until 1990). The income from the appeals, although going into capital funds, is not earmarked specifically for capital expenditure and the objective is that it should build up a source of operational income for each trust (through investment). Other separately recorded 'capital' income is money given either for reserves' purchases or for specific spending projects *outside the usual range of trusts' planned activities* (e.g. for the 1987–88 storm damage appeals, for which separate funds were established). Since some of the Wildlife Appeals' income is also earmarked for particular land purchases but the amount is not specified, it is impossible to calculate the total amount of capital raised for reserves' purchase as compared to that raised to build up a fund for future income generation.

In 1988/89 the NCC granted £394 521 to Wildlife Trusts for reserves' purchase, almost exactly one-third of the estimated costs of reserve purchases by the trusts in this year. Throughout the period 1971–77 a large share of reserves' purchase costs were met by WWF grants (20 per cent of total costs; SPNC, 1978), but this share has been declining since then and by 1988/89 the proportion of estimated reserves' purchase costs met by the WWF was

only 6.9 per cent. Comparing the average price per hectare
paid for reserves with that recorded in 1978 (SPNC, 1978),
this has fallen in real terms by almost 50 per cent. The
reasons are difficult to ascertain, but are likely to include
falling agricultural land prices throughout the 1980s.

It may also represent a shift of trust priorities away from
buying reserves in the cases where this will cost them a
great deal, and towards using a greater proportion of
capital resources to establish reserves' maintenance funds.
In the period 1975–77, reserves' purchases had accounted
for around one-quarter to one-third of the combined total
expenditure of all trusts. During 1988, estimated capital
expenditure on land purchase accounted for just under
one-sixth of gross expenditure by them whilst increases to
separately recorded capital funds accounted for approximately one-third of the gross income of the trusts in this
year. This indicates the relative importance to the Wildlife
Trusts of the money they build up in capital funds, and
suggests a decline in the relative importance of capital
expenditure on reserves' purchase. However, these data
present only one year's activities – it would be necessary to
examine a series of accounts over the years to ascertain
whether the change in emphasis is a consistent trend.

Also in this context it may be significant that a number
of trusts have recently renamed their 'Reserves' Acquisition Fund' as a 'Reserves' Acquisition and Maintenance'
fund.

Trust problems

Of all 47 trusts who replied to our 1990 request for information, 33 addressed this question specifically. Each listed
on average two main problems. As Table 7.8 shows, by far
the most pressing concern of trust management was the
lack of a sound financial base from which to fund their
ongoing commitments and their developing workload. In
particular, the problem of finding the money to pay
enough staff was highlighted. As one respondent put it,
raising money for specific reserve acquisitions is often
easier than raising money for people's salaries. Even those
posts which were grant-aided by the NCC, Countryside
Commission, UK2000 or WWF were aided for a limited
period only, and often on a declining percentage

Table 7.8 Principal trust problems, 1990

	Respondents	
	No.	%
Core funding	26	78.8
(specifically for staff)	(14)	
Reserve management resources	14	42.4
Too much administration pressure*		
general	3	7.7
from demand growth	4	10.3
from outside factors	2	5.1
Membership small or declining	5	12.8
Lack of decent HQ premises	6	15.4
Skills shortage	2	5.1
Specific local campaigns	2	5.1
Lack of money for everything	2	5.1
Other**	3	5.1

* 'Demand growth' refers both to demand for trust services from other bodies and demand associated with membership expansion, and 'outside factors' refers to replying to questionnaires and the increasing need to 'market' activities commercially.
** Competition from other trusts, VAT liability, and merger with another trust leading to short-term uncertainty in planning.

contribution, with the understanding that the trust uses this support to create a post which will gradually be funded from its own resources. In fact, there are many instances of these posts simply ceasing once the initial grants dry up – albeit often only temporarily, until another grant source can be tapped.

As things now stand, very few trusts generate sufficient income directly from their own activities to support more than a handful of staff. Their current range of growth and development activities still rely heavily upon grant-aided posts. However, the comment is relative: it must be remembered that ten years ago most trusts would not have been in a position to even contemplate this kind of work.

The second most commonly expressed problem was that of generating sufficient resources to manage reserves. This comment was often accompanied by comments such as 'the demise of MSC schemes has been a serious problem', and may reflect 1990 preoccupations with this particular responsibility because of the CP–ET change. One trust said that building up equally effective and skilled volunteer·

management resources required much time and effort, while another commented that *long-term* management costs were a particular concern.

The other issue which lies behind many of the trusts' problems is a more general one of settling upon the most appropriate form of development for a national assemblage of such varied local organisations. The delicate balance which exists between competitive-style expansionist aims and peaceful co-existence was touched upon earlier and is considered further in Chapter 14. In explaining their main problems, several trusts hinted that they felt they were spending too much time on administration and management and too little on practical conservation. One trust representative proposed that this problem could best be solved by a major 'rationalisation' of the movement involving mergers and restructuring, centralising management as far as was possible in order to reduce administration costs and leaving the local groups free to 'get out into the countryside'.

While this might appear attractive from a financial viewpoint, other trusts would no doubt find the idea worrying because it could mean an accelerated 'corporatisation', of a movement which has traditionally maintained a grassroots, locally-based image. One of the problems cited on another questionnaire was 'growing pressure to become more of a business, less of a voluntary organisation', and corporate 'rationalisation' could easily appear as another such pressure.

One is drawn to the similarities between the Wildlife Trust movement and the older co-operative movement. Several theorists (reviewed by Le Vay, 1983) have examined the forms of growth and development of co-operatives in different countries which, like the Wildlife Trusts, all share common non-commercial objectives (in addition to commercial ones). Le Vay (1988) describes how one form of national co-operative development, typified by France and West Germany, has been to 'corporatise' into a strong national organisation, while another has been to remain as large numbers of small and dispersed groups without a single national structure, as has been the case in the UK and USA. In the case of 'corporatisation', growth seems inevitably to involve the progressive transfer of day-to-day decision-making away from members and towards professional managers, in return for greatly increased stability and financial turnover. The individual member becomes progressively less 'a crucial and active part' of the organisation and more a passive 'consumer' of its services. In the second more 'individualist' case, however, the national co-operative movement is often viewed as a relative failure because each co-op tends to be more concerned with its own day-to-day survival than with any wider aims and objectives, and many co-ops are short-lived.

The county trusts are clearly not as vulnerable as the latter sort of co-operative; their record of survival so far has demonstrated their durability as organisations. However, the issue of corporatisation, and its implications for the nature of the trust movement, is certainly of current importance to them. The movement as a whole might do well to consider in exactly what ways it hopes to develop over the coming decade, and the roles that trust members, staff and the different state and private funding bodies will assume in determining this development.

Today, it could be claimed that the Wildlife Trusts fill a 'local' niche by comparison with other national organisations such as the RSPB and, in a slightly different context, the National Trust. If the movement opts for greater national corporatisation in future, it could perhaps mean that they create a niche for still smaller, more opportunist and grassroots trusts to be established within their areas, dealing with more localised and individual concerns. There has been a great deal of activity and interest in the field of specific local initiatives (e.g. Civic Trust, 1989), suggesting that such a niche has been emerging. However, would a more strongly corporatised Wildlife Trusts Partnership complement or compete with the other clearly national groups? On the other hand, if the Wildlife Trusts retain their 'local' image, will this seriously restrict their ability to influence the growing national and international environmental debate?

The 'middle path' between top-heavy corporatisation and fragmented individualism may be a form of comprehensive 'networking' between all the individual trusts; and also perhaps within individual trusts, between their local members' branches, their urban and rural groups and their central offices and professional staff. The concept of networking embodies a respect for the relative political autonomy of the units who make up the network, as opposed to the hierarchical organisational structure implied by corporatisation. It also emphasises the benefits of 'free and fair exchange' of information and resources between these units, as opposed to competitive exploitation of comparative advantage and the increasing commoditisation of nature conservation benefits which are then traded for other resources, as is implied by competitive individualism. It therefore appears to be in line with aspects of Wildlife Trusts' philosophy.

In theory networking, particularly by making use of modern information and communications systems, could make it possible for the trusts to co-ordinate activities and exchange resources without inevitably developing an increasingly centralised administration, losing their local autonomy or the active participation and support of local members. However, in the current political and economic climate, it remains to be seen how feasible and effective such a system can be in practice.

Notes

1. Compilation of statistics on trusts' reserves' tenure in 1989

Complete reserve-by-reserve tenure details were given for 1989 by thirteen trusts (holding 24.4 per cent of the total area of all trust reserves). For three trusts complete reserve tenure details were given for 1986 or 1987 and were almost complete for 1989, so were grossed up proportionally to add up to the total reserves area held in 1989 by each trust.

Nine trusts (holding 44.8 per cent of the total area of all trust reserves) supplied details of total area of reserves plus total area owned in 1989. For these, the 1982 RSNC *Reserves Handbook* states the tenure of some of their reserves, and some newer reserves' tenure is detailed in trust newsletters and annual reports. Together, these sources supplied an incomplete 'sample' of tenure information for each trust, so to make up the total reserves' area held, the 'sample' totals for leased and agreed reserves' area were grossed up proportionally.

Twenty-two trusts (holding 30.8 per cent of the total Wildlife Trust reserves' area) only detailed the total area of all their reserves in 1989. For these, RSNC handbook and trusts' reports again supplied tenure details for an incomplete 'sample' of reserves' area and for 21 trusts the sample figures were grossed up proportionally to estimate the 1989 areas held under each tenure type. The 'sample' for which details of tenure were known accounted for over 50 per cent of that trust's total area in 1989 for all these trusts except Suffolk and Derbyshire. In the latter cases only, grossing-up therefore involved multiplying the sample figures for each tenure type by a factor greater than two, and the reliability of these particular trusts' figures is therefore particularly suspect. For one trust, the Ulster Trust, their 1989 Annual Report states that very few of their reserves are owned, so the two owned reserves that had been traced were assumed to be their only owned reserves (out of a total of 19 reserves).

2. Tests on correlation of tenure details with other information

The following showed no clear relationship:

a) Area leased or agreed with total area owned by National Trust in that county area, or area owned by NT and Woodland Trust together.
b) Area leased or under agreement with proportion of county held by NT, RSNC, WT, RSPB and Wildfowl and Wetlands Trust, added together.
c) Proportion of trust reserves leased and agreed with total area owned by NT in each county.

3. Details of trusts' access arrangements for their reserves

Of those reserves for which a permit is required, it is not possible to say whether permits are charged for or available to members only in each case. Generally, permits will be mostly for members only and may involve a small fee, but a certain proportion will be for interested members of the public as well, and some will be issued free to members. Prior agreement will usually be given to members only, but again in certain cases it may be given to non-members who contact the trust office or a local warden.

Of those reserves with public access, the majority have this by default because public footpaths cross the reserve. For a number of these sites access is only along the public paths. In some cases the trust says that the public should keep to rights of way but members may walk wherever they like, in other cases both members and public are asked to keep to paths, and in other cases both are allowed off the paths. However, since few reserves are carefully policed, this may make little real difference to where people go once they are in a reserve.

4. Accounting conventions

In the accounts, the convention among trusts is to give the details of movement in these funds separately to the presentation of income and expenditure for general operations.

Ironside and Silverdale AONB. Reproduced by permission of Countryside Commission/Pete Burbridge

Single-objective-led success: the Royal Society for the

8 Protection of Birds

Introduction

The Royal Society for the Protection of Birds (RSPB) holds a unique position among conservation trusts in the UK. It has one of the largest memberships – over 890 000 – and is one of the largest landowners among conservation organisations, managing 92 900 hectares of open land. Its financial influence is considerable, with a gross income of around £30 million in 1993/94: over three times the combined income of all the Wildlife Trusts in the same year. The RSPB has also been described as the most influential international voluntary conservation organisation, campaigning throughout the world to further its cause. And yet it is a charity with a remarkably clear, single objective for an organisation so large: the protection and conservation of bird species and their habitats. It is perhaps this singularity of purpose which gives the organisation its distinctive approach to the acquisition and management of rural land.

History

Like the National Trust, the RSPB is one of the oldest British conservation organisations. It began life in 1889 as a single-issue pressure group, formed by one woman in protest against the use of exotic bird plumage for ladies' hats and other clothing. The initial campaign of the Society was highly successful, significantly reducing the demand for exotic plumage and leading to government legislation to regulate the trade within the space of twenty years. This first victory set the tone for the future development of the organisation. For over a hundred years since then, the

RSPB has worked influentially on several fronts, campaigning, researching and acting directly to conserve bird populations under threat.

The RSPB is perhaps particularly privileged as a society whose past and present membership have given it a good measure of financial stability, rarely apparent among its fellow conservation trusts. It benefited greatly from the receipt of a significant number of substantial legacies and gifts early on in its development, and from a major capital gain made on relocation from a central London office to Sandy, Bedfordshire, in the early 1960s. Also, it may be that its relatively early development as a landholding conservation trust allowed the Society to capture a particular 'species refuge' niche in land management which has proved to be an extremely durable and popular role.

The RSPB's involvement in land management began relatively early on. In pursuit of safe havens for breeding bird colonies, its second principal campaigning issue, the Society recruited wardens at several sites across the country in the late 1890s. These people were volunteers, monitoring and managing the control of access to sensitive breeding areas, with the tacit consent of the landowners concerned. The number of these wardens grew steadily as their responsibilities increased. As an extension to this policy, the RSPB began to acquire its own land in 1930, when the Society purchased one small site and was given two more; most acquisitions were of important areas for breeding or migrating birds. Thus land management and landownership have been a central element in the Society's strategy from its early days.

The estate of the RSPB

The RSPB has over 130 reserves spread right across the United Kingdom. The strategic importance of the RSPB's landholdings is still recognisable today, reflected in the attitudes of staff and in the administrative structure of the Society. Reserves' management is a clearly identified and particularly well-resourced area of its work. The traditional view survives, in that reserves are seen as important primarily for their role as refuges for threatened bird populations. However, this primary role is now coupled with others – reserves are also increasingly seen as tools for experimentation, for research into optimal management, and for education: teaching others about birds and their ecology.

As might be expected from the character of the Society, which clearly meets our definition of a primary conservation CART, its landholdings are almost exclusively sites of high value for nature conservation, either internationally, nationally or occasionally at a more local level. The reserves include many designated National Nature Reserves or Sites of Special Scientific Interest.

Unlike the National Trust, the RSPB has no special powers which set it apart from other voluntary bodies. Perhaps partly because of this, it has adopted a wider variety of means to gain control over land use and management in key areas. The Society is landlord, owner-occupier, tenant and contracted manager at different sites, reflecting its desire to influence management by whatever means available in those places where it recognises a strong interest.

Site acquisition policy

The RSPB prepared its national reserves' acquisition strategy in the late 1980s. This exercise signalled a change from a more adaptive and reactive stance to reserve acquisition, to the pro-active pursuit of ownership or management of sites which fulfil its objectives most fully. The strategy assesses areas according to a list of the most important and threatened bird species and related habitats. A sites inventory, collated at RSPB headquarters in Bedfordshire, assesses which kinds of land area are most valuable in the conservation of these birds and their habitats. Target sites within each region can thus be identified, and acquisition policies developed accordingly. As might be expected, actual site acquisition tends to be slightly more opportunistic than this would suggest, because of the nature of the land market. RSPB knows its priorities, but it is generally constrained to wait and see what becomes available.

The national reserves' acquisition strategy translates into both a consolidation and a new site strategy, consolidating around the sites already obtained and seeking other acquisitions where the Society would like a new involvement. For this organisation, with its relative financial stability and large membership among conservation trusts, the availability of grant-aid from public bodies is not always a critical factor in the ability to acquire a site. However, over the past decade grant-aid from the various countryside agencies in England, Scotland, Wales and Northern Ireland has been offered to help the Society to acquire key sites.

The RSPB prefers to go for landownership wherever possible. Ownership is seen as the best option for site safeguard, because it gives the greatest control and therefore allows the Society to make the greatest impact upon land management. With leases, it seeks as long a lease as possible. Management agreements are seen as the weakest form of protection, and the RSPB sometimes views them as expensive and fragile in the short-term. However, they are acknowledged by staff to be useful in building up the advisory role of the RSPB in a local area: using the management of land held under agreement as a show-case to influence the management practices of existing owners and neighbours.

Regional variations in bird habitat may lead to slightly different priorities for acquisition. For sites in the uplands, for instance, the habitats of most value for rare species are large expanses of extensively farmed land, on which the traditional agricultural management may be optimal for birds. Here, it may be easier to maintain bird numbers relatively cheaply without outright land purchase, through simple management agreements with traditional farmers. Sometimes, such a policy is linked to RSPB ownership of a small reserve among the land managed under agreement, which is then developed as an information resource for surrounding landholders.

In principle, RSPB seeks control over detailed management. It would rarely take on land with a full agricultural tenancy already operating. Nevertheless, the Society does have a number of reserves over which such tenancies exist. This is usually as a result of inherited tenure systems. RSPB staff do not see themselves as landlords in any comparable fashion to the image espoused by many staff within the National Trust.

Generally speaking, RSPB will keep any land of conservation value that it is given. Very occasionally it sells small pieces of land with minimal conservation interest to generate extra funds. This mostly happens if a single lot of land is bought of which the major part, but not all, has high nature conservation interest. But unlike the National Trust, whose powers of inalienability can sometimes hinder the disposal of land of low landscape or heritage value, the Society does not have problems of being burdened with uninteresting land.

Land management

The straightforward objectives and relative financial security of the RSPB may make land management easier to plan than it is for other conservation groups. By virtue of the land itself, the conservation of birds is always the main objective, but management will also be designed to enhance the intrinsic value of the site as a whole for wildlife. The income-generating potential of a site is assessed, but is not a critical factor.

RSPB's management strategy, like its acquisition policy, is therefore unashamedly professional. The Society was one of the first CARTs to adopt comprehensively a structured procedure for management plan preparation. Each plan can take up to 18 months to prepare, in a process which is begun by the reserves' warden at each site, but which then involves detailed consultation at headquarters and with other organisations. The management plan process is co-ordinated by a small team of reserves' ecologists. The planning procedure, begun in the mid-1980s, replaced a former arrangement whereby the reserves' warden – often a highly skilled biological scientist – would tend to be almost wholly responsible for site management planning and implementation. RSPB management plans have been likened to Nature Conservancy Council procedures for SSSI management and it is likely that by adopting this 'plan' approach they have provided the necessary means to keep government agencies involved in management planning with them.

Some illustrations from interviews with regional reserves' managers in Wales, East Anglia and the north of England, demonstrate this approach.

> In addition to the work of the wardens, management
> is mainly purchased from contractors or employment

training services (managed by other agencies, not themselves). The choice of which labour source to use depends largely on the specifications laid out in the management plan and its cost-effectiveness.

Volunteers are used where appropriate, either under an RSPB work scheme or through local community or RSPB members' groups. A member group may get involved with management at its local site, as well as fundraising for it – these funds raised actually on a reserve can later, in some cases, be attached to specific work at that reserve.

BTCV [British Trust for Conservation Volunteers] people may be used, but usually only if BTCV contacts RSPB because they've got a work party in the area on a certain day – the warden at the reserve might get a phone call and in response, ask BTCV to do one or two specific jobs on the reserve while they are there. The jobs would be things which were already on the management plan, and the warden would simply be taking the opportunity of a bit of free assistance when it is on offer. Similar opportunities may be offered by Heritage Coast labour resources, Woodland Trust or local trust volunteers, or National Rivers Authority technical teams.

Contractors are used for most of the more technical jobs such as large-scale dyke clearance, earth moving, cutting hay, making silage or other farm work. When there is a need for specialised equipment, a contractor is hired. These will usually be local people known to the wardens if the work is something like dyke clearance, but for much larger projects RSPB will put the work out to tender. Contractors are then chosen on a value-for-money criterion. Reserve monitoring work is also often contracted to other organisations.

RSPB is quite a 'developer' at some of its sites rather than just a holder – although the management plan always depends upon the current status or value of each site and upon its potential for enhancement. The Society uses its reserves to promote its own preferred management techniques in the hope that this kind of management will develop more widely. For example, in Glan Conwy, the Welsh Office was planning a tunnel under the estuary, and sought to deposit the spoil somewhere further down the estuary. The local Borough Council was interested in developing the area for nature conservation, so the RSPB took on the lease of the site – 80 acres – from the Crown Estates Commission. They are aiming to restore it as a wetland, developing it as a major educational reserve and visitor attraction. The local proximity of visitor traffic was an asset in this respect: the site is on a major tourist route. But the Society is confident that this kind of site can withstand heavy visitor pressure with proper planning.

RSPB farms reserves mostly by managing other people's stock, from which it recoups some income directly, but also indirectly through government schemes such as Environmentally Sensitive Areas and Countryside Stewardship in which the Society has been a keen participant. In 1991 the RSPB bought an area (450 acres) of arable land to revert to heathland, adjacent to an existing reserve at Minsmere. The reconversion to heathland, with Countryside Stewardship assistance, represents an important experiment for the Society. At its Berney marshes reserve, the RSPB has sought to encourage surrounding landowners to enter the higher-tier ESA scheme to maintain the water-table. The Society is re-flooding some bits of its own site.

The RSPB also has a few herds of its own cattle and sheep to help with the management at some sites. Reserves' managers try to get graziers in wherever possible, but in some places there are not any local livestock farmers left, or the appropriate terms cannot be agreed with local livestock graziers. The Society always makes sure that stock can be bought or sold very quickly, as local management requirements change.

Shooting is sometimes a difficult issue: RSPB policy generally is not to allow shooting on land over which it has control of the sporting rights. There are some exceptions where shooting is traditional and limited licences are granted to approved individuals or organisations where RSPB feels a net gain to conservation can be demonstrated. Often this involves the licencees agreeing to warden larger areas than they actually shoot. Red grouse is a Red Data Book species; its conservation is of international importance. However, the RSPB recognises that traditional grouse shooting has in many places maintained the heather management that proves not only suitable for red grouse but for a range of other upland breeding species.

Several RSPB reserves have shops, visitor centres and hides, educational displays and in-house interpretational staff. Some of these, in contrast to the majority of less developed reserves, are profit-making. Members have free admission to reserves. There are three tea-rooms at reserves, and refreshments are already sold in many reserve shops.

Access to RSPB reserves

The Society welcomes access wherever possible, because it is good for membership recruitment and for disseminating conservation information to the wider public. However, wildlife conservation at each site always comes first, and the interests of neighbouring landowners must also be taken into account. Public access may therefore be restricted only to certain more durable parts of reserves. The Society gives no publicity to the most sensitive sites as a matter of policy, but elsewhere visitors are encouraged through local and national promotion.

The Society encourages visits by members and non-members, but acknowledges that large numbers of casual visitors would not be welcome at some sites, for example where there are particularly rare or sensitive species breeding. They do have some areas within larger reserves which will be completely closed to access, for these kinds of reason. The results of RSPB surveys show that visitors to its reserves include a large number of people on holiday, but many local people also visit. Wardens may organise special local open-days for schools and other groups and individuals. A high percentage of visitors to the more remote, specialist sites are members, but elsewhere there is more of a mixture.

In areas of high population growth, RSPB considers ways of better visitor management, such as putting ceilings on the numbers of visitors to certain sites where pressures are very heavy, or looking at the possibility of managing certain areas of reserves for a larger number of visitors in order to relieve pressure on other more sensitive parts of a reserve.

Educational reserves – a new development

RSPB has an established tradition of using its reserves for teaching and field study – 35 reserves now offer these facilities and 50 000 children visit them each year. In the 1990s, the Society has identified four of its reserves as Educational Development Centres, with a special role in education and training. The Centres are all near to major conurbations in Scotland and England. They develop new teaching programmes and serve as training centres for educational staff from other RSPB reserves, as well as demonstrating the Society's field education to key national and international visitors.

Education on RSPB reserves is offered to schools for a charge which goes to pay the costs of the 70 part-time teacher–naturalists working at the reserves. The emphasis of the teaching is activity-based work, designed to integrate into the national curriculum in each UK country. This venture has proved very popular with corporate sponsors, and through their support the Society has been able to place a new emphasis upon demonstrating the benefits of field education to an increasing range of schools.

Future priorities for reserves

Both habitat action plans and species' action plans have been prepared, which set out the best ways of pursuing priority tasks for each of these. This helps guide the use of current and future resources, and decisions on how reserve acquisition and management should be balanced against other demands for resources for lobbying, information provision, etc. For instance, if an important species has a large range which includes a mixture of habitats, trying to protect it through site acquisition is likely to be ineffective, whereas promoting better management by all landowners within its natural range could be more cost-effective. By contrast, a rare species which depends on particular habitats or features could be best provided for by targeting and acquiring areas where these can be specially maintained or created.

In order to raise the public's awareness of land management issues in conservation, the Society must use its reserves effectively. It is now seeking to do more to develop interpretation at reserves, but always in a way that is appropriate to the reserve. Some regions did very little interpretation until quite recently, perhaps because as conservation experts first, they did not have the in-house expertise or the local-level resources for this.

Another related issue for the Society's future development must be its relations with other local interests and local communities. Although undoubtedly some local wardens were extremely effective in liaising with other local groups over the management of their sites, in other places there have been some serious obstacles to RSPB site acquisition and/or work caused by local community resentment of the 'intrusion' of what they have seen as a specialist, nationally and internationally-focused organisation into their local sphere. Again, the Society is aware of this issue, and it is a subject of concern which it is addressing.

RSPB administration: private organisation and central control

Unlike the National Trust, whose active membership has caused significant debate on land-use policies over the years, the RSPB's membership remains apparently staunchly supportive of the society's acquisition and management programmes. Notwithstanding the large membership and the considerable regional staff of the RSPB, their reserves' policy is largely professionally and centrally directed, although since the early 1990s the line management of the reserves' mechanism has been delegated to the regions. This contrasts somewhat with the National Trust's longer-standing, broad regional autonomy. However, at ground level, much responsibility is vested in the individual wardens at each site, a body of well-qualified and experienced conservation land managers, who also serve as the principal spokespeople for the Society among local communities.

When budgeting for reserves' management, site wardens put in a bid for the work set out in their reserve's management plan for that year through the regional network. The bids are then prioritised at national level. In the process of allocation, all reserves' managers discuss

Table 8.1 Major sources of RSPB income, 1985 and 1994

Source	1985		1994		% change 1985–1994
	£000s	%	£000s	%	
Membership	3258	47	10 529	34	223
Income from land	227	3	745	3	228
Investment income	364	5	1018	3	180
Enterprises	218	3	2654	9	1117
Grants and donations	1630	23	7492	24	360
Legacies	1279	18	8397	27	556
Total	6976		30 835		342

Sources: RSPB Annual Reports, 1985/86 and 1993/94.

their needs collectively with staff at headquarters, so compromises can be struck. Through this process, wardens know well in advance the funds that will be available to them for the coming season. All the funds generated at each reserve (through visitor fees, sales, refreshments, etc.) are accounted for centrally, again allowing maximum central flexibility, with no resources tied to any one site or area.

The strong profile of headquarters in RSPB management also means that a lot of basic enquiries about information are passed to the centre, reducing the public relations pressure on regional staff. The RSPB members' magazines and annual report are widely read and contain a great deal of up-to-date material concerning RSPB activities in the regions, which contributes to this process.

Finance

As Table 8.1 shows, the income of the RSPB has more than quadrupled in nominal terms over nine years since 1985. This overall figure masks some interesting shifts in the contribution made by each major income source to the total. Although membership income has trebled over the period (as membership numbers have grown), its relative share of total income has fallen from just under one-half to one-third. While the contributions of income from land, investment income and grants and donations have remained proportionally similar, the relative contributions of both enterprise income, and income from legacies, have grown significantly. The most marked increase is in enterprise income, which increased over ten-fold, but from a relatively low base in 1985.

As with the figures given in Chapter 6 for the National Trust, these do not record the contribution of labour offered by volunteers, some highly skilled naturalists and scientists, who work for the Society each year. In 1992, over 15 000 volunteers contributed their time and effort to RSPB work.

Future issues for the Society

The changes of the 1980s within the conservation movement, with the advent of a more market-orientated approach, have made the RSPB more efficient on the marketing side. Its membership has grown, and general awareness of the organisation among the general public has grown. However, retaining members has been difficult, particularly through the recession.

When asked about occasional bad press, possible causes are variously suggested by staff: perhaps the Society's image is not very well-developed among non-members, and people remain unaware of the internationally influential conservation work that RSPB does. Despite its large and broad membership, the organisation has been most successful in recruiting middle-class and frequently older people, thus it may perhaps have alienated others – one officer noted that they have not examined urban ecology at all, which might appeal to different kinds of potential member.

Notwithstanding these issues, the RSPB clearly plays an influential role in policy at national and even international levels (through active membership of the 'Birdlife International' umbrella organisation). It produces a steady stream of policy documents which promote its objectives and are widely recognised as important contributions to current environmental and related policy debates. It also plays a valuable innovative role through localised experiments in new forms of land management, through giving specialised advice to others, and by commissioning and publishing scientific research relating to the needs and the status of birds and their habitats. Given this strong 'top-level' profile it is perhaps inevitable that at a local level it may be the subject of some envy and possibly some mistrust by other groups, as we have occasionally detected when researching this book.

In future, with the advent of more European and global environmental policy, the Society will doubtless continue to build upon its national and international successes. It remains to be seen how far this work will continue to sit comfortably alongside its equally distinctive role as landowner and manager around the country, with all the responsibilities and resource demands that this inevitably brings.

Blà Bheinn, Skye. Reproduced by permission of Dr T.E. Isles

Private land trusts: philanthropy or survival?

In the course of researching this book, we discovered a huge variety of organisations which come within our definition as Conservation, Amenity and Recreation Trusts. In Chapters 6, 7 and 8 we examined three of the largest and most influential organisations. In Chapters 9, 10 and 11 we attempt to give a flavour of the many others in existence by looking at the principal forms and origins of different kinds of landholding trust. In this chapter we examine how trusts have been set up from former traditional country estates. In Chapter 10, we look at examples of trusts originating from the local concerns of groups of individuals, most of whom were not traditional landowners. In the final chapter of this part of the book (Chapter 11), we look at the particular example of trusts formed largely through the initiative of the public sector.

A sector in decline

In Chapter 2, we described the decline of the 'country house estates'. These had been a major influence on the pattern of countryside development in the 19th century, but experienced rapid and extensive decline in the early parts of the 20th century. Those which have remained have often faced considerable difficulties in keeping the house and land intact and in the physical upkeep of the property. Sometimes this has been achieved by selling off certain assets and sometimes by introducing new activities onto the estate, often based on the tourism potential of the house itself. Sometimes, too, estates have been transferred to new owners who have the necessary capital to invest in the estate to keep things going. But this kind of purchaser has often not been easy to find, and estates have instead been split up and the main house has either been transferred into separate, often institutional ownership, or fallen into disrepair. In recent years, the heavy tax burden on these kinds of property has been significantly reduced by successive governments, thus reducing the need for estates to be split up in order to meet a tax bill, upon the death of an owner. But the high maintenance costs remain a problem and thus in many cases fragmentation is still the most likely outcome upon sale. The decline of country houses and their collections has been surveyed by Sayer (1993). In the fourteen years from 1979, some 250 family estates have been sold in the United Kingdom.

Various arrangements are possible which may keep an estate together. As we described in Chapter 6, one is for estates to be passed over to the National Trust. But this is only possible for property of national significance and where it is possible to raise a sufficient endowment. The Trust will then ensure the long-term maintenance of the estate, allowing the continued residence of the donor and his or her family. An alternative, which may end up with a similar result, may be possible where the owner faces a substantial tax bill and the property can be handed over to government in lieu of taxation. Such properties have then often been handed over to the National Trusts. This practice has in the past been facilitated through the National Land Fund, which is discussed in Chapter 13. In this chapter, we consider two further different arrangements. First we examine the question of tax relief on heritage property, but primarily we concentrate on privately endowed charitable land trusts. In the first type of arrangement, an owner is given relief from tax and, as we see, it seems that in at least some cases in the past, little has been given in return. The second arrangement requires the owner to give up any financial return from the estate.

Tax relief on heritage property

The state provides assistance to the owners of land and property of particular scenic, scientific or heritage value in the form of relief from inheritance tax. Where an estate can be regarded as part of the national heritage by virtue of its outstanding historic or wildlife interest or landscape value, legislation allows such assets – together with an optional maintenance fund as an endowment to pay for their upkeep – to be free from inheritance tax. Exemption can apply both to works of art and other chattels and to land and buildings. In the case of land and estates, exemption is conditional upon a management plan being adopted which provides for the long-term maintenance of the valuable features of the estate, plus reasonable public access. In England, this plan will be negotiated with the Countryside Commission, English Nature or English Heritage (depending upon the principal heritage interest). Most plans will require improved public access and strict control over any development which might be proposed on the estate. Once granted, conditional exemption remains in force indefinitely, provided that the management conditions detailed in the plan continue to be satisfied. In a sense, by allowing this relief the state is implying that the owner is holding the property in trust for the nation, and the public good. However, it does not fall within our definition of a CART because the property is still owned by private individuals.

Inheritance tax relief for heritage property has not been widely publicised and the total cost in terms of tax forgone is not known. The Inland Revenue has estimated that £36 million was forgone as a result of new agreements on land and buildings between 1 April 1986 and 31 March 1992 (National Audit Office, 1992). This mechanism has been criticised, most particularly for failing to publicise the arrangements which have been made for public access. The degree of secrecy has been particularly criticised by Shoard (1988) who was able to discover officially the number of cases which had been involved, but nothing at all about them. Given the public access requirements in the agreements this seemed wholly inappropriate and meant that there was unlikely to be any effective monitoring of the implementation of the management plans. More recently there has been some public discussion of the agreements (Davies, 1992). For instance, agreements have been made on the Duke of Devonshire's estate relating to 12 000 acres at Chatsworth and a further 6000 acres near Buxton. At the other extreme, tax relief was allowed on 760 acres of herb-rich pasture and woodland in Dorset. In 1991 arrangements for publicising access to land were strengthened in that owners are required to inform the Central Council for

Physical Recreation and in Scotland the Physical Sports Association about the relevant access arrangements on the land in question. Since 1992, the information has been passed on by the relevant government agencies. This information is then passed on to member organisations. The requirement, however, only applies to applications for exemption which were received after January 1991.

This type of arrangement is also subject to a variety of other criticisms. Management plans may be insufficiently detailed in their specification of requirements in contrast, for example, to the details which are incorporated into management agreements on Sites of Special Scientific Interest or scheme agreements in Environmentally Sensitive Areas or Countryside Stewardship. The level of tax saving and hence the incentive which an owner has to offer any public benefit depends upon his or her individual financial position (which determines the marginal rate of tax) rather than on the potential public benefit (Whitby, 1993), and the level of the saving is not made known to the countryside agencies which negotiate the management plans. There is also a limit from both a public and a landowner's point of view in that the land has to be of national significance; so sites of only local importance do not qualify.

Private land trusts

For other landed estates, an option which is in principle more widely available is for the owner to establish a private land trust – a CART formed to take on the ownership of the land and property of the estate. These meet the definition of a CART because they provide public benefit, but they are usually privately endowed, having their origins in an established landholding whose main form of use is often maintained upon formation of the trust, with the previous owner or family keeping some involvement in the land, even though the ownership of the land is itself given up to the trust. Abecassis (1989, p. 6) defines a land trust as 'a charitable trust or non-profit making body which is created by a landowner in order to hold his land in perpetuity for the public benefit'. Some form of conservation, amenity or recreation is often included amongst the objectives of such trusts. We call these 'private land trusts' to differentiate them from other independent CARTs which have their origins in the public sector or in a collective iniative. However, we should, of course, note that all of the CARTs which we are considering are private and own land! A number of the best-known country houses, including Arundel Castle, Burghley House, Chatsworth and Harewood House, are held by privately endowed charitable trusts (Sayer, 1993).

Land trusts generally have charitable status. Once this has been achieved, there will be considerable tax advantages, being completely free from capital and income taxes, and a trust may also become eligible for grants which would otherwise not be available. In order to gain these advantages, the property must be fully and permanently owned by the trust (or, exceptionally, at least to be leased to the trust for a long period of time, such as 99 years) and the trust must have charitable objectives which are acceptable by the Charity Commission. Acceptable objectives generally fall within four headings:

1. The relief of poverty.
2. The advancement of education.
3. The advancement of religion.
4. Other purposes beneficial to the whole or a sufficiently important section of the community.

Notably in our present context, it was accepted by the courts (re Verrall 1916) that 'the permanent preservation for the benefit of the nation of lands and buildings of beauty or historic interest and also with regard to land the preservation of their natural apsect, features and animal and plant life' constituted a valid charitable purpose, provided that it was for general benefit and not only for the benefit of the donor family (Nuttall, n.d.). The decision is therefore based upon whether there is sufficient public benefit to justify the acceptance of the trust as a charity; preserving land in an estate is of itself not enough. Land in a trust established solely for its preservation as a single estate would have to demonstrate some public benefit arising from its scientific or historic interest or outstanding natural beauty.

To be viable, the trust has to have a sufficient endowment to support its obligations as a landowner. This may be from assets which are themselves conserved or there may be a maintenance fund, such as can be set up for the maintenance of national heritage assets. A maintenance fund may include land or other assets which can be managed in any chosen way, but from which all income is devoted to the support of the charitable objectives of the trust.

The trust will be managed by trustees who are often drawn from the donor and family and others who offer professional expertise or represent the interests of the other beneficiaries of the trust. The donor family may continue to farm the land, as a tenant to the trust, but rent must be paid at the full market rate. Thus the family must not benefit financially from the value or the income of the trust.

Private land trusts in practice[1]

The concept of a landowning charitable trust is a very old one. The Hospital of St Cross in Winchester is an almshouse charity dating from 1136. It exists to provide accommodation to the poor who are housed in a set of mediaeval buildings. The charity also owns surrounding parkland, including a small dairy farm. In this century the Stornoway Trust, another private land trust, was established in 1923, and another, the Ernest Cook Trust, dates from 1952. But most private land trusts are considerably more recent, the majority having been established since the late 1970s.

Sometimes the trust is set up to preserve a tradition which has lasted for generations – for example the Clan Carmichael Charitable Trust, which was established from an estate which had been in Carmichael ownership for 700 years. This Trust has the aim of preserving local buildings and countryside, agricultural improvement and provision for the welfare of members of the Clan Carmichael and local residents. In other instances the land has been

1. We are grateful to the Land Trusts Association and in particular to Mr James Ruddock for help in providing contacts and information on many of the trusts which are referred to here (with the trusts' permission).

acquired only recently, such as in the case of the William Scott Abbott Trust, established in 1964, which owns a 533-acre farm first acquired by the Abbott family in 1923. The Trust's objectives are to advance agricultural education and promote sound and reasonably stable agricultural systems, and it operates a centre which had 25 000 visitors in 1991.

Many factors are usually involved in the establishment of a private land trust. Sometimes the estate is not generating any income or is threatened with being broken up under financial pressures, and the tax savings offered by trust status may enable it to be maintained intact. But there is usually some further associated context or motivation. Some trusts are established to commemorate somebody, or to protect an estate where a landowner has no direct heirs. In some cases the owner wishes to pursue some charitable objective or the preservation of some specific element(s) of the environment, and some or all of his or her assets may be directed towards this aim. Each trust will have its own individual characteristics and some examples are given below.

Community and estate preservation trusts

Wadenhoe is a small village in north-east Northamptonshire. Much of the village, together with an area of farmland and woods, comprise the Wadenhoe estate. The estate was owned by Major and Mrs Ward-Hunt, having been owned by the Ward-Hunt family since the early 18th century. Major Ward-Hunt's father was killed in the First World War and since that time the upkeep of the estate has to a large extent depended upon all the profits from the estate being ploughed back in maintenance and improvement. The Ward-Hunts have no children and, being concerned to ensure the survival of the estate as a single entity, they decided to establish the Wadenhoe Trust. In 1981 they set up a private land trust which became the owner of about 1000 acres, including 600 acres of farmland let to two tenants, over 200 acres of woodland let on a long lease to the Forestry Commission, together with Wadenhoe House and 29 of the 47 houses in the village. These include the village post office/store and public house.

The primary objectives of the Trust are:

(a) to preserve the village properties as an entity, as part of the national heritage;

(b) to conserve, maintain and improve for the public benefit the architectural and aesthetic qualities of the village properties;

(c) to conserve and enhance for the public benefit the natural beauty of the village surroundings;

(d) to advance the education of the public in the architectural and aesthetic merits of the village and the desirability of preserving the village and villages of a similar character for the benefit of the nation;

(e) to preserve and encourage the study and dissemination of knowledge of the archaeological sites and the indigenous flora and fauna to be found in the village and its surroundings.

It is a principle stated in the trust deed that 'every endeavour shall be made to ensure that the social character of the village as a live and continuing local community is preserved.' It is notable that neither the house nor the grounds are open to the public. The Ward-Hunts are trustees, together with four other local people. It is planned that the Ward-Hunts will leave further property to the Trust on their deaths.

The objective of village conservation is shared by the Guiting Manor Amenity Trust. The Guiting Manor estate in the Cotswolds was bought in a run-down condition in 1958 by Mr Cochrane, comprising an agricultural estate of about 1000 acres and nearly 50 houses. The property was in fact offered to the National Trust, but was turned down. It was argued that the village was not in danger, although the value of the estate was regarded as sufficient to justify preservation (Gaze, 1988, p. 221). Initially the houses and subsequently the whole estate were transferred into a private land trust. The first concerns of the Trust were to improve the physical condition of the houses which had been allowed to fall into disrepair. However, as this was achieved, the demand by outsiders for housing in the village grew, raising property prices above those affordable to many local people. The emphasis of the Trust then shifted in response to this by restricting access to the houses to people belonging to local parishes. It is the aim of the Trust to continue building houses so as to return the population to around 600, close to its 19th century level.

The agricultural land is managed to generate income for the Trust, but there is also a concern for wider amenity. Public access is allowed over the land and a 17-acre nature reserve on the estate is managed by the Gloucestershire Trust for Nature Conservation. There is also a ban on growing oilseed rape in fields adjacent to the village since the yellow flowers clash with the limestone walls and roofs. The organisation is described by Mr Cochrane as 'neo-manorial', but 'one run not for the benefit of the Lord but for that of the community'.

A large charitable trust, incorporating two major estates, was established by the Earl of Ancaster in 1978. It has been described by Clarke and Ruddock (1994). The Grimsthorpe and Drummond Castle Trust includes both Grimsthorpe Castle, located within a 12 500-acre estate in south Lincolnshire and Drummond Castle in Perthshire. The Lincolnshire estate comprises 25 let farms and 200 houses and cottages in three villages, as well as 1500 acres of commercial woodland. The Drummond estate covers a further 1500 acres. In addition to the properties, there is also an investment fund which generates about 25 per cent of the Trust's gross income.The main purpose of the charity is to preserve the properties, their historic contents and surroundings for public benefit. The specific objectives of the Trust also emphasise the educational potential of the Trust in respect of such subjects as history, natural history, agriculture, art, architecture and literature. The Trust is administered by a Board of Directors, including two family members, together with appointees made by a number of art and conservation bodies, including the National Trusts, the Lincolnshire Trust for Nature Conservation and Lincolnshire County Council. Perhaps a little counter-intuitively, Clarke and Ruddock point out that the change from a privately owned property, where the commercial objective is not necessarily the primary aim of policy, to a commercial basis operating within the guidelines of the Charity Commission can have unfortunate repercussions on the local community. For this reason a management plan is being formulated in which, for instance, certain properties have been identified to be used for local people at affordable rents.

Focusing exclusively on housing, the Lockinge Village Housing Charitable Trust owns houses in Lockinge and Ardington in Oxfordshire. This was created in 1974 by a settlement which vested 46 houses in the Trust. Since then some have been sold and others built. The aim is to provide accommodation to those who would otherwise be unable to live in the area, particularly to old-age pensioners and young people.

At a rather different scale in many respects, but with similar aims, is the Stornoway Trust. In 1918, Lord Leverhulme acquired the ownership of the Island of Lewis, off the west coast of Scotland. He decided to give this up in 1923 and, in doing so, offered the island to its people. Any crofter who wanted to become the owner of his land was given the chance to accept it as a gift (Thompson, 1986). However, the offer was refused for fear that, as owners, they would end up paying more in rates than they paid in rent and that they would also lose their eligibility for crofting grants. In place of this a Trust was established to administer the 64 000-acre estate, including Lewis Castle, the Parish of Stornoway, all the large farms and the sporting and fishing rights. Trustees are elected from the community by those owning or occupying land on the estate, providing for community control. The objectives of the Trust go beyond simple administration to the promotion of the material and social welfare of the community, through social, recreational or educational activities, improving communications, and promoting industry, agriculture, forestry, higher education and medical services. Despite this, due to a lack of funds, little had apparently been done beyond acting as the caretaker for the estate. However, recently the development of oil-related activity has provided funds which have been used for the development of salmon farming and other educational and social activities for the people of the island.

The Weston Park Foundation was established by the Earl of Bradford in order to ensure the upkeep of Weston Park estate and to make the house and park available for public access. The Trust owns the House itself, together with other buildings and about 1000 acres of surrounding farmland and woodland. The farmland and grazing in the park are let to tenants and the Earl of Bradford leases back the woodlands and sporting rights at a commercial rent. The house and park are operated as a commercial enterprise by Weston Park Enterprises Ltd, managed by Lord Bradford, the profits from which are paid to the charitable Trust.

Educational trusts

Education commonly features amongst the objectives of private land trusts. The Edward James Foundation is a charitable educational trust established in 1964 when Edward James vested West Dean Park House and its 6000-acre estate in West Sussex and a large collection of modern art, establishing West Dean College. Edward James himself led a colourful and somewhat eccentric life, spread between England, the United States and Mexico. He was a great sponsor of the arts and took a particular interest in surrealism. He was painted by Magritte and commissioned work by Salvador Dali. He was also noted for the estate which he created in Mexico, filled with surrealist constructions (Kernan, 1994). He died in 1984. The West Dean estate had been bought by William James, Edward's father, and some of it was sold at the time of his death to pay death duties. After the Second World War, it became clear that it would not be possible to maintain the house and estate in the face of the prevailing levels of taxation and increasing costs. Thus, the basic reason for founding the Trust was for their preservation as an entity. The college offers residential courses providing training in the visual arts and opportunities for high-level craftsmanship. These are aimed both at those wishing to develop a career and at amateurs. The college also accommodates conferences and seminars. There are eleven farms on the estate, six leased to tenants, and the income from these and from cottages and commercial woodlands is used to maintain the educational activities of the Foundation. Two areas on the estate are set aside as nature reserves, one leased to English Nature and the other managed by the Sussex Wildlife Trust.

Similar in many respects is the Lamport Hall Preservation Trust. The hall and its estate were formerly under the ownership of the Isham family for 400 years. The 12th Baronet, Sir Giles Isham, in the absence of direct family heirs, established in his will a charitable trust with a broad aim of promoting historic and aesthetic education, vesting the hall and 2250 acres in the Trust.

During his lifetime Ernest Cook acquired a number of landed estates; between 1931 and 1951 he purchased over 37 000 acres (Collins *et al.*, 1989). His prime objective was to preserve the estates for all time and to manage them 'in the best traditions of the old Landlord and Tenant system'

(Gaze, 1988, p. 184). He was particularly keen to preserve the connection between the estate and the previous owners, if at all possible (Collins *et al.*, 1989, p. 7). Several of these properties later represented important donations to the National Trust, including Montacute in Somerset and the Assembly Rooms in Bath, transferred during his lifetime, and Coleshill and Buscot in Oxfordshire and Bradenham in Buckinghamshire, transferred on his death. When these three latter properties were purchased, Cook made a covenant that they would be assigned to the National Trust on his death.

When he died, an attempt was made for other estates also to be accepted by the National Trust, but it was reluctant to take them. So, a separate trust was established and the remaining estates were transferred into it. The Ernest Cook Trust was set up in 1952 as an educational charity to establish or support any educational institution or initiative except agricultural colleges; to endow scholarships, fellowships, lectureships and prizes in connection with any school or university; and to pay school or university fees (Collins *et al.*, 1989, p. 37). But the primary objective was to establish a means of holding and preserving the estates. In the preamble to the trust deed, the trustees are enjoined to manage them in accordance with 'the great traditions of English landed estates, to uphold the landlord–tenant system, and to encourage "the manly sports of the countryside"' (Collins *et al.*, 1989, p. 38). Over the years, the Trust has given considerable sums towards various educational causes. Annual disbursements rose from about £4000 in the early 1960s to between £80 000 and £90 000 by 1972–75. In 1987, the figure exceeded £500 000. Amongst many other things the Trust funded the Ernest Cook Chair in Countryside Planning held jointly at University College and Wye College by the late Professor Gerald Wibberley.

The Parnham Trust is a specialised educational charity concerned with teaching design, production and management skills for the establishment of new enterprises using timber. It was set up in 1977 by John Makepeace, a furniture designer and maker, to run The School for Craftsmen in Wood based at Parnham House in Dorset. In 1983, the Trust bought Hooke Park, 330 acres of mixed woodland three miles from Parnham. This site is used by the School for Woodland Industry, providing graduates

with skills enabling them to establish their own manu-
facturing enterprises based on the supply of domestic
timber, and also for the Working Woodland, which is open
to the public.

Environmental conservation trusts

While several private land trusts have subsidiary environmental objectives of various sorts, and some even reserve
areas for nature conservation, there are others which have
a primary environmental goal, thus making them primary
conservation CARTs, as discussed in Chapter 5. A good
example is the Elmley Conservation Trust which protects
over 3500 acres of the Elmley Marshes on the Isle of
Sheppey in Kent. The Trust was established by Mr Philip
Merricks in 1987, with the funds given under a management agreement with the Nature Conservancy Council
(now English Nature). The land represents some of the last
unimproved stretches of grazing marsh in north Kent and
it had originally been planned to drain it for cereal production. Instead, the land is now actively managed as a
nature reserve. The management of the reserve has been
developing systems of grazing which can be advantageous
both from a socio-economic and from a nature conservation point of view. The Trust itself has wider aims,
including to purchase, for positive management for conservation purposes, further land of conservation value, and
to undertake further practical conservation works.

The Sir Alexander Lawrence Woodlands Trust was
established in 1985 by Sir John Lawrence and named in
memory of his father. Its purpose is to preserve an area of
55 acres near Bristol, primarily of woodland thought to be
over 500 years old and never to have been ploughed. The
objectives of the Trust include the permament preservation
and improvement of the existing land for the benefit of the
public generally and especially for the inhabitants of
the Parish of North Stoke and the village of Upton
Cheyney (Boddington *et al.*, 1989, p. 32). Conservation
work at the site was undertaken by labour funded by the
Manpower Services Commission. Since this is no longer
available, the trustees hope that future management work
may be undertaken by the British Trust for Conservation
Volunteers.

The prospects for private land trusts

It is important to make a clear distinction between the provision of tax relief for heritage property which was discussed at the beginning of the chapter and the private land trusts which we examined subsequently. In the first case, the owner receives an effective subsidy from the Treasury in return for which certain requirements are made, primarily concerning the maintenance of the asset and public access to it. However, in the past these requirements have not always been very publicly specified, nor apparently especially onerous. By contrast, in establishing a private land trust, even though all requirements for income and capital taxation may be avoided, the owner has to give up all claims to the property. Any dealings with the trust have to be entered into on a commercial basis and the trust has to demonstrate that there will be wider benefits enjoyed by the public in some way and this undertaking will be subject to the scrutiny of the Charity Commissioners. This is not to say that the owner ceases to gain any benefit from the asset. Often the critical element to the owner lies in the security which the arrangement gives for the preservation of the estate in the future. This concern commonly applies not just to the physical fabric of the estate but also to the community within which it is set. Thus where an estate has generated little or no surplus income to the owner, the financial loss may not be great. However, where the estate generally operates at a loss it may not be possible to establish a financially viable trust at all.

The creation of trusts depends upon the existence of landowners with significant holdings who are either under some degree of financial pressure or who see no other way of guaranteeing the long-term protection of their interests, particularly where there is no immediate member of the family to take over the running of the estate. It seems unlikely that owners would otherwise decide to place their land in a trust. It is therefore an approach which will only appeal to certain kinds of landowner; primarily those at the margins of long-term viability and for those without direct heirs. It is difficult to make an estimate of the public cost involved. We simply do not know what arrangements might have been entered into, if the trust option had not been available. It is probable that higher levels of tax would have been levied. In many cases a sale of estate land in small parcels would be likely to give future owners smaller total holdings and thus a smaller total liability to capital taxation, so the tax cost could be relatively short term. On the other hand, a private trust is inherently a long-term arrangement, so that public benefits should, in principle, continue. There have been some instances where the National Heritage Memorial Fund has made a financial contribution to the establishment of trusts, presumably subject to an agreement as to the specific objectives of the trust and in return for a right to nominate trustees. This may well represent an effective mechanism for the generation of environmental and social benefits for the public. However, there is considerable scope for more detailed study of the costs and benefits of these rather specific arrangements.

Of the range of organisations which meet our definition of CARTs, these private land trusts are probably closest to conventional private ownership. There is commonly a strong element of self-interest in their establishment, not only in the pursuit of the preservation of an estate but also in the preservation of a family role in the management of an estate; the element of survival. And yet they do generate clear public benefits; there is also an element of philanthropy. This reflects our general theme: the support and redirection of private incentives towards wider public goals.

Lavethan Wood, Blisland, Cornwall. Reproduced by permission of The Woodland Trust

10 Local community inspired CARTs

Trusts formed from local communities or local interest groups are perhaps the most diverse group of CARTs we have encountered. They range from organisations set up specifically to acquire land and/or to manage it for environmental ends, to others who have almost become involved in this by accident, as a by-product of their other principal aims, which may include a range of local interests and pursuits. To discuss these trusts in more detail, therefore, we have made this distinction in terms of their original intentions. However, in looking first at trusts whose activities grew out of the concerns and activities of local amenity societies, and then at their perhaps more modern counterparts – trusts originating from local campaigns, we can see common threads which we will return to at the end of the chapter.

Local amenity CARTs

There is a small group of CARTs which have a specific focus on the protection of a local area which has an established status and reputation. They are a subgroup of a much larger number of amenity organisations which are active in seeking to maintain the character of a local area, generally of high nature conservation, landscape or historic value. While they are involved in a range of activities they have a particularly active involvement in the local and sometimes national planning system. Most publish a newsletter and have a membership. Those ones which have included the ownership of open land within their activities fall within our definition of CARTs, although it should be pointed out that landownership is often a relatively minor element in the societies' overall activities.

The number of CARTs which we have identified within this group is quite small; we have obtained details of eight. But given the very large number of local amenity organisations nationally, it seems quite likely that some which would fit into this category have been missed. Lowe and Goyder (1983) record that in 1975 there were some 1250 local amenity societies, although their grouping included the County Wildlife Trusts, and very many other societies which are primarily concerned with the urban environment.

Local amenity trusts include some of the oldest CARTs which we have identified – the Dartmoor Preservation Association was established in 1883 and the Selborne Society in 1885 – dating from a first phase in the development of environmental groups as identified by Lowe and Goyder (1983). While neither was the oldest national environmental group (Lowe and Goyder propose that this was the Commons, Open Spaces and Footpaths Preservation Society established in 1865), both preceded the foundation of the Royal Society for the Protection of Birds or the National Trust.

The Dartmoor Preservation Society has as its first object 'The protection and enhancement in the public interest of the landscape antiquities flora and fauna natural beauty and scientific interest in Dartmoor'. Its second indicates 'The acquisition of land and rights over and interests in land for the purpose of object (1)'. It has acquired land at a number of sites, currently owning around 250 acres, mostly land of high nature conservation interest or else land threatened by afforestation.

The Selborne Society was founded (as the Selborne League for its first few months) in 1885 to commemorate Gilbert White (1720–1793), the curate of Selborne in Hampshire and the author of the well-known *Natural History and Antiquities of Selborne*, published in 1789. In this respect, it was perhaps not strictly conceived as a local amenity CART; it might perhaps better be described as a 'memorial' CART similar to that established recently to acquire Wheat Fen in Norfolk in memory of Ted Ellis. However, the Selborne Society has a focus upon the location about which White wrote and was established with broad concerns for the protection of birds and their plumage and the preservation of forests and places of popular resort.

In the first sixty or so years the Selborne Society operated at a national level, with a London office and several regional branches. In 1902, one of these, the Brent Valley Branch, in Ealing, established a bird sanctuary at Perivale Wood. The land was purchased in 1920 to mark the bicentenary of White's birth. Since the 1950s this reserve has been the major focus for the Society's activities.

Lowe and Goyder (p. 17) indicate the second period of the organisational expansion of environmental groups as the inter-war years and, amongst the local amenity CARTs, this saw the establishment of the Cambridge Preservation Society (1928), The Friends of the Lake District (c.1935), The Oxford Preservation Trust (1927) and the Society of Sussex Downsmen (1923). These are contemporaries, for example, of the Council for the Protection of Rural England which was established in 1926, and indeed some local societies, such as the Suffolk Preservation Society, were initially constituted as a local branch of the CPRE.

The inter-war years were a period of substantial and largely unplanned urban development and the Oxford and Cambridge organisations were founded very much in response to this. Before the Second World War, the Cambridge Preservation Society bought land strategically in order to arrest the spread of housing from Cambridge, particularly to the west of the city, given that substantial development had already occurred to the east. This effectively established a green belt in that area. Since the war some of this has been sold, but sold subject to covenants which prevent building from taking place. In the 1930s, the Society similarly extinguished development rights over some 150 acres of Grantchester Meadows. The Society has also acquired other property, including two mills and Wandlebury – over 100 acres of nature reserve in the Gog Magog hills, which is managed in-hand by the Society.

The basic policy of the Oxford Preservation Trust is to 'retain for future generations the delights of unspoilt countryside within easy reach of the city'. The first land purchased, the Old Berkeley Golf Course, was, as in the case of the Cambridge Preservation Society, also in response to the threat of building development. Other land nearby, bought in 1929, is now managed by the Berks, Bucks and Oxon Naturalists Trust (BBONT, one of the County Wildlife Trusts). Several sites were purchased in the late 1920s and

1930s and the Trust currently owns about 300 acres. The Trust has a number of area committees and associate groups which have an interest in a particular local area.

The Friends of the Lake District is not primarily concerned with land ownership. It does, however, own Hows Woods in Eskdale which was purchased from the Forestry Commission in the mid-1980s and this draws the organisation into our definition of a CART. But generally, as with practically all of the organisations in this category, the organisation is actively involved in a wide variety of issues which affect the quality of the local environment. It maintains an active participation in the planning system, for instance, in resisting the expansion of the nuclear industry in Cumbria, fencing on common land, and the development of wind farms or road proposals. It also gives grants for environmental improvement, giving money to other CARTs such as the Woodland Trust; and grants for research into topics of local interest, including rural housing and land management.

The Society of Sussex Downsmen was established for the preservation of the beauty and amenities of the Sussex Downs for the public benefit, and amongst the seven types of activity to be taken in furtherance of this objective is included 'To acquire and hold any lands, buildings and hereditaments situate in or in the vicinity of the Sussex Downs'. As with others in this group the Society pursues its aims through a wide range of activities. For these purposes, it has divided the Downs into twelve districts, from Petersfield in the west to Eastbourne in the east, and each district has an officer. The Society manages three sites in the Downs, one of which has particular archaeological interest.

In contrast to most other categories of CART, there appear to be fewer recently established local amenity CARTs, perhaps because most local areas of conservation significance already have well-established amenity societies. One more recent example is the Chiltern Society which was founded in 1965 with an interest in an area of 500 square miles bounded by the River Thames, the River Colne and the Chiltern escarpment. The Society owns a 37-acre wood near Stokenchurch. It takes a wide interest in land use, and has itself established other organisations. For example, it has set up separate companies, one which runs an open-air museum and Chiltern Woodlands Ltd.

The final CART which we will describe in the category is rather different from the others, but it is perhaps best described here as it is something of a hybrid between a local amenity and a private land trust, as discussed in Chapter 9. This is the Isles of Scilly Environmental Trust, founded in 1985. The Trust leases all the untenanted land of the Islands from the Duchy of Cornwall, including all the uninhabited islands and most of the Heritage Coast. The Trust manages this land in order to conserve the terrestrial and marine wildlife, the landscape and the archaeological and historic remains for the benefit of the public. It also has the objective of furthering public education about the Isles' wildlife, landscape and historic remains. The land managed by the Trust comprises just over 1000 acres on four of the five inhabited islands together with some 200 further uninhabited islands, islets and rocks scattered over an area of 106 square miles. A Management Plan has been prepared for the area and approved by the islands' Council and other local and national bodies. It is a specific requirement of the Trust's lease agreement that it shall manage the land in accordance with this plan. The Trust has a professional director and ten Scillonian trustees. While it has received financial support from the Duchy of Cornwall, it is the aim that the Trust should gain the bulk of its income from the general public and other independent sources.

Trusts from grassroots campaigns

Threats and perceived needs

The oldest UK conservation trusts were formed almost without exception in response to perceived threats to wildlife or the countryside. As previously described, both the National Trust and the RSPB began life in this way, and the pattern continues to the present. Of the 71 primary trusts identified in our survey, around 20 per cent had been formed in response to an immediate threat to, or a perceived need to protect, a specific feature or area of land in the countryside. It is this impetus which is particularly common in the recent grassroots formation of trusts by non-landed individuals and by local community groups.

One clear example of a grassroots trust born in this way is the Buchan Countryside Group, which arose after a group of local people from the Buchan area in north-eastern Scotland had come together to fight the proposed destruction of an avenue of old beech trees for a road-widening scheme. In the process of fighting the campaign, which was eventually successful – the road was re-routed around the side of the avenue – the people began to value the community activity which had been engendered, to a point where they decided to continue their conservation work beyond the campaign, and turn their energies towards the wider enhancement of the Buchan country-side. More than ten years on, they now work on a range of schemes, including tree-planting and woodland manage-ment, planning, and local environmental education through schools and community organisations. During the early 1990s they did a lot of work on paths and cycle routes which has now been taken on by the regional council. This pattern of growth and varied involvement in a range of activities is repeated by trusts in many other parts of Britain.

Another type of grassroots trust formation is a more opportunity-led process, often initiated by the particular inspiration of an individual or small group of friends with common values. In this instance, the people forming the trust again perceive a need for their work, but this is not in direct response to a specific local threat, more a recognition of an opportunity to create something of value. The following two examples of this kind of growth into a trust illustrate the kinds of circumstance in which they may arise.

The Scottish Tree Trust (STT), based in Glasgow, was the vision of one man, Greer Hart, and a small group of friends and former pupils. Greer Hart taught economics in an inner-city school in Glasgow, but had a longstanding and far-sighted interest in environmental and ecological issues. His enthusiasm has encouraged many pupils and former pupils of his school to join him after school hours to attempt to do something positive for the environment, in both a local and a global sense. When he proposed the formation of the Trust in 1980, the idea was that a group of them would work together and raise money for wildlife. When they heard of an estate in Argyll being sold very cheaply in small lots, they decided to buy a piece of rural land to manage as a nature reserve and as an inspirational 'green lung' area for young people from Glasgow. They bought 30 acres and planted trees on the site. They later decided to build a hut on the land where the boys could stay when they went up to work on the site. Cement was donated by Blue Circle, they laid the foundations themselves, and with help from the corporation, a local joiner and architect, the hut was erected by the boys. A £1200 grant from Shell (through the Better Britain Campaign) helped them to complete the work.

This first experiment has been followed by other small land purchases and larger projects on other rural sites, where again they manage land for trees and other wildlife. The STT is also developing a scheme for tree-planting on farmers' set-aside land, expanding its management responsibilities beyond its own landholdings. And the Trust has recently been working with the Forestry Authority at Loch Awe, developing an old farm as an outdoor centre for those interested in studying the oak woodland.

In Glasgow itself, the STT rented some derelict allotments behind a large housing estate, where it created a tree nursery, a shrub and flower nursery, and an organic vegetable area. At one end, the team designed a small ornamental garden for local people, with a mixture of trees and shrubs. The aim was to get young people involved in practical work close to home, to give them the chance to learn about how to grow things and gain an appreciation of the environment. The vegetables are given out at the school, and the trees and shrubs are used in other STT project work. This project was helped by gifts in kind from local people (gardeners, police stablemen, truck drivers). In a larger urban project, the Trust has now successfully raised £100 000 to create a people's park for Eastwood housing scheme in Glasgow, with a children's play area, football pitch and nature reserve.

As well as managing land, the STT has successfully made contact with young people in a wide range of other countries with similar environmental concerns and interests, and a series of sponsored exchanges of pupils has arisen. In 1991 Greer Hart received a group from Russia, and sent some of the Glasgow young people to the 1992 Earth Summit in Rio. Since then, they have had youth exchanges with Hungary, Romania and Bulgaria. The visits abroad are mainly funded through British Council and Foreign Office 'Charity Know-How' Grants, some Cadbury Trust Grants, and Onoway Trust Grants. And a future aim is to raise funds to found an international centre for the environment in central Scotland.

Another opportunity-led trust – although 'trust' is not a precise term in this case, since the group is not a registered charity – is Heritage Conserved, a woodland initiative centred in mid-Wales. Heritage Conserved was the inspiration of Graham Stroud, a man whose love for native Welsh woods sustained his two-year recovery from cancer in the early 1980s. He describes how the visualisation of one of his favourite woods played a significant part in his convalescence, but how, upon recovery, he discovered that it had been entirely cleared. Since a good friend of his had recently negotiatied the purchase of a small plot of land which he intended to use for horticulture, Graham persuaded him to change his plans and use the land as the starting point for a new native wood, to replace the one that had been lost. The scheme has succeeded, to the extent that in 1991, 10 acres had been planted, and the site had been enhanced by a pond and several footpaths.

Organisation

Grassroots trusts reflect a diversity of organisation which reflects their diverse formation. However, many are clearly sustained by a single individual or small group, who may be either those who originally conceived of the trust, or one or two crucial employees (or a 'project director') whom members have raised funds to support and who then carry the responsibility for sustaining and developing the trust's initiatives. And like individually run small businesses, although characterised by a very high level of voluntary commitment by other people, these trusts also exhibit some of the most individual and entrepreneurial styles of business management.

Heritage Conserved succeeded through the concept of multi-ownership of its woodland: offering the public the opportunity to buy (freehold) small plots of land on the site, each of which will be planted with a native tree dedicated to themselves or a friend or relative. The funds generated gradually, through selling more and more of the plots on the site, fuel the planting and management costs on site, which are incurred by the partnership. The concept has proved very attractive to a wide range of buyers from the UK and from abroad who have learned about it from magazine and newspaper articles. Graham Stroud and his business partner spent a year investigating the possibility of grant-aid for planting, and discovered that in the most part they were not eligible for any. They prepared a plan for the Clwyd Development Agency, but were refused a grant. They have avoided charitable status because they felt that it would mean the two of them losing control over the operation. But they do not feel they lose out because of this; they still pay no corporation tax because they make no profit.

Heritage Conserved's money for land management comes from individual capital investments in new plots with trees, giving them two main options for sustaining it into the future. Either they must keep planting new areas, to maintain a throughflow of money, or they must find alternative funds. Whilst relying on the first of these strategies, Heritage Conserved used to be very wary of approaching larger organisations in search of funds. However, by 1991 it had some sponsorship interest from an advertising company, which it was considering.

The Scottish Tree Trust raised all its initial funds through several years of running discos in and around Glasgow, netting over £30 000 profit. This initial financial independence perhaps made STT more opportunistic in its attitude towards grant-aid than some of the more established CARTs. For instance, on the first site there was trouble with cattle grazing out the tree seedlings, so the Trust applied to the Nature Conservancy Council (NCC) for a fencing grant. The NCC refused the application, so Greer Hart wrote a letter of complaint to Margaret Thatcher, and he reports that, in due course, STT was given £4000 to fence the land. Another of its sites is a miniature *sphagnum* bog. The raised bog has some Scots pine growing in it, but the trees never grow high Greer Hart believes it is too waterlogged for them ever to make headway. STT again applied to the NCC for a fencing grant. The NCC wanted STT to cut down the Scots pine, so STT refused the grant. The Trust simply wants to fence the site and put a stile in, removing some birch scrub but leaving the pines. This stand paid off in due course, since in 1991 the Trust won £1000 from Glenfiddich Whisky for this particular project.

Heritage Conserved bought its first site through a bank loan, which was very costly, but the amount is steadily being repaid. In 1991, the partnership remained wholly independent of grant-aid: Graham Stroud feels it has tended to get a bad reaction from other more conventional conservation organisations, who may have thought the scheme was a con, or that it was not a 'pure' enough approach. The partnership had no contact with the NCC or its successor Countryside Council for Wales (CCW) – both partners felt it would be too time-consuming an exercise.

Other grassroots trusts may subsist for several years on minor funds and a lot of voluntary input, and it may be only an attempt to market themselves through seeking major project sponsorship from private and public sources which will develop their commercial and strategic business planning. The Buchan Countryside Group has successfully tapped a range of different sources of grant since its foundation. The Group's commercial support began with local oil companies. It then became aware that many companies specifically look for local-area grassroots initiatives to sponsor, in preference to larger and more established groups. Both BP and Shell have supported the Group for these reasons. And also the Group has won sponsorship by locally-based industries, because this kind of support can improve a company's local image and indicate a concern for social as well as environmental values (e.g. improving the quality of life of its workforce and their families).

These styles of fundraising hint at an 'independence' which is often a tightly held value among grassroots trusts, despite their frequent need to tap funds from other sources. It may be reflected either in an unwillingness to accept anything but the most basic management interference by funders, or in a wariness about being 'taken over' by other, larger trusts from whom help may occasionally be needed. These attitudes were evident in all three of the organisations discussed here. It may be that this independence, born of the individual or collective commitment of trust founders, plays a major part in determining their entrepreneurial management style. The parallels with small business are clear. But the flip side to this coin can be relative instability, and a temptation to change priorities to match the targets of any newly identified potential funds.

The attitudes towards growth among grassroots trusts also vary. Those that have a clear local focus are unlikely to aspire to grow beyond their spatial boundaries but the range of work undertaken within that area may well broaden. For instance, Heritage Conserved were not keen to go out and buy another site outright. By 1991, however, they were considering another site in Scotland near Crianlarich/Tyndrum which had been offered to them. And the Buchan Countryside Group was clearly focused upon work within one local area.

For trusts with a broad and inspirational objective, however, their growth is potentially national and inter-national in influence, even where their own organisation remains small. The STT can be seen to have some such aspirations. However, even among these kinds of grass-roots initiative, the concept of widespread networking through a multiplicity of autonomous local 'cells' is perhaps the most commonly expressed aspiration.

The Woodland Trust – a unique grassroots initiative

One grassroots organisation which has established a national role for itself is the Woodland Trust (WT). The WT was quick to perceive the national potential for a single group clearly focusing on this popular and historic form of land use. Perhaps the prior success of the RSPB inspired their own strategy, or perhaps it was the popularity of other organisations' woodland campaigns. Whatever the case, this Trust devoted to the acquisition, ownership and sustainable multi-purpose management of small British native woodlands, with a management team of con-siderable business acumen, has been a powerful and rapidly expanding force in the UK conservation market.

The founder of WT was originally the Secretary of the Devon Wildlife Trust with a particular interest in woods. Initially, from 1972 to 1977, he and a group of friends ran WT in the West Country on a voluntary basis. However, early support for the Trust by the Countryside Commission and strong initial marketing and sponsorship planning were critical in getting the WT moving. In 1977 the

Countryside Commission agreed to fund the appointment
of a National Development Officer for the Trust. This
individual is now the Executive Director of WT: a professional businessman, with a strong commitment to
conservation work. He was principally recruited in order
to fundraise to develop WT as a national rather than local
trust. The original trustees had always intended that
WT become a national charity in time. The WT now takes
the view that the Development Officer's appointment
and early work marked a crucial phase in the Trust's
development.

Other funding agencies have been, and still are,
important sources of help: throughout the 1980s, these
agencies covered an average of 50 per cent of purchase
costs for all WT's new woods through a mixture of grants,
in order of decreasing importance, from the Countryside
Commission, local authorities, English Nature (formerly
NCC) and WorldWide Fund for Nature. Occasionally, the
WT receives some help from the National Heritage
Memorial Fund. Grant-aid has been less significant for WT
for staff posts, though there is limited core assistance in
grants from the Department of the Environment and
Scottish Office. For planting and management funds, the
WT uses the Forestry Commission's Woodland Grant
Scheme.

WT strategy

The WT's two-pronged strategy is both to safeguard and
enhance existing woods and to create new woods through
acquiring woodland or bare land for tree-planting. In the
last few years, WT's woodland creation work in particular
has grown substantially. This shift reflects a general long-
term decline in agricultural profitability, increased public
support for environmental matters, and the opportunities
created by the government's Community Forests initiative.

WT spent around £2.8 million on land acquisition in
1994. In this process the Trust is essentially reactive; the
majority of woods come onto the open market before
the WT offers to buy them, or else the wood is offered
to the Trust privately without any prompting. With woods
donated to the Trust, all are considered and, in principle,
the WT will not ultimately turn down a woodland simply

because there are too many offered. The only occasion for refusal would be if there is a reason why the situation would be very difficult – for instance if there was no likelihood or opportunity for public access or access for management – but this seldom occurs. However, the WT must have priorities because the Trust may have more offers in one year than it can take at that time. Opportunities for public access are a very important consideration, as is the landscape conservation value of the wood. The wildlife habitat value of woods is the third main consideration, and the WT aims for 50 per cent of the acquisition budget to go towards ancient woodland.

More than a decade ago, the WT developed its own original Community Woods concept. More recently the Trust has widened the range of options for community involvement from informal working groups to whole-community woodland managment plans agreed with the Trust. The Trust uses personal contacts and public meetings to generate local interest in a wood, and then a series of activities follow. At different sites these developments work in slightly different ways according to local interests. At some sites the WT may simply organise one-off events and institute voluntary wardening, at others a much more planned style of management is implemented. The Forestry Commission now offers a Community Forest Supplement payment within the Woodland Grant Scheme.

WT has undergone major reorganisation during its development. In 1989 it had eight Regional Officers who were both wood managers and wood acquirers. Since then, the organisation has grown and was in need of some further managerial input into the regions. By 1991 it employed 26 staff in the regions. In 1995 the Trust employed four regional managers: North; South East; South West and Midlands (including Wales) and an operations director for Scotland. These staff have responsibility for managing both people and resources, with a total of 30 Woodland Officers working under them.

The independent streak in this grassroots Trust persists, despite its formidable growth. WT staff say that the Trust tends to go it alone because it has its own specific objectives. However, it consults with others over acquisition, especially with County Wildlife Trusts, RSPB and the National Trust. The WT would not want to compete with other bodies like these for sites which come onto the open market, but if sites are privately offered, consultation may not be felt to be so necessary. On wider forestry and woodland management issues the Trust liaises regularly with other conservation CARTs through fora such as Wildlife and Countryside Link.

The WT is not involved in woodland consultancy, although this may develop in the future. However, it has played a role in creating demonstration sites and providing a focus of planting activity, especially in the early stages, of the Countryside Commission's National Forest and Community Forest programmes. WT works in close co-operation with the Countryside Commission on these programmes and the Commission funded new WT Woodland Officers in each of the target areas.

Use of resources

Financially, the WT basically divides funding into three areas:

1. Support services (administration) – all centrally budgeted.
2. Acquisition – from central and local sources, raised in advance of purchases, often in conjunction with local people and communities together with grant-aid.
3. Management – determined largely by each wood's management plan, organised by bidding from the Woodland Officer to Headquarters, balanced nationally at HQ.

By 1995 the Trust had 700 sites, all owned or held on long leases. It also has a licence planting scheme where it takes out a twenty-five-year licence to plant new woods on private land, and through this it had built up over 800 acres in 300 different projects by 1995, across Great Britain. The majority of woodland management work is undertaken by professional contractors.

Many commentators have questioned the Woodland Trust's ability to sustain and to manage its rapid rate of growth and development, but, as yet, the Trust appears to have coped both politically and administratively. A further consolidation of its local and regional structure, its staffing and its land management planning will undoubtedly be needed as it grows, but the place of this Trust among the frontrunners at a national level now seems assured.

Overview

There is undoubtedly something exciting about grassroots trusts – with their individuality, their entrepreneurism and their often impressive achievements. In this analysis, they perhaps appear very different to the local amenity CARTs described previously. However, both groups have shared a local focus in their land management activities, coupled to a much wider interest in conservation and public enjoyment at national or even international levels. Just as the Selborne Society had a very influential role in helping to inspire the foundation and growth of national interest in conservation in the 19th century, perhaps the new grassroots trusts of today will inspire another kind of environmental approach which reflects the views and needs of the late 20th century. However, the common contemporary phenomena of individuality and the willingness to take risks that we have highlighted here may be weaknesses as well as strengths for these trusts, in that they render their growth and development a rather sporadic and opportunistic business, by contrast with the more gradual and perhaps more financially stable development of the local amenity societies. Such small organisations rise and fall periodically, and it is only those most tenacious and adaptable ones which persist and develop to influence others. Nonetheless, the few examples discussed here, from the small initiatives in Wales and Scotland to the fastest-growing CART in England, represent some of the newest examples of an enduring and important tradition among voluntary initiatives in the UK conservation movement.

Community tree-planting day at Colnbrook, Slough.
Reproduced by permission of Colne Valley Groundwork Trust

Trusts from the public sector

11

Since the early 1980s, the public sector has been a main source of new trusts for conservation and amenity. There is clearly a link between this trend and the policies of the government throughout the 1980s, with its support for the privatisation of public assets and services and for the growth of charitable giving among the private sector.

Trusts as entrepreneurs

Many new conservation and amenity trusts from the public sector adopt landownership or land management roles, with a strong focus upon conserving or achieving a better environment through local, practical action. The largest group is probably the urban-fringe trusts, usually formed by local authorities, acting alone or in partnership with government agencies. Tracing the growth of these kinds of trust, one can find examples of all stages between pure 'public' to almost pure 'private' organisations. Deciding at what stage these organisations can be called CARTs is not simple: is an independent management structure sufficient, or must the trust or project be entirely supported by private funds? Considering that many of the old, established CARTs discussed in earlier chapters also rely on a degree of public grant or subsidy, perhaps even a wholly publicly funded trust should be called a CART, if it acts as an independently managed body.

From the point of view of the public bodies who set up these trusts, the overwhelming importance of a trust for them is its ability to be seen as an independent body, usually of charitable status, with its own management and its own objectives. This distances it from the sometimes negative popular image which may bedevil local authorities, and should give it the ability to react quickly to new opportunities, unhampered by the bureaucracy of the public service. Because of this view, the fact that a trust is perhaps almost entirely funded by public bodies, or is housed in public offices, need not mean that it is the same as a public body (although these circumstances could perhaps affect its public image, if widely known) – and it can assume the image of a true 'entrepreneur'.

Countryside management projects

Starting at the most 'public' end of the scale, Countryside Management Projects are publicly funded schemes to improve the local countryside, set up by a partnership of local authority and Countryside Commission funds. Although these projects are mainly intended to work by helping or encouraging other landowners to make the countryside more attractive and enjoyable for local people, some of them have begun to take a longer-term responsibility for land management. But they remain public-sector funded projects. To date, there are over 30 Countryside Management Projects in England. To illustrate the kind of activity and influence that they can develop, we have drawn material from a visit to the East Cumbria Countryside Project.

The East Cumbria Countryside Project (ECCP)

This Countryside Management Project was set up in the late 1980s. The local authorities saw ECCP as a way to set up a small and active group which would be independent of public-sector bureaucracy and could directly attract the support of local people. The initiative grew out of a rural economic development project, fostering economic regeneration by means such as farm tourism and other village-based schemes. This had been funded by central government, via the Rural Development Commission, English Tourist Board and Countryside Commission, while local authorities gave it office space. When the development project ended, the local authorities assessed its effects and from this they developed the idea of ECCP.

In 1991, ECCP had a manager, four project officers and administrative staff. The Countryside Projects Manager is funded by the Countryside Commission. The Project is overseen by an Executive Committee, members of which are all appointed by parent committees, usually from the particular local authority departments with an interest in this sort of work: planning/economic development/ environmental services. The executive meets about five times a year, and is closely involved in the management of ECCP.

The Countryside Commission supports 50 per cent of ECCP's work. Initially this support was intended to be on a tapering basis, but the taper ceased because the local authorities have had problems in maintaining their share of the budget. The project was never intended to have a major financial input from the private sector – this would have taken too much time and effort to build up. Officially, ECCP is not a charity, and all staff are employed by Carlisle City Council, which relieves ECCP of employment responsiblity. It spent in the region of £180 000 in 1991.

ECCP's main work has been:

1. Woodlands advice and woodland management – targeting farmers. English Nature was grant-aiding this work, because the woods they are trying to enhance act as buffers for Sites of Special Scientific Interest. ECCP approaches landowners to encourage them to make use of the English Nature money which is available to improve the quality of their woods. ECCP also administers a small Landscape Conservation Grants scheme (local authority and Countryside Commission funded) for gill woodlands, whereby they can offer up to 90 per cent grant on some schemes. This scheme was initiated at ECCP's request, having pinpointed a specific need for such assistance.
2. Paths and rights of way work – to get a good geographical spread of unobstructed and maintained routes throughout the area. ECCP has close relations with all the Parish Councils; it always intends that the Parish Council should take on long-term path management responsibility once ECCP has helped get work started. Also, parishes generate ideas for new schemes, on which ECCP will advise or offer help as

appropriate. The Project also has a joint initiative with the British Horse Society – filling in the missing links in the bridleway network.

3. Publications and interpretative work – ECCP wants to improve these services, targeting the average family. It has a specific series of events planned to build up the public appreciation of the role of farming and woodland management in maintaining the country-side. It has a series of offshoot activities, with traditional workers demonstrating woodland crafts, and arts-related activities. It also ran a storytelling initiative with local people. ECCP sees it as important that interpretative work should be for the local people as well as for visitors. Recent schemes have involved schools, local craftspeople and older people in broad community development works.

Land management responsibilities ECCP is the acting local agent for the Woodland Trust, managing all WT's woods in the area. Also, it is the Countryside Commission's chosen subcontractor for the Pennine Way in East Cumbria, and other major trails and bridleways. It thus has a number of important land management responsi-bilities, without owning any land. ECCP also monitors local Countryside Commission schemes, such as tree-planting. With each grant-aided landowner, ECCP staff follow up any planting closely for three years or so, and then make occasional visits. Their work to develop circular footpaths also involves long-term commitment to manage-ment, in contrast to the parish-held responsibility for parish paths.

Labour ECCP mostly uses local contractors, with one or two forestry companies. For footpaths work, it has a list of local contacts and an informal system for tendering locally. It prefers to involve smaller local firms rather than bring in bigger outside companies; continuing the economic devel-opment theme. ECCP has its own estate team for any work which would take too long to set up through contract. In its use of material and other resources, it also tends to have a local bias. Local businesses advertise in the ECCP magazine, so they nominally 'pay' to support ECCP, and this is good for maintaining local involvement. ECCP also gets help in kind from local people, and volunteers for certain work – probably not as much as they might if they were a registered charity, but it is still useful.

The estate team and all other project work except the project officers and the administrative staff are costed into programmes of work, funding for which is split between work on contract for highway authorities, Woodland Trust, English Nature and others, and mainstream work funded by the parent bodies. ECCP sees contract work as a means of tiding itself over, financially, because it has to strike a balance between what people will pay for and what their main objectives are. ECCP has no formal 'friends' or similar supporters' group.

In interview in 1991, the Director of ECCP (now sadly deceased) described how she valued the local authority support that it has in managing its work and that this was an advantage over being a wholly independent trust. As a semi-public organisation, ECCP has the rein to try out new ideas. In that sense, it undertakes things such as arts events which others might view as peripheral, but it sees them as part and parcel of raising local awareness about the countryside. She believed ECCP could have a real effect upon people's attitudes and understanding, and appeal to ordinary people who did not already have an interest in the environment.

There are some 'constraints' for the organisation as a result of close links with local government. ECCP will not become involved in local planning issues, but works to ensure that footpaths and other facilities are protected properly. With planning issues, it usually tries to deflect these to another CART such as Cumbria Wildlife Trust, encouraging them to take action if this is needed.

Groundwork trusts

Countryside Management Projects, as a special kind of initiative, began in the early 1980s. A similar development at a similar time was the Groundwork Trust movement, which has since grown into a network of local trusts with a central foundation and core funding from the Department of the Environment. Groundwork was spawned from a suggestion made by the then Secretary of State for the Environment, Michael Heseltine, in 1979, as an alternative

to public urban regeneration schemes. He envisaged a
'catalytic environmental trust' to bring various partners
together, especially including the private sector, to co-
ordinate a programme of action. After discussion with the
Countryside Commission, the first Groundwork Trust was
set up in St Helens in late 1981.

Unlike Countryside Management Projects, Groundwork
has a more overtly private-sector bias in its financial and
operational structure, and focuses exclusively upon urban
and urban-fringe areas, often in places where the landscape
has been seriously degraded by industrial and urban
development. There may be a link between the financial
balance and the location, in that private-sector funding
may be easier to secure in an urban-fringe location than in
the 'deeper countryside' areas in which Countryside
Management Projects may be sited.

Groundwork Trusts are now spread all over England
and Wales; a network of local trusts assisted by a central
headquarters in Birmingham. The channelling of public
funds from the Department of the Environment through
Groundwork HQ allows the network to be nationally co-
ordinated. This gives it added strength; HQ can assist with
advice, training and finances (both public and private) in a
way that local trusts could not co-ordinate alone. They
function as a network, not a hierarchy, although Groundwork HQ requires formal co-operation from the local
trusts. Groundwork has a trainee environmental manager
scheme which is run nationally and each local trust has a
quota of trainees allocated from this scheme to work with
them. HQ pay for them, and it operates like an industrial
placement, with trainees going off for more training at
intervals throughout their time with a local trust. Again,
we look more closely at one example, Merthyr and Cynon
Groundwork Trust, and follow this by notes on the Central
Scotland Countryside Trust, a similar though independent
body in Scotland.

Merthyr and Cynon Groundwork Trust (MGT)

MGT was originally a charitable trust called Merthyr
Greenspace, which later developed into a Groundwork
Trust. When it became MGT, it was offered a five-year
funding package: 50 per cent Department of the

Environment (which comes via Groundwork headquarters in Birmingham), 30 per cent local authority, and 20 per cent Trust earned, initially, with the grant-aid from government designed to gradually decline over that period. This basic core of funds has paid for four or five staff posts.

MGT has over 30 staff in all: seven or eight of which are core staff, while the rest are funded privately for specific work. Most staff are on short-term contracts, although a small number are on three-year appointments paid for by the Countryside Council for Wales (CCW) or Welsh Development Agency (WDA). Where staff are employed entirely on MGT-earned income, they have only a one-year contract.

The CCW is a member of the MGT company board, and this gives the Trust a lot of public support. In the first two years of Greenspace, the MGT set-up was very informal, with one fulltime and one part-time worker. Once incorporated, it took on six staff. By 1991, for every new work programme the Trust would cast around to find the funding necessary to organise and staff it properly, tapping WDA, CCW and Welsh Office funds.

Their major projects have been many and varied, and some examples are given below.

1. The Taf Trail: developing a 50 mile path from Cardiff to Brecon.
2. Developing a Cynon Valley extension of MGT, which involved finding funds for four more staff.
3. Developing an effective training system, for particular Groundwork skills. MGT has trainees funded jointly by Groundwork HQ and the European Commission, plus a few people on student placements during a 'year-out'.
4. The 'Brightsite' campaign, to improve the environmental and amenity quality of industrial sites. The Trust has been strongly supported by all local authorities in this scheme, and has been pro-active in seeking new projects. It has been able to look at whole industrial estate areas, rather than single-plant project work.
5. 'Greenstreet'. This policy works to develop a co-ordinated environmental approach on key routes into and out of a town. It targets all the major approach roads, integrating landscaping and environmental

work on these sites into local community areas, as well. In developing this work, MGT liaises closely with the local authority to determine how far it should extend its operations from landscaping into nature conservation and the development of local amenity facilities.

6.   Environmental education. MGT runs a yearly programme with children, involving regular simple activities. Some of this is done in conjunction with local schools. This work is funded via headquarters, from a private-sector source.

Some projects are initiated from MGT's own ideas, some are supplied by the local authority, and some arise out of local community/residents' requests for assistance. Quite a lot of work has arisen as a result of previous project work. For example, in 1991 MGT had a contract with a local housing association which grew out of previous local authority work.

Land management responsibilities MGT does not own any open land sites, and most work is project-orientated. However, it leases two areas: one site leased by the Borough Council as part of an urban-fringe development project, and the other much smaller site, to develop as a play area. MGT works quite a lot on publicly owned land, such as formerly Welsh Water land, and Forestry Commission and some County Council land. Some Brightsite schemes have involved large areas of privately owned land. All MGT's work is environmental, so its Director does not see a distinct boundary between which of its work is commercial and which is purely community work: as she put it, MGT does not set out to make a loss on any of its community projects. Through this work, the Trust has built up a surplus which can help to finish off non-profit-making projects where necessary. Initially, all projects had to pay their way.

To choose contractors, MGT started from scratch by building local individual contacts. The nature of the project partnership often determines which labour sources are to be used. The Trust uses some volunteers, but this is not easy because there is no tradition of volunteering in Merthyr like there might be elsewhere. Generally the Trust would use a mix of own staff, outside contractors and volunteer teams where possible. The bulk of work is done professionally, while volunteers may be used to finish up project work – usually the more simple, but interesting work. MGT has some international volunteers who come to work on its projects. In the early years it had some large Manpower Services Commission Community Programme schemes, doing work both on the ground and in the office.

The sources of projects and funds are very heavily biased towards the public sector. MGT has some private-sector projects, but the Director feels that there has been enough public money around for this kind of environmental work for her to feel that relying on public projects is probably the best use of time. However, the private sector has provided a great deal of important help in kind. Both the Borough Council and County Council are represented on the MGT board. MGT has the freedom to mix and match funding in a way which the Director feels would be impossible for the public sector to do on its own.

Asked why people used MGT, as opposed to anyone else, for the jobs it does, the Director felt it was partly because MGT is the only group doing this kind of work, locally. Initially, people thought that it would be very hard for Groundwork to get local people involved, but the availability of Community Programme resources in the early years and the fact that environmental issues are now much more commonplace combined to make local people gradually far more interested in practical conservation. From the point of view of prospective partners, MGT's strengths are that it is professional, can organise things, can help raise funds for work, is locally committed and is non-profit orientated. The biggest problem identified by the Trust in 1991 was maintaining its level of activity, maintaining involvement, interest and community participation.

MGT gives some advice on an *ad-hoc* basis to other organisations and individuals, but usually its advisory work is a preliminary to developing a project with someone. If no project seems likely to come out of some advisory work, the Trust tends to pass it on to another organisation fairly quickly. MGT is offered more projects than it can accept. Popularity is a measure of the extent to which MGT is now seen as one of the major players in local environmental matters. It can be difficult to avoid getting tied up in related bureaucracy.

The Director of MGT gave the opinion that in a rural setting, where there are fewer large private industries and local authorities, there would be less money for this kind of work and Groundwork would be a less viable option: the fact that you would not be in an urban programme area like Merthyr could be a major handicap.

Central Scotland Countryside Trust

In Scotland, a similar kind of body exists in the Central Scotland Countryside Trust (CSCT) – a trust set up in 1985 to improve the industrially scarred environment of Central Scotland. Informal efforts to enhance this area through tree-planting, bing reclamation and other environmental improvement, led by the local authorities and the Scottish Development Agency, began in the 1970s, and a million trees were planted by 1985. The CSCT was then set up to formalise these efforts, beginning as a small, low-profile, tree-planting charity. Since 1989, it has become a key partner in the government's 'Central Scotland Forest' project, alongside the Scottish Office, seven District Councils, three Regional Councils, four local enterprise companies and Scottish Enterprise, Scottish Natural Heritage, and the Forestry Commission. The Trust plays a pivotal role in implementing the Forest, acting as a promoter, co-ordinator, facilitator and broker. Turnover now exceeds £2.5 million a year, and the Trust employs 45 people.

CSCT began by small-scale tree-planting, but it has now developed a more holistic approach to environmental improvement – often working on whole farm or whole property schemes. It sees itself as having a dual role, both planning and implementing works through its own resources, and helping others to do so. Its staff are grouped into seven main teams:

1. Development unit – developing policies and strategies for the Forest and identifying targets for new projects.
2. Community liaison – seeking the public's views, raising awareness and encouraging local involvement in woodland projects.

3. Landscape architects – helping clients and Trust staff to design planting projects, particularly used to enhance new business premises in the area (a parallel with the 'Brightsite' initiative, perhaps).
4. Operations unit – small teams of foresters, managing CSCT's own planting or helping others to plant and manage new woods.
5. Workshop – producing signs, benches and other wood products for use in the Forest and for sale.
6. Direct labour team – actually carries out planting and management work.
7. Nursery – provides and maintains a plant store for CSCT's use.

CSCT has strategic priorities in finding sites, and therefore can be pro-active in some instances. It owns several properties and in some cases by exchanging its own land with neighbouring landowners has enabled a major restructuring of the local landscape through new planting and management. But the bulk of its work is in partnership with local authorities, and many of the projects worked on have been on public land.

The Trust's early tree-planting was all amenity planting rather than commercial timber production, but this has broadened into a more fully multi-purpose strategy in recent years. For labour, CSCT uses its own team and also many self-employed subcontractors (a lot of whom used to work for CSCT under the Community Programme, and whom CSCT then helped to set up in genuine businesses). The Trust also uses some major contractors on occasion (e.g. Tilhill Forestry) and sometimes volunteers, mainly Scottish Conservation Project teams. CSCT once had 300 people employed on the government's Community Programme, but there was a feeling among some staff that this was far too many people to organise properly, and the smaller number of more skilled people working on its sites today is perhaps more effective.

In addition to public support, the Trust charges fees for environmental reports, for some project work, and it is part-funded by private sponsors. It is seeking to widen its funding base to include other charitable trusts, more private business and public donors. CSCT, working in the industrialised belt between Glasgow and Edinburgh, is reasonably well placed for sponsorship. As well as visitors to the big cities, there are lots of large industrial companies in the local area who have been keen to sponsor this kind of work. The Trust has a commercial subsidiary to avoid any problems of charitable status. The subsidiary carries out minor contracting operations (such as the resurfacing of a car park in connection with a wider landscaping project). But it is not designed to generate regular income: CSCT just decides when it is better to use that than to do work directly as a charity, so the subsidiary's turnover varies greatly. Often the Trust finds that with environmental enhancement work agreed to as part of a planning-gain negotiation, it is best to have the trading subsidiary doing the work.

CSCT has no membership, although this was considered in 1989. However, it may develop a 'support group' in future, as part of its work to promote the re-creation of a 'forest culture' among local people, so that they will be able to maintain their new woods well into the future.

Trusts as stewards or benign landowners

In contrast to these non-landowning, 'enterprising', dynamic and project-focused groups, a number of other trusts from the public sector have begun life as major or minor landowners, or long-lease tenants. In these instances, one of the main reasons for forming a trust seems to have been a political desire to dispose of publicly held land, but to do so in a way that would protect the landscape and amenity value of that land in perpetuity. A trust can be set up specifically to protect open and accessible areas of land for public enjoyment and appreciation. In our investigations, we came across examples of trusts formed from former water authority land, from parish-owned land, from former national health service land, local authority land and the open land preserved during the development of new towns. In each case, nature conservation and landscape enhancement and a desire to maintain local amenity figure strongly in the objectives of these trusts.

These kinds of estate-based trust are often at the other end of the scale from community projects. Virtually all seek to be entirely independent of regular public-sector funding, although, as with many other independent voluntary bodies, they may get a stream of grant-aid for specific activities, from a variety of different public sources. Most of their land will be managed by professional staff and contractors, and management is funded through the income of other trust assets (where avilable). They rarely, if ever, engage in active environmental campaigning work.

To illustrate the most contrasting form of this sort of trust in comparison with the other categories described in this chapter, we include the example of the Welsh Water Elan Trust in Mid-Wales.

The Welsh Water Elan Trust (WWET)

The Elan valley area, in Mid-Wales, was bought by Birmingham Corporation in the 1890s in order to develop its water storage potential. In 1974 responsibility for the area passed to the newly formed Welsh Water National Development Authority. The land area was mostly tenanted to farmers. WWET was set up in October 1989, to take on all the tenanted land from Dwr Cymru, which retained only the reservoirs, the reservoir fringes, the woodlands, Elan village and the visitor centre. When visited in 1991, WWET was appointing someone to prepare a management plan for the Trust, and inviting local conservation interests to help to form an advisory committee. All of the trustees are nominees. Until recently they included an independent chairman nominated by Dwr Cymru, nominees of Powys and Dyfed County Councils, and nominees from Dwr Cymru and the Development Board for Rural Wales. The DBRW are no longer represented on the Trust and a nominee from the Countryside Council for Wales will soon be confirmed as a trustee. The former Nature Conservancy Council in Wales had refused because it was apparently unsure of the Trust's financial viability, and had voiced concern about possible conflict of interest since much of the land concerned is designated as a Site of Special Scientific Interest. This concern has now clearly been overcome.

In the local agent's view, the Trust came about through privatisation pressures on water authorities. The public was worried that when Dwr Cymru was privatised they would lose access onto the land – possibly more a perceived threat than a real one. Dwr Cymru saw the creation of a trust as an opportunity for good public relations, in that they were setting up an organisation entirely independent of the new water company which would specifically aim to safeguard the future status of the valley.

The income of the Trust comes from an original endowment, plus agricultural rents on all the tenanted land, plus a fairly substantial in-hand farming operation, and grant-aid. In the past, the landowners had been fairly lax about rents from the land, but rents were reviewed in 1982, then in 1986 and comprehensively in 1989. In the estate manager's view, some longstanding tenants were relatively suddenly brought into a modern world of commercial tenancy, and there were quite a lot of disputes in this period. However, by 1995 the Trust reported that a further rent review had been completed and all rents had satisfactorily been settled by negotiation.

The farms are holdings of an average of more than 1000 acres, all hill land, the majority of which is unenclosed. Most of it is not common land, but it operates very similarly, with different farmers' stock settled in different places on the hill but not fenced apart; and some holdings have grazing rights on adjoining commons. The Water Act stated that the whole area must remain open to the public, so WWET's ability to enclose more land is limited. All the Trust land is in an Environmentally Sensitive Area. This was a major factor in the most recent rent review of 1992 – those farmers eligible for ESA payments may have improved their incomes as a result of entering the scheme, and a recent estimate was that about 80 per cent of farmers in the valley were involved.

The Trust has no expansion plans, and no other income-generating facilities. Dwr Cymru owns a visitor centre and a shop in the valley, but the Trust receives no money from these enterprises. Considering the future, the nature of the Trust's land makes it difficult to think of possible developments, primarily because Dwr Cymru has retained all the land around the reservoirs. The land is all held on a 999-year lease, because Dwr Cymru wanted to retain freehold ownership. In the lease, there is a provision that Dwr Cymru can regain 10 000 acres of the land if it needs· it for water supply purposes.

Before the creation of WWET, the Dwr Cymru estate was just about breaking even, with the income from the visitor centre. But without this, the Trust was not fully viable at the start. With the recent rent increases its financial position is now on a much sounder footing, but it remains vulnerable to potential rent reductions should government or European Union support for hill farming be reduced or removed. For administrative support, WWET has been almost entirely dependent upon Powys County Council, and it remains to be seen how the creation of a new unitary authority for Powys may change this situation. WWET has also received some help from CCW such as grant-aiding the post of a countryside ranger for Trust land, and support for the Trust's management plan. The Trust is perhaps much more likely to attract grant-aid from public agencies than the privatised water company would have been, if it had held on to the land.

Apart from being a landlord, WWET has additional responsibilities for fencing, and it is solely responsible for the management of 3500 acres 'in-hand', stocked with its own sheep. It employs shepherds on contract or on a day-work basis, always using either neighbouring tenants or adjoining landowners. Some of the 'in-hand' land was a legacy from the Dwr Cymru holding, but more has been acquired since then. It is kept because it generates an income and it gives a comparative basis for setting rents on the tenanted land. It may offer more opportunities for conservation work too – to try out ideas that could later be adopted on tenanted land.

Most of the tenants are very longstanding local farming people, with a few incomers, all of whom are farming, and Welsh. The Trust has a written commitment to maintain the local community. In 1991 the agent felt that local farming people did not really know anything about the Trust, since they had had little direct contact with it. However, there is now an annual meeting with tenants which has helped to promote the Trust's identity, and the Powys County Council-nominated trustee is a well-known local person.

Other estate-based trusts including New Town Trusts

As already explained, the Welsh Water Elan Trust is at one end of the spectrum of these kinds of 'privatisation process' CARTs. Others traced in this study include the

Nene Park Trust, the Shetland Amenity Trust, the Deadwater Valley Trust, the Ivanhoe Trust, the Milton Keynes Park Trust, the Severn Gorge Countryside Trust, the Shenley Park Trust and more.

New Town Trusts

New Town Trusts are an interesting phenomenon. When the New Town Development Corporations began to be disbanded in the early 1980s it was the Department of the Environment that promoted the idea of endowing non-productive community assets with income-earning assets from other parts of the towns, in order to ensure their longer-term survival. Initially vested in local authorities, these self-supporting units came under pressure during the financial squeeze of the late 1980s, and as a result the notion of transferring them to charitable trusts was born (Land Trusts Association, 1994). Since then, parkland trusts have been set up in Milton Keynes, Telford and Peterborough, and the model has also been used for smaller areas of public land such as the former grounds of a hospital, in Shenley, Herts.

The New Town Trusts each look after former Development Corporation areas of open or wooded land. In these cases, the Trust is endowed with significant income from associated developed land which was also formerly owned by the corporation – this land may still be held by a public body but, where this is the case, that body is obliged to give all the income from this property to the Trust. A variety of structural models have been used; the Telford and Peterborough Trusts ('Severn Gorge' and 'Nene Park') have a limited membership of particular interested organisations, while the Milton Keynes Trust has the ability to have a paying membership of up to 250 people. Land management responsibility also varies – Nene Park Trust manages a single, albeit quite large site, Severn Gorge has an area of closely grouped woods, and Milton Keynes looks after a whole suite of parks and gardens. While the Severn Gorge Countryside Trust's objectives are centred around nature conservation and education (and it supports the Green Wood Trust, which develops training and useful outlets for small roundwood products), the Milton Keynes Trust focuses on public amenity.

These trusts were created to facilitate the transfer of land from the public sector to a conservation and amenity CART that is endowed with some other source of income to support long-term site management. The income from property development would seem to be relatively more secure than that from marginal farmland. However, because of the recession and some uncertainty in the viability of the chosen endowments, these CARTs have in their early years shown a preoccupation with land management responsibilities and the need to ensure sufficient income to maintain them. This is in quite sharp contrast to the community projects and trusts previously described, where a mixture of direct public funding, public contracts for specific work, and private contracts and sponsorship appear to have given these organisations more confidence and an impetus to build upon their existing, relatively lower level of land management responsibility. The contrasting financial structures of CARTS from the public sector will be returned to in Chapter 13.

In sum, the recent trend to create CARTs from the public sector has clearly been related to changing government perspectives about the particular pros and cons of public versus private-sector management and the public interest. However, this common perspective has led to a wide variety of structures with very different financial, managerial and operational behaviour, and an impressive array of new ideas and approaches for the voluntary sector in conservation management.

Part 3:
Land management:
problems and potential

Conservation Volunteers Lothian Group dyking at Achnacon, Glencoe.
Reproduced by permission of The National Trust for Scotland

Actions for the
12 environment

Land management is at the centre of CART objectives and activities. But it is in many ways a means towards the broader goal of improving the environment. CARTs engage in a range of activities which are either aimed at promoting environmental quality or raising funds in order to allow them to pursue this aim. In this chapter we concentrate on the former, while fundraising is covered in the next chapter on Finance.

We could begin by asking: what is the potential for environmental improvement by CARTS?

To answer this, we need to be clear what we mean by environmental improvement: an increase in the quality of the environment as perceived by society at large; locally, regionally, nationally or globally. We can define environmental quality in its broadest sense – including the opportunities offered for species and habitat preservation, for improved landscape quality, for better environmental equilibrium or sustainability (in soils, water, etc.) and for any changes leading to an improvement in the quality of life of people in terms of employment, recreation or amenity, and social, cultural and educational activity.

Potential through holding land: CART action in the land market

Land is acquired by CARTs through a variety of means. While some land is put into trust by an owner or is donated to an existing trust, much is also acquired by purchase on the market. This can present a CART with particular obstacles, because it is looking for land of quite specific attributes and yet as a voluntary organisation it cannot perhaps afford to be seen to be too choosy. Only a small proportion of open land in the UK comes onto the market at any one time, so although CARTs may establish a detailed plan of the types and locations of sites which they wish to acquire, they will in practice have to take advantage of whatever opportunites arise. Also, it may not be wise for them to be too public as to their precise targets. If it becomes known that a trust is keen to acquire a particular site or even a particular sort of site, it may encourage owners to hold out for a higher price.

In theory, if CARTs' targets were widely recognised, speculators might be encouraged to acquire these types of land in the knowledge that there would be a ready demand for them and in the hope that the pressure to acquire these types of land will increase. It is possible to conceive of an environmental equivalent of a ransom strip. Builders sometimes hold on to small areas of land which will be needed if a larger area of land is to be developed. This is usually a strip across which access is necessary, referred to as a ransom strip. The developer of the whole site may then be prepared to pay a large sum in order to gain access to the site. Environmental organisations may want to acquire particular sites, such as to complete contiguous stretches of land along the coast, nature reserves which are large enough to support wildlife populations or connecting sites for long-distance paths. An owner of the last few sites not in CART ownership might hope to achieve a higher price for his or her land than that generally realised by this type of land.

In practice, there are several ways in which this kind of behaviour is mitigated against, in the UK. Firstly, few land purchases by CARTs take place without some element of public grant being given to secure the purchase. Where this is the case, public agencies will only fund a fixed percentage of the District Valuer's guide price for the land – hence there is a strong incentive for CARTs to attempt to purchase at or very near this price wherever possible. Secondly, it is perhaps quite rare for CARTs to be so specific about what sites they particularly want: usually there will be room for choice between several possible sites. Thirdly, in many cases CARTs are targeting land which otherwise has a relatively low commercial value – it is often because the land has a low earning potential that it has retained the kinds of environmental value that make it a CART target. In these circumstances, owners may often feel that selling to a CART offers them a way out of ownership of an unproductive or relatively costly burden, in which case they are unlikely to play too 'hard to get' for fear of failing to secure the sale. Of course, this factor may diminish in future if predicted falls in agricultural land values occur while the landholding influence of CARTs continues to grow. For the time being, however, purchase by a CART is unlikely to be seen by the majority of sellers as the most lucrative option for their land.

The best purchase deals will generally be struck when a CART can act quickly, taking advantage of opportunities as they arise, without publicity. But with the exception of the largest groups like RSPB and the National Trust, most CARTs do not have funds readily available with which to operate in this way. In practice, it is more common for a CART to identify a possible acquisition and then to embark upon a lengthy campaign to raise the required money. Indeed, in some instances CARTs have been established in order to acquire specific sites only when they come onto the market.

Large CARTs may be much better placed to respond rapidly to opportunities to purchase land. For instance, the Nature Conservancy, a large conservation trust in the United States, has not infrequently purchased land which it has subsequently sold to the federal government, on the basis that as a private organisation it is able to reach decisions and to take action more quickly than can government agencies.

What does land purchase by a CART contribute, in terms of environmental quality? In essence, such a purchase represents a transferral of the responsibility for management of the site from a private owner, who may have a variety of objectives for land management, to a body which has specific conservation or amenity objectives for land management. But the land purchase does not provide the CART with the funds with which to secure these objectives through land management. It thus represents a kind of public commitment – land bought by a CART should, wherever possible, be managed for public benefit, whereas land held by a private individual may or may not be so managed. People who donate money to help CARTs buy land are really buying a guarantee of benign or positive environmental aims in management – whether or not these aims can then be met by appropriate funding.

Choices for landholdings

Clearly, most organisations will hold land of varying environmental quality and of varying relevance to their objectives. Land might be donated which is of little conservation potential, or CARTs may have some land which was accepted in the past when objectives were somewhat different. The environmental value of land held might be lost; storms might destroy stands of trees, pollution might damage wetland habitats, or the CART may simply have found itself unable to meet the costs of optimal environmental management of that site. In these circumstances, what should be done with the less useful land? Should it be sold or retained?

If retained, there may be opportunities for various forms of development, such as building, leisure development or extracting natural resources (e.g. forestry, minerals or energy reserves). All these developments can generate funds which can be applied to further a trust's objectives in other ways. An active approach to asset management would suggest that the less useful assets should be sold and/or development opportunities be undertaken whenever the money realised could be reinvested in ways which have the potential make a greater contribution towards the objectives of the organisation. But to some members or supporters of CARTs, any development or disposal of assets is anathema, seeming to represent a breach of trust both with those people who have made donations to the organisation, and with future generations who might value assets differently.

Anderson and Leal (1991) argue that a key characteristic of voluntary bodies which act to conserve the environment is that they are able to reach rational and well-informed decisions about how best to manage their assets, balancing conservation and development objectives. They cite (pp. 90–91) the experience of the National Audubon Society in the United States. The Audubon Society is a voluntary organisation focusing primarily on bird conservation and owning reserves across the United States. The Society allows oil extraction in its Rainey Sanctuary in Louisiana, an area of coastal marsh providing habitat for alligators, wading birds, fur bearers and wintering waterfowl. Oil wells have operated there since the 1960s, paying royalties to the Society. The Society imposes strict conditions on how the oil can be extracted and, because of this, the level of royalties paid is lower. Thus the Society gains a financial benefit from development while its primary conservation interest is protected.

In 1975, Mobil Oil sought permission to explore for oil and gas in the Bernard W. Baker Sanctuary, owned by the local chapter of the Audubon Society in Michigan. This proposal failed to achieve the necessary majority in a vote of the membership and was therefore turned down. However, five years later it was decided to allow Michigan Petroleum to explore using directional drilling from a pad half a mile from the marsh, again subject to environmental constraints. The Society received royalties of $1 million.

Also in the United States, the Nature Conservancy has been the subject of criticism for its policy of accepting 'trade lands'. This is land donated to the Conservancy which may subsequently be sold. While donors can gain tax benefits from giving land, the Conservancy is reluctant to hold land unless it is of high conservation value. It argues that in preserving land of low conservation significance from development, it is in effect raising the pressure for the development of land of higher value. Therefore it makes sense to sell less valuable areas, either privately or to government agencies in order to raise the funds which can then be directed towards the acquistion of more valuable reserves.

This approach appears to be in stark contrast with British CARTs, such as for instance the National Trust's emphasis on permanent preservation and its declaring land inalienable. But the contrast is probably less marked in reality. While all such organisations have the goal of the permanent preservation of important conservation values, nothing can be absolutely guaranteed for ever. Circumstances change. For instance, external factors can destroy the particular attributes for which a site may have been valued. Alternatively, it may not be within the power of the organisation to prevent development, such as land being acquired compulsorily by the state in the national interest perhaps for a new road. Again, new information may indicate better ways of achieving conservation objectives, thus rendering current landholdings less critical. CARTs have to balance their responsibility for long-term protection against their responsibility to operate in a cost-effective way. A failure to do this will mean a failure to achieve as much for conservation as the CART could otherwise do, and may even threaten its own survival.

Clearly the image which an organisation presents to the public is important. It ultimately depends upon the public to fund its operation and often to donate important assets. It must have the public's confidence otherwise it may not be able to survive. But it can be difficult for a CART to explain the sometimes complex issues involved in decisions about whether development should be permitted, or whether land should be sold. Where an organisation is expected to operate with clear and unambiguous principles, bad publicity over complex development decisions may threaten its credibility. In consequence, it is likely to shy away from taking controversial actions, even when they may well be consistent with conservation goals. In practice, much will depend upon the influence which a membership or the wider public has on decision-making and the organisation's ability to make its case in public. We return to these organisational issues in the next chapter.

Potential benefits through land management

Landownership and management by CARTs can contribute directly to environmental improvement in a number of principal ways:

(a) the protection or restoration of semi-natural habitat, valuable landscapes or historic features in the countryside;
(b) the creation of new habitats/features of value;
(c) education on-site – developing a site as a resource for environmental education;
(d) developing examples of good practice – demonstrating what can be done to enhance the environmental quality of land in a particular area or of a particular kind, and promoting this so that other landowners and

managers can be encouraged to apply these methods elsewhere;
(e) honeypots for income generation – using some more durable sites to generate income from visitors, which is then used to cross-subsidise other environmental work by the CART.

This variety of uses shows considerable potential to generate a range of benefits – more than just benign land management – and demonstrate that the particular strategy of owning and managing land as a conservation or amenity trust gives that trust many opportunities to influence the quality of the wider countryside beyond its own landholdings.

Different trusts adopt different approaches to site management, depending upon their objectives and the assets which they have available to them. The preservation versus creation range is perhaps illustrated by the National Trust at one extreme, most of whose assets have been acquired on the basis of their already having a conservation value of national importance, to a CART like the Woodland Trust which has on occasion bought whole farms in order to put most of them down to create new woodland. If the interests of conservation are to be advanced, against an inevitably declining inheritance of heritage assets, then the relative importance of environmental improvement and habitat re-creation must rise. The efforts by the Will Trust to re-create the Caledonian pine forest or the Countryside Restoration Trust to restore overintensively farmed land may be illustrative of this.

Another contrast is evident between those trusts for whom public enjoyment, education and therefore access is a large part of their work, such as the Wildfowl and Wetlands Trust, and those for whom access can threaten the future value of sites, such as Butterfly Conservation, whose sites may be kept relatively secret in order to protect rare species from overzealous collectors.

However, among those CARTs with several sites and fairly broad conservation objectives it is often the case that landholdings represent a more or less balanced portfolio of site management objectives, covering most of the list given earlier. Sometimes several of these objectives can be realised on the same site; in other cases they are clearly divided between sites of different quality and location. In many instances, both the purposes of site management and the techniques used will be very varied both within and between a CART's different holdings. Perhaps the main danger with this kind of approach, as has been suggested by our analysis of CART records and literature, is that it tends to encourage a sometimes inappropriate level of site diversity within a relatively small local area, in relation to the wider national or international relevance of the habitat or landscape context of each site.

An emphasis upon land management has particular relevance to the concept of striking a socially desirable pattern of land use within a localised or larger area. However, land management is neither the only way nor a sufficient condition for CARTs to achieve environmental improvement; this may be brought about by numerous direct and indirect means separate from the formal ongoing management of land areas by the group. We should therefore perhaps consider why it is a central theme in the activities of all those groups which we have decided to study.

Lobbying for change

While CARTs, by definition, are directly involved in land management, many also promote their goals by seeking to influence the actions of others, most notably by lobbying central and local government to achieve changes favourable to their objectives. Indeed for many CARTs, lobbying and seeking to influence the planning system are primary activities. The priorities attached to these alternatives differ considerably between organisations. While many, especially smaller trusts, concentrate exclusively on the management of their land, others take a considerably broader view of their objectives. The National Trust, although it was in its early stages active in pressing for reforms, now no longer campaigns for changes in policy, tending rather to avoid confrontation (Strong, 1988). A recent exception has been where policies have direct and specific impacts on its properties in the public criticism of the government's roads programme. It has, however, recently been argued that the National Trust should adopt a more aggressive stance in the protection of its interests (Weideger, 1994).

On the other hand, the Royal Society for Nature Conservation, representing the Wildlife Trusts, has resolved to adopt a more campaigning role in the 1990s (Micklewright, 1993), having to date become involved in issues such as water shortages, environmental damage from peat digging and the conservation of ancient woodlands and flower-rich meadows. The Royal Society for the Protection of Birds has an active programme of research which is directed towards attempts to influence policy. It has, for instance, been a keen critic of the Common Agricultural Policy, particularly promoting reforms based on cross-compliance, which would require that farmers achieve certain conservation objectives as a condition of receiving agricultural subsidies. Following the reforms of the Common Agricultural Policy or CAP which we outlined in Chapter 1, there are now more opportunities for this approach to be adopted since a greater proportion of agricultural support is now by means of direct payments to farmers, rather than by market price supports. On the other hand, it might be argued that this does not represent the best potential method of securing environmental goals and that a more direct approach is generally to be preferred (Hodge, 1992).

There may, however, be conflicts between a more radical campaigning role and that of a landowner. It is perhaps notable that the landowning environmental groups appear to adopt rather less extreme positions than do some other campaigning groups such as Friends of the Earth or Greenpeace. Effective lobbying tends to depend upon the pursuit of clear and straightforward principles. But as we have seen, land management often involves making difficult compromises in specific circumstances. It would, for instance, be quite easy for a CART to campaign for rigorous laws against development on the coast or against blood sports, only to find itself compromised with respect to the management of its own particular properties. For example, the maintenance of a coastal estate may only be possible from funds generated by a small unobtrusive development such that a failure to undertake the development could mean a failure to conserve other aspects of the estate. Alternatively, important land for conservation might be offered to an organisation provided that fox hunting can be continued, and an organisation which opposed fox hunting in principle would be unable to accept it. Even in the case of environmental groups, landowners tend to be on the side of stability and incremental change. We noted in Chapter 6, for instance, the controversy over stag hunting on National Trust land, and the RSPB has faced similar, if less well-publicised, disputes over the issue of shooting on its reserves.

The wider impacts of CART actions

The key element of CARTs need not be in their ability to improve the environment of sites themselves, but the ability to use their sites and their local administration to influence environmental quality in the wider locality. Being local landowners gives them a certain degree of influence over land-use decisions in general, and the possibility of influencing other landowners by ripple and knock-on effects.

For example, having a reserve sensitive to local water-table levels makes a trust instantly aware if these are falling, and to tackle such a problem it will need to work with other landowners. Having a reserve for wild species sensitive to pesticides necessitates the same vigilance and co-operative relations with others. In the process of court-ing the attention of other landowners to tell them what damage their activities are doing, CARTs are providing a source of information which landowners may not have previously had. Because the CART owns or is itself responsible for land, a private landowner may be more inclined to acknowledge its right to fair treatment. But this depends heavily upon the trust having a benign and respected image in the eyes of the local community: if it is seen to be too extreme or unrepresentative of publicly-held values, then its credibility will fall and its influence is likely to be less.

In theory, the presence of landowners within the locality who own land for environmental as opposed to com-mercial reasons should mean that environmental concerns are appreciated by a wider sphere of local people, and that resulting land-use decisions incorporate a greater degree of environmental sensitivity than they would otherwise have done. However, there is no particular reason to assume that the degree of environmental influence achieved by the presence of these groups will in any sense be 'optimal'. We have already argued that the existing market incentives to produce environmental outputs are limited.

While the activities undertaken by CARTs are generally beneficial, they are not necessarily regarded as such by all who may be affected by them. Perhaps the most typical concern relating to CART activity is that their objectives of environmental preservation tend to prevent development, so causing a loss of income and employment. Concerns about the growth of CART ownership in the Highlands have been expressed by Wigan (1995). Where a trust owns a substantial amount of land within a local area this can have a marked impact on the local economy. But this need not always be the case. There may be circumstances when conservation can have a more positive impact on local economic development. The issues which arise here represent a microcosm of the much broader debate about the general conflict between environment and development.

CARTs will often acquire and manage property to prevent certain developments from taking place. Similarly they may operate land at a lower level of use due to their greater concern for environmental impacts. We have discussed many examples of this: protecting habitat against agricultural development or preserving coast and countryside against urban developments. Almost by definition, CARTs give a greater weight to non-market values than do those owners who have a more central concern for financial returns. However, the economic impact of this emphasis is not always negative. Sometimes, a concern for conservation becomes a source of economic development potential. The most obvious example is the impact of environmental management on tourism where it is possible for visitors to come to an area to experience the environmental qualities which are conserved by the trust. And it is not only the landowners who benefit. While visitors may have to pay an entry fee to the owner of the site, they are also likely to spend money on other local services: meals, accommodation, transport, souvenirs, and so on. They may also be encouraged to visit other sites and to spend money there. At the same time, the trust operating a site will itself pass on some of the income which it receives in buying goods and services from the local economy. There may be a more general effect too. In preserving or enhancing some aspect of the local environment, the area may be made more attractive to potential inmigrants, itself increasing the size of the local population, raising property values and stimulating the demand for local services.

What is clear is that CART activity is likely to lead to a different pattern of local economic activity from that which would otherwise have occurred. The larger the area owned, the larger the likely impact on the local economy. As a result, some people will gain and others will lose, as is the case with any form of development. And, as in other areas of life, we may not be surprised if those who lose tend to make more noise than do those who gain. We may therefore anticipate that we will hear more of the negative impacts than of the positive ones.

Further horizons for CART action

New mechanisms

As we have seen, CARTs are involved in a variety of different actions although their direct actions generally concentrate on the management of land. There may be alternative actions for CARTs in the land market. Rather than acquiring full ownership of land, it could be possible to acquire individual rights, such as rights to prevent the draining of wetland areas or the application of chemical fertilisers or pesticides in particular places. The scope for private organisations to do this is limited under current law and we discuss possible changes in Chapter 15.

Global action

The great majority of the trusts which we have examined have confined their attentions to local issues and operate within the UK. Perhaps the main exception to this is the RSPB, which has established contacts and joint projects overseas. The long-distance migration of birds gives an immediate basis for international co-operation in bird conservation. The launch of Birdlife International has given form to these mutual interests. Clearly there is great scope for other organisations to expand their vision, recognising mutual interests in conservation.

In the United States, the Nature Conservancy has an active International Program. This recognises the global interests in protecting habitat and biodiversity: as a potential source of drugs, as a source of genetic material for improvements in the production of food and other valuable items, and as a potentially critical component of the earth's life-support systems. The Nature Conservancy's work is founded on a network of some 82 Conservation Data Centers across the Western Hemisphere, fourteen of which are in Latin America, which develop inventories of a region's flora and fauna in order to identify the most threatened natural areas and to establish priorities for action for conservation. Locally, the Conservancy works with partner organisations in each country, lobbying for protected area status, seeking voluntary protection from private landowners, or buying land outright.

The US Nature Conservancy has also helped to pioneer debt-for-nature swaps. Many less developed countries suffer from very high levels of debt, which they owe to foreign banks. Pressures to pay interest and repay capital force debtor countries to take actions which can quickly generate the necessary funds to make payments, but often do so at the expense of environmental quality, clearing forests, mining in sensitive areas or constructing dams which require an initial social upheaval in the area flooded, and which may in any case soon silt up meaning that any gains may be short-lived.

Debt-for-nature swaps attempt to redirect this pressure towards environmental conservation. A non-profit organisation can buy part of a country's debt from a creditor, usually a commercial bank. Because the creditor often has little expectation of the loan ever being repaid in full, it can be purchased at considerably less than its face value; a $1 million loan might be acquired for $100 000. The debtor country then owes the face value of the loan to the non-profit organisation. With the agreement of the debtor country and its central bank, the debt can then be donated to a local conservation organisation. Arrangements can then be made to pay the conservation organisation in local currency and this can be used to support conservation projects. There is an advantage to the central bank in being able to pay its loan in its own currency rather than having to find, say, US dollars, hence reducing the pressures to expand exports to generate foreign currency.

For example, a debt-for-nature swap was used to establish the Blue Mountain/John Crow Mountain Forest Preserve, protecting nearly 80 000 hectares in Jamaica from logging, poaching and squatting (Williams, 1992). The Nature Conservancy raised $300 000 from the US Agency for International Development and the Puerto Rico Conservation Trust, and with this was able to buy $437 000 of Jamaican debt which was trading at 68 cents on the dollar. These funds were then used to establish the Forest Preserve. By 1992 nearly $109 million of commercial bank debt had been acquired with conservation objectives in less developed countries. This generated nearly $70 million for conservation projects, mostly in Costa Rica, Ecuador and the Philippines (Williams, 1992). While these amounts are minimal in relation to the total debt burden carried by less developed countries, they can make a valuable contribution to conservation objectives and they indicate a possible mechanism for funding conservation on a greater scale. But of course, the initial funding still has to be met by a donor of some sort.

Conclusions

So CARTs' land management objectives should lead to environmental benefits in a variety of ways. Collectively individuals can achieve environmental improvements which they could not achieve alone. Some of this is done directly and practically through actions in acquiring and managing land. But this means that often difficult choices have to be made; taking out loans against an uncertain prospect of future donations to secure the purchase of property, balancing a concern for environmental protection against financial pressures, recognising the wider implications that actions have for the local area. This feature characterises a wide range of actions from the efforts by a small village group to purchase land for public access to the complex international financial transactions involved in debt-for-nature swaps to protect the rainforest. But they have an essential element in common: they represent efforts by groups of individuals to band together to achieve improvements in the environment for the general good. This is the essence of CART activity.

However, we are also interested in the degree to which these benefits represent a real improvement on alternative forms of landownership and management – the 'additionality' element of CART landholding and management.

In order to assess this, the following points need to be established:

1. To what extent do the combined activities of these organisations reflect the interests of a wider public at different geographical levels, and to what extent do they 'redress the balance' of rural land-use patterns determined otherwise largely by commercially orientated groups and individuals, to bring the overall pattern of land use more into line with public environmental improvement objectives?

2. To what extent can these groups *achieve* aims consistent with the improvement of environmental quality, within the current policy framework, and are there alternative institutional arrangements which could achieve improvements more effectively (either through these organisations, or independently)?

Question 1 is one which will focus our analysis upon the activities of CARTs, their objectives and their ability to represent the public interest. Public interest must be distinguished here from members' interests – not all members will identify strongly with the aims of a CART (Bull, 1986) and their joining up may have little to do with any wish for their interests to be directly expressed in many areas of CART activity and policy.

Question 2 is one which must focus upon CART finances, links to government policy, group structure and management, as these factors influence the whole spectrum of what we term as environmental improvement. It must also look at CARTs' integration with other landowners to see how balances are struck between different interests in rural land, and whether the current balance of control would conform to what is assessed by the public to be high environmental quality.

These two questions influence the form of the remaining chapters in this book.

Opening the Timotei Grange Meadow, 1991. Reproduced by permission of Plantlife

13 Finance

Finance and CARTs

CARTs are non-profit-making organisations, and as such their ability to aquire land and manage it for conservation or amenity objectives depends critically upon the extent to which revenue and capital can be raised externally. The main sources of such funds are through private sub-scription, donation and legacy, and through public-sector departments and agencies who support the work that the CARTs do, at both local and national levels. In this chapter we attempt to distinguish the factors which influence a CART's choice of external funding sources, and the ways in which this then affects their behaviour as organisations. We have drawn our conclusions from a mixture of published accounts and discussions with many trusts across the UK.

Table 13.1 shows recent figures for sources of oper-ational income for some different CARTs: independent CARTs, the Wildlife Trusts and the National Trust. The differences in accounting conventions make detailed, direct comparisons difficult. In particular, the National Trust and Wildlife Trusts record appeals income and legacies in quite separate accounts, whereas other trusts may count them among general donations or investments. In 1990, for the National Trust, these two sources comprised some £24 million, equivalent to 30 per cent of their general oper-ational income. Notwithstanding this, the table indicates the relative importance of membership and admissions charges to the National Trust, in comparison with the other organisations.

Among the independent CARTs, the largest portion, approximately 27 per cent of combined income, came from

Table 13.1 Percentage sources of operational income

	Independent CARTs*	County Wildlife Trusts**	National Trust***
Membership	8	22	37
Admissions	–	–	10
Donations	11	13	1
Public-sector grants	27	31	10
Enterprises	26	25	8
Rents	17	-	14
Investments	8	9	20
Other	3	–	–

* 1989/90 accounts of 41 CARTs for which data available.
** 1988/89 accounts for 47 trusts.
*** 1990 accounts.

the public sector in the form of grant-aid and this figure rises to over 30 per cent for the Wildlife Trusts. Other significant sources of independent CART income include membership subscriptions, the profits of associated sales (e.g. shops and mail-order services selling promotional and educational materials), fundraising events, income generated from CARTs' landholdings and environmental improvement work (agricultural and other rents, income from contract work for other landholders and the sale of produce from the land), and income from separately held capital (investment funds, legacies, commercial property).

It is important to remember that the variation between the proportional sources of funds for individual trusts is extremely wide – for example, almost half the primary trusts have no income from a subscribing membership because they do not have one. Likewise, a small number of relatively large trusts obtain income from renting most of their land to tenant farmers, whilst many other CARTs do not act as landlords in any respect.

Income from membership

Income from membership appears to be relatively important (around 20 to 30 per cent of total operational income) for those trusts who have subscribing members. However, the charge for membership is remarkably uniform across a very wide range of primary trusts, ranging from around £5 to £30 for one individual for one year: a relatively modest sum by comparison with the membership fees of many more overtly user-orientated clubs and societies, which may be several hundred pounds annually. This would suggest that membership of a primary CART is viewed by those who join more as a demonstration of tangible commitment to its environmental objectives than as a fee related directly to the services the CART offers to its members.

Sales of goods and events

Proportional income from the sale of goods and from fundraising events appears to be very variable between trusts and between years. A well-established sales outlet can contribute a significant and regular amount to CART funds from year to year, but not all CARTs are equally able or well-placed to offer this kind of facility, which requires suitable premises, stock and careful management, and which must be attractive to the purchasing public. Some trusts, for example the Wildfowl and Wetlands Trust, have developed considerable expertise in running their own sales outlets, while others sell through the outlets of larger trusts (e.g. Cambridge Preservation Society had such an arrangement with the local Wildlife Trust for some years). Fundraising through one-off events and through commercial sponsors is a more flexible option for trusts because it requires less consistent financial commitment, but, perhaps even more so than sales, it is very sensitive to any fluctuations in the wider economy which have a significant impact upon the 'climate for giving'.

Income from the land

All those CARTs managing areas of semi-natural habitat with traditional methods can generate some income from the produce of management at established sites – such as coppice-wood, hay, stock reared at low densities on grazing marsh, and/or the rents from conservation tenancies or licences (agricultural leasing but with conservation clauses written into agreements by the landowner). However, these practices are rarely economically viable: indeed the unprofitability of such management regimes is usually the reason why they are now undertaken increasingly by charitable trusts rather than commercial landowners. CARTs who realise income from their sites in these ways are rarely able to meet their management objectives in full from this source, and further fundraising or the acquisition of other income-generating assets remains an important part of their survival and growth.

Many heritage CARTs are in possession of considerable capital assets associated with the land areas which they seek to preserve as a heritage resource. The income from these assets can therefore cross-subsidise heritage management costs. For example, where a heritage CART is set up on a large, formerly public or private estate, the management of heritage areas can be subsidised by the income generated from, say, a commercial business based in the former stately home or some of its outbuildings, or from rental income associated with other non-conservation lands and properties on the estate. But here too there will generally be a net deficit to be covered from other sources.

Some conservation and heritage CARTs operate rather like museums or wildlife parks, generating income by charging visitors for access to part(s) of the land and/or buildings held: the Wildfowl and Wetlands Trust is a well-known conservation example. This operation does not render the CART commercial in the same sense as a golf course, zoo or leisure centre would usually be – CARTs retain charitable status because they are not motivated to make profits. But also, their charitable objectives stress the preservation aspect of their role, such that visitors are not the primary or sole beneficiaries of the public goods and commercial retailing businesses they provide. These services are merely a means to the end of maintaining the heritage or conservation value of the land itself, which is seen to be of broader, indirect public benefit.

Institutionally, income generation from visitors is usually managed in a similar way to income generated through the sale of goods. The CART's charitable status is protected by establishing a separate commercial trading subsidiary to handle the commercial aspects of its work. Any profits are then covenanted back to the trust.

There are also attempts to 'sell' other aspects of the

CART's activities directly. For example, we have described in Chapter 10 the approach taken by Heritage Conserved (HC) whereby contributors buy small freehold plots of land for tree-planting. Initially, each plot was priced at £12.50, but this has been raised towards £25 to keep pace with rising costs. Publicity for the scheme began with small advertisements in newspapers, then an article appeared in the *Daily Post*, and one or two followed in the local papers and subsequently in the national press. The greatest response came from an article in *Homes and Gardens* magazine, where the article had been placed at the front of the magazine and was quite long. About three-quarters of sales are as presents for someone else and about three-quarters of the buyers are women. About 20 per cent of trees are bought for children, in trust, while another 18 per cent are bought in memoriam. Oak is the most popular tree, accounting for 55 per cent of all trees. Ash is the least popular. Very few people send donations with their purchase money. HC is unable to distinguish between people who buy for the novelty of the idea and those who buy for broader conservation aims. A map is sent showing the plot where their tree is planted, and each tree is marked with a plaque. HC has had buyers from all over the world (e.g. Zimbabwe, South Africa, the US and Europe), who hear about it through international magazines. About 5 per cent of the trees have been bought by local people.

However, in some cases this kind of approach may have been abused and brought into disrepute on the grounds that the scheme is suspected of being used as a means of making a profit. Traditional British Broadleaf Heritage Limited offered a similar scheme in which they offered long leases (75 or 110 years) to plots of land on which trees were planted. They operated two sites, one in Cornwall and one in Surrey. They were not a charity, but emphasised that the shareholders had agreed that in the foreseeable future profits would go towards the purchase and planting of further woodlands. They were, however, the subject of unfortunate comparisons in *Which?* magazine, where they were judged to be very expensive, charging between £30 and £186 per plot. The magazine also questioned the permanence of the scheme, given uncertainty as to what would happen after the end of the lease. Traditional British Broadleaf Heritage Limited have subsequently become bankrupt.

Selling services

A different type of income source is from contract work, where the CART offers its expertise and equipment to other landholders at a competitive rate, allowing it to make a surplus from this activity which can cross-subsidise its own environmental improvement work and land management. Contracting out their often highly specialist services to other organisations is a growing form of income generation for CARTs. However, it is one which can cause problems for the CART if it becomes too significant. Alternative views of the increasing role of consultancy in local Wildlife Trusts have been expressed by Shirley and Knightbridge (1992). Firstly, providing commercial services to others may be in conflict with the charitable status of the CART – making the formation of a separate organisation necessary. And once a consultancy or other service is begun, its growth demands continuing input of time and energy by trust staff, which can sometimes compromise their ability to continue to service the loss-making activities of the trust adequately. Also, trusts which too obviously operate successful commercial wings may find that their other sources of finance are withdrawn as public and private sponsors judge that there are other, more needy causes to support. There are also potential conflicts of interest between the lobbying and campaigning activities of the organisation and its commitments as a consultant. This will depend in part on the degree of commercialism with which consultancy activities are pursued. It is possible to limit the range of organisations for which consultancy will be undertaken, but this will limit the level of income which can be generated.

Income from the public sector

Among other sources of funding, the grants offered by public agencies and departments are clearly very significant for a large number of CARTs. The main grant-aiding bodies are government agencies, notably the Countryside Commission, English Nature and some of the Rural Development agencies, the National Heritage Memorial Fund (see below), the Department of the Environment, and local government, including both County and District Councils and National Parks. A large proportion of trusts receive such income for specific management tasks or development projects, usually tied to a fixed period of five years or less. But a small number of trusts have also entered into longer-term arrangements for public funding, with grants agreed on the basis of an annual work programme approved by their sponsors. The third pattern of public subsidy is one-off grants for land acquisition by CARTs, on the understanding that purchase and subsequent management of the site will generally be in the public interest.

In looking at how these grants change over time, it is evident that they may be significant factors in trusts' growth. Consider the varying grants paid to the Wildlife Trusts over past years. In 1976/77, the Nature Conservancy Council (NCC) paid out £15 533 to the Trusts through its Section Three grants for general management (SPNC, 1978). By 1988/89 the NCC paid £418 702 in grants to the Trusts, which represented 6.9 per cent of their total operational income that year. £105 000 was also given to the Trusts by UK2000 in 1988 (RSNC records). Then in 1992 English Nature announced that from 1993/94 its land purchase grants would be temporarily suspended to allow more to be spent on supporting better management of existing sites (National Audit Office, 1994). Local authorities have funded Trust activities for a number of years. In 1976, they gave a total of £45 000 towards specific Trust activities, and grants rose during the 1980s but have tailed off somewhat since then. And in the late 1980s and early 1990s the Countryside Commission became a significant source of support for specific, amenity-related work by the Wildlife Trusts.

The National Heritage Memorial Fund and related funding

The National Heritage Memorial Fund is an increasingly important source of finance for CARTs. It has its roots in an earlier fund (the National Land Fund) established in 1946. And since 1994, its purpose has been copied in the establishment of the Heritage Lottery Fund.

The National Land Fund

In the 1946 Finance Act, Hugh Dalton, then Chancellor of the Exchequer, established a £50 million fund, the National Land Fund, in order to encourage landowners to give property of outstanding interest to the government in lieu of death duties. Property was to be judged as pre-eminent for its national, scientific, historic or artistic interest. Provision for this had already been made in the Finance Act 1910, but it had been very little used. Under the 1946 Act, property received would be handed over to some non-profit-making body, such as the National Trust or the Youth Hostels Association, and the National Land Fund would be used to reimburse the Inland Revenue for the tax forgone. Properties given could also be transferred to government departments under a slightly different mechanism. It was not possible for the Fund to be used to buy property during the lifetime of the owner (although this was possible for the Ulster Land Fund, established in 1949). Dalton's intention was that property protected in this way should be seen as a memorial to those who gave their lives in the war and that it should be established from the sale of army surplus. In fact it was created by a single payment from the Consolidated Fund.

In subsequent legislation, the types of item which could be accepted in lieu of taxation were extended, in 1953 to include objects kept in buildings which were also accepted in lieu, in 1956 to works of art of pre-eminent aesthetic merit or historic value, and in 1973 to any item pre-eminent for its national, scientific or historic interest. Also, in 1953, the Historic Buildings and Ancient Monuments Act enabled the use of the National Land Fund to re-imburse government expenses incurred in acquiring buildings and objects, and for grants to local authorities or to the National Trusts in connection with such buildings. Further, this Act provided for cash endowments to be made to the National Trusts for buildings that had received grants, although the provision was never used. It was only inserted into the Act under back-bench pressure, and the government made it clear at the time that it did not intend to apply it.

In practice much less use was made of the Fund than had been anticipated in 1946. Total expenditure up until 1977 was about £11 million, averaging something over

£300 000 per year. This compares with the Fund's income from investments of about £1.7 million. In 1957, in the light of this low level of expenditure, the Government decided to reduce the capital to £10 million. Nevertheless, over the period to 1977, it had facilitated the transfer of nearly 70 properties to the National Trust, including Penrhyn Castle, Ickworth House and Petworth, including over 40 000 ha of land. This represents about one-third of the total area acquired by the National Trust over that period. Much smaller amounts of property had been transferred to the National Trust for Scotland, the Youth Hostels Associations and to government departments. No other private non-profit organisations received properties, although there appears to have been no reason in principle why they should not have benefited.

The National Land Fund operated with little publicity and with little public awareness of its existence until 1977. For at least two years before this, negotiations had been under way between Lord Rosebery and the government over the possible transfer of Mentmore Towers and much of its contents (Jones, 1985). The property was offered for £2 million together with an undeclared amount of tax relief, but after lengthy negotiation the government announced, in the face of much criticism, that it was not willing to allocate funds for the acquisition and for the large endowment that would have been necessary for the maintenance of the property. It was widely felt that the National Land Fund should have been used for the preservation of Mentmore and that decisions on expenditures from the Fund should be made independent of government controls over public expenditure. A sale of the contents was subsequently held at Mentmore in May 1977 which raised about £6.25 million.

The National Heritage Memorial Fund

This episode prompted a House of Commons Select Committee inquiry into the operation of the National Land Fund which reported in 1978 (Expenditure Committee, 1978). A variety of concerns were expressed in evidence to the Committee, including the limited use made of the Fund, and Treasury interference with decisions concerning Fund expenditure. The National Trust in particular indicated the problems that had arisen from the Fund's failure to provide endowments to cover the costs of managing and maintaining properties received from the Fund. While the National Trust had been the recipient of a large number of very significant houses, it had incurred a substantial deficit in their management which had to be covered from its own funds. Annual grants had been introduced for the maintenance of properties but they had been insufficient to cover the deficits involved. The National Trust indicated that it had had to find £650 000 from its own resources in connection with properties received from the National Land Fund, and it was also unwilling to become dependent on regular government grants for maintenance.

The Select Committee recommended that payments from the Fund should not be regarded as public expenditure, on the grounds that the expenditure from the exchequer had already taken place in 1946 when the Fund was initially established, so that subsequent expenditure was beyond controls over public expenditure; a view contested by the Treasury. It also recommended that the Fund should be renamed the National Heritage Fund and empowered to make grants or loans to non-profit-making organisations for the preservation of exceptional elements of national heritage, including the countryside. The Fund would thus no longer be limited to situations where property was offered to the government in lieu of taxation.

The Select Committee's report was followed by a Private Member's Bill to implement the proposals, a White Paper produced by the Labour Government, a National Heritage Bill, introduced by the incoming Conservative Government in 1979, and finally the National Heritage Act 1980. This Act established the National Heritage Memorial Fund; the name was extended to emphasise Dalton's original purpose for the Fund. The new Fund, under the control of independent trustees, was empowered to give financial assistance towards the cost of acquiring, maintaining or preserving land, buildings, works of art or other objects which are of importance to the national heritage. The Fund was established from the bulk of the balance remaining in the National Land Fund and receives an annual vote from parliament. The provisions for accepting property in lieu of taxation continue, but responsibility for this was

Table 13.2 Grants, loans and acquisitions from the National Heritage Memorial Fund, 1980–1994

	£000 (%)	No. (%)	Average grant (£)
Land of scenic and/or scientific interest	21 975 (16)	195 (21)	112 700
Buildings and associated contents	43 492 (32)	96 (10)	453 042
Paintings, drawings, watercolours and museum objects	52 766 (38)	404 (43)	130 609
Industrial, transport and maritime history	6363 (5)	94 (10)	67 691
Manuscripts and archives	12 453 (9)	144 (16)	86 479
Total*	166 142** (100)	936*** (100)	177 502

* Includes three specific grants of £29 million for Kedleston, Nostell and Weston.
** Excludes £7000 loan to Cornwall Trust for Nature Conservation converted to grant in 1993–94.
*** Number of grants in 1993–94 excludes grants authorised in previous years and payable in instalments.
Source: National Heritage Memorial Fund, Annual Report 1993–1994.

transferred from the Treasury to the Secretary of State for the Environment and the Minister for the Arts.

The National Heritage Memorial Fund is seen as a last resort where items of outstanding importance are under threat; where art objects are likely to leave the country or where inappropriate uses threaten the conservation value of land. Applicants are expected to raise whatever funds they can from alternative sources before being allocated money from the Fund. However, in emergencies, the Fund is able to respond quickly. The range of interests assisted by the Fund is very broad. The pattern of expenditures over the first fourteen years of the Fund's operation is illustrated in Table 13.2. Some 16 per cent of funds have been allocated to the protection of land of scenic or scientific interest.

The establishment of the National Heritage Memorial Fund has also increased the variety of organisations receiving funds. Amongst CARTs receiving funds within the first two years of the Fund's operation were the

National Trust, the National Trust for Scotland, the Cambridge Wildlife Trust, the Wildfowl Trust and the RSPB. The grants to CARTs in 1993–94 are listed in Table 13.3.

The Heritage Lottery Fund

Part of the proceeds from the operation of the National Lottery are now being allocated for projects to preserve the national heritage (Newbould, 1994). Twenty per cent of the funds available for 'good causes' will be directed to the Heritage Lottery Fund to be administered by the National Heritage Memorial Fund. It is anticipated that about £150 million will be available in 1995, rising to a plateau of about £300 million by 1998 or 1999. The guidelines for allocating funds are similar to those for the Heritage Fund. The Heritage Lottery Fund may not solicit specific applications and there must be an element of partnership funding, although the percentage is not specified. Primary emphasis must be on capital expenditure, although, exceptionally, endowment or revenue grants may be allowed where they are necessary for a capital project to go ahead. Eligible projects include:

1. The acquisition, preservation, restoration and enhancement of important landscapes, sites of special scientific importance, historic landscapes and parks and gardens.
2. Major works of improvement or restoration to assist management of or access to sites in 1.
3. Acquisition of land which is not itself of recognised importance to protect the setting of or access to 1.
4. The building of appropriate visitor facilities.
5. Once-for-all surveying and recording projects on such sites, to improve their management or enhance public access.

Like the National Heritage Memorial Fund mechanism, the recipients of funds cannot be private individuals. Assuming that the pattern of allocation for this Fund is thus similar to that established by the Heritage Fund, this could represent a substantial opportunity for CARTs.

The first round of grants was announced in April 1995 to be met by almost universal criticism. £13 million were

Table 13.3 Grants to CARTs from the National Heritage Memorial Fund, 1993–1994

Recipient	Property	Amount (£)	Description
Carstairs Countryside Trust	Thorganby and West Cottingworth Ings	24 522	Flood-meadow in Lower Derwent valley – part of this payment may be refunded
Cornwall Trust for Nature Conservation	Sylvia's Meadow	7000	Converted from a loan
Essex Wildlife Trust	Tollesbury Wick Marshes	90 000	175 ha of grazing marsh, sea wall, borrowdyke and saltings in the Blackwater Estuary
Herefordshire Nature Trust	Hampton Meadow and Big and Little Million	24 600	24 ha of meadow at the confluence of the rivers Lugg and Frome
John Muir Trust	Sandwood–Oldshoremore Estate	25 000	Remote 4500 ha estate in Sutherland south of Cape Wrath under pressure from visitors and overgrazing
Leicestershire Wildlife Trust	Loughborough Big Meadow	4250	2 ha Lammas meadow alongside River Soar
Montgomery Wildlife Trust	Dyfi Estuary Saltings	35 000	Purchase of 30 ha of saltings
National Trust	Gibside Estate	309 000	Acquisition of further elements of the estate, including 140 ha of woodland
National Trust	Prior Park	250 000	Grant for maintenance fund for 11 ha landscape park on south-east edge of Bath which had been donated to the National Trust

continues overleaf

Table 13.3 (*continued*)

Recipient	Property	Amount (£)	Description
National Trust for Scotland	Dunbeath Estate	500 000	Castle, gardens and farms on 18 000 ha estate on the east coast of Caithness, Scotland. Proposed transfer was withdrawn and grant repaid
Sussex Wildlife Trust	Manxey Level, the Pevensey Levels	70 000	89 ha of gravity-drained grazing marsh to form a hydrological unit for water-level maintenance
Weston Park Foundation	Weston Park	146 191	Further payment towards repair of house on Weston estate
Woodland Trust	Ledmore and Migdale Woods	95 000	Estate covering 710 ha on the northern banks of Dornoch Firth, including 95 ha natural oak wood

Source: National Heritage Memorial Fund, *Annual Report* 1993–1994.

allocated towards securing an archive of Winston Churchill's papers for the nation. This is not the place to consider the pros and cons of this particular decision, but it was clearly not a popular start for the Fund. The second largest grant, of £10 million, was used primarily in order to establish an endowment fund to enable the National Trust for Scotland to acquire the 77 500-acre Mar Lodge estate in the Cairngorms. Amongst the nine grants announced there was a grant of £8000 towards the improvement of Ryeclose Wood by the Northumberland National Park Authority. No CART other than the National Trust for Scotland received a grant. It is clearly not appropriate to judge the potential value of the Fund on the basis of these grants alone. However, while the two largest grants were both made in respect of contentious problems that had remained unresolved over several years, the practice of handing the bulk of the funds to a few of the very largest organisations (in this case two projects which received 95 per cent of the funds) is somewhat questionable.

Sponsorship from the private sector

Sponsorship from the private sector is a volatile and image-linked prospect, if assessed by reference to interviews with the staff of different CARTs. Many of the corporate sponsors of individual CARTs choose to do so because of a particular local link – for example, the oil companies who support the work of the Buchan Countryside Group, and the Wildfowl and Wetlands Trust which received some assistance for its new Llanelli reserve from adjacent industries. Alternatively, there may be some attribute of a particular project which offers a sponsor an attractive image. An example of this would be Plantlife's Timotei Meadow Project. The makers of Timotei hair shampoo provided funds enabling Plantlife to acquire four meadows in Yorkshire, Suffolk, Buckinghamshire and Gwynedd. The reserves are now all managed by the local Wildlife Trusts. The association with wildflower meadows was clearly one which the makers of a herbal shampoo found attractive, and offered an opportunity for Timotei to promote its product. CARTs therefore experience a degree of restricted access to these sorts of funding simply because of the need to be 'in the right place at the right time'.

Of those private companies which regularly support environmental initiatives at local or national level, many award grants very much on a one-off basis each year, operating an annual competition for their funds. Amongst the more prominent are Shell and British Petroleum. Some exhibit a preference for new trusts, or for local community-based projects, while others appear more willing to support only the best-known groups, albeit for increasingly novel themes from year to year. Trust staff generally agree that sponsorship funds diminish enormously in any period of economic decline, and the relatively low level of sponsorship which was detected in an analysis of independent trusts' income in 1989 probably reflects this tendency. Many trusts have newly recruited sponsorship and promotional staff, often themselves supported by government grant-aid, but, as yet, few appear to have been able to establish a firm line of such support.

Some well-known trusts have a particular status and it may be possible for them to use this in their fundraising. The Wildlife Trusts expected to receive £200 000 for endorsement of a 'green' range of household cleaning products. These would bear the Trusts' logo, and the Trusts would receive £160 000 together with further funds based on a donation from the company for each item sold bearing the logo. It was planned to spend the money on a campaign for wetlands conservation. There is an obvious risk in such deals that the CART may lose some of its status by entering into such deals, and the Wildlife Trusts' arrangement was a source of controversy within the partnership.

Some CARTs have made a particular effort to support themselves through sponsorship. The Groundwork Trusts are a clear example of this phenomenon. Supported initially through a mixture of local authority and Countryside Commission core funding, the Trusts were intended to become self-supporting through private sponsorship and contract work within a relatively short space of time. But although many have made the transition away from being dependent upon core funds, it is noticeable that among their sponsors and the purchasers of their contract services, public bodies, particularly local authority schemes, often figure prominently.

There has been little systematic analysis of the types of private donors who contribute to the work of conservation trusts. One American study of corporate donations to the Nature Conservancy (Griffith and Knoeber, 1986) suggests, with some support from a statistical analysis, that firms for which genetic diversity, advertising and reputation for environmental responsibility are more valuable are more likely to contribute.

Fundraising

Campaigns to buy land can be an important component of CART fundraising activities. It is in general easier for organisations to raise funds when there is a specific goal; people would rather contribute to protect a particular site from development than towards the general operations of an organisation. Thus a threatened area of land is an important financial lever in soliciting donations.

The Magog Trust

By way of illustration, we can consider the behaviour of a small trust deciding to acquire land. The Magog Trust was established solely to buy and restore a particular arable site in the Gog Magog Hills near Cambridge to flower-rich chalk grassland. At Easter 1989 163 acres were first put on the market. It was part of a private estate, which was being sold in lots and had planning permission for a golf course. However, three local people, stimulated by the late Colin Davison, the local vicar, conceived the idea of buying the site for public amenity and set up a trust with the intention of buying the land. The initial appeal was run by offering people notional plots of land, termed 'Gogs', raising £40 000. South Cambridgeshire District Council offered £90 000 and the City and County Councils also made smaller contributions. The deadline for raising the asking price of £327 000 was September 1989, and by this time the target had not been reached, although money was still coming in slowly. The situation was retrieved by Edmund Vesty, a local businessman, who agreed to underwrite the Trust for £100 000, at the same time persuading it to buy the whole area of land on that site. He gave a £100 000 interest-free loan for twelve months, and the Trust took out a bank loan to cover the remaining amount. This allowed it to purchase the site.

After that point the needed build-up of support was very difficult to achieve, partly because local businesses had been hit by the recession. In 1991, the Trust had achieved a 40 per cent reduction in the initial £170 000 debt. Also the private loan was extended for up to ten years. The Trust continued to offer Gogs, and a membership scheme was established as was a scheme to sponsor trees, asking minimum donations of £5 per tree. Several areas of woodland have been planted, one of which has particularly been identified as a memorial wood, where all trees have been planted in memory of different individuals. The land is being returned to extensive grassland and facilities have been provided for visitors. It is estimated that some 25 000 people are using the downland in a year. But the constant pressure has been to reduce the level of debt. Various initiatives have been taken and a fundraiser was employed. There has been a link with a local estate agent who enrols all housebuyers as members of the Trust. The area was officially 'opened' to the public in June 1993 with more than 20 000 trees and shrubs planted and the debt reduced to £90 000. Public agencies have also been vital to the success of the venture. Besides the grants received towards the cost of land purchase, land has been placed into the voluntary set-aside scheme, the Farm Woodlands Scheme and the Countryside Premium Scheme.

By 1995 the debt had been reduced to below £60 000 and the Trust is on target to repay the loan by 1998. By this stage the membership had reached over 700. But the financial pressure and uncertainty continues. Concern has shifted towards the arrangements for the longer-term management of the land. At the end of the five year set-aside scheme, there is the opportunity to move into another scheme which will continue funding for at least a further five years. But some £25 000 per annum will need to be found on top of this income to continue the improvement of the site, and donations for continued management are less attractive to potential donors. And continuing changes in agricultural and land policies mean that the potential for public support for land management must be insecure. There is clearly a requirement to engage a large local population in the support of the area in order to keep the management of the land on track.

It is difficult to see any clear way around the difficulties faced by small trusts as illustrated here by the Magog Trust. Success has depended upon a variety of factors, beyond the deep commitment of the numerous individuals involved; the grants from government, the availability of the large private interest-free loan, and the coincident availability of agricultural schemes. In general, funds cannot be raised until an opportunity arises, but action cannot be taken until funds have been raised. In order to avoid CARTs competing amongst themselves when appropriate sites do become available, there is a need for organisations to maintain close contacts. It will not usually be the case that a beneficent private donor of immediate funds can be found. There could be a possible role for government here, perhaps offering cheap loans in addition to grants so as to give organisations the time required to mount campaigns for land purchase. But then there is the question of the long-term management of the area and its continuing source of funding. We return to this issue in Chapter 15.

Incomes based on other assets

Income may also be obtained from capital investments entirely unrelated to the land which CARTs manage. This continues to be a very significant resource for a number of trusts. Often, the investments have been bequeathed to the trust upon the death of one of its members, or they have been made as a result of a cash legacy. The magnitude of this source of income for trusts is highly variable among the privately formed trusts, though among the younger, publicly formed trusts it is usually relatively small. On the other hand, a number of the most recently established amenity trusts generate income from holding other capital assets derived from other sources, for example receiving rents from developed land adjoining their open land, in the same way as heritage trusts. The parkland trusts arising via the initiative of New Town Development Corporations (Milton Keynes, Peterborough, Telford) are notable examples.

Balancing sources and security

In considering the various ways in which CARTs seek and acquire finance for the work that they do, the question of the influence of funding sources upon CART activities naturally presents itself. For any voluntary organisation dependent upon external sources of finance, the balance between funding sources and the consequences of this for the future freedom of action of the organisation are very important considerations.

As already touched upon at the start of this chapter, in the last decade there has been a noticeable link between shifts in the main sponsoring agencies and departments, and the kinds of CART activity supported. As a result, many trust staff express a frustration with the way that government funds seem always to be available only for new initiatives, with different policy preferences from one year to the next. They feel that there is an element of 'flavour of the month' in the grants offered by government for conservation trust activities. However, it is also notable that many trusts seem nonetheless to have been able to adapt to these changing demands and continue to exploit this funding source to significant effect.

An organisation with a large proportion of its income from a subscribing membership may enjoy relative freedom from the short-term changes in funding policy which can be observed in both public and private charitable sponsorship. However, members will usually expect to see results for the money which they give to their organisation, and they may also wish to influence its policies and practice to some degree. For a small organisation where members and 'staff' are almost synonymous, this need not cause any tensions. Where the organisation is much larger, with perhaps a close-knit team of professional staff, the strong desire of a large or relatively distant body of paid-up members to have a say in policy development may sometimes lead to conflicts in management.

There is a third major alternative, whose attraction is increased in periods when public-sector funding is particularly difficult. This is income from investments, acquired either through generous donation of legacies or lifetime gifts, or through the original set-up of the trust. Where these capital endowments are both large and well-bolstered against recession, they undoubtedly offer the most secure and independent source of CART funds. But they are of course susceptible to market change. For example, for several older CARTs, capital is held mainly in the form of agricultural or wooded land, from which maybe fifty or more years ago, a reasonably secure rental income could be derived. This is certainly no longer the case with declining levels of farm rents. Of the newer CARTs, some have capital assets in the form of developed land and property, which could be at risk from a slump in property prices or in industrial growth. Nevertheless, the evidence from a range of CARTs does indicate that more fluid forms of capital investment provide the trust with a particularly valuable basis upon which to grow and develop as it pleases; if it can get them.

The safest strategy, it would therefore appear, is to seek

to fund the CART in an amoeba-like fashion, taking what is on offer in return for modest changes to short or medium-term objectives and the frequent generation of 'new initiatives', but aiming never to become so dependent on a single sponsor or government agency or department that it can radically overhaul the CART's operations overnight, nor so dependent upon the constant support of members that management efficiency is greatly impaired, and to maintain a varied investment portfolio.

Fritillary. Reproduced by permission of Countryside Commission/F.B. Pearce

Competition or co-operation: an ecology of CARTs

14

Introduction

We have up to this point largely concerned ourselves with CARTs as individuals. In this chapter we examine issues arising from the interrelationships between them; and consider how they match the range of potential actions for the conservation of the countryside. In doing so we adopt an ecological analogy which appears to capture a number of aspects of CART behaviour.

As has been seen, there is a considerable diversity of CARTs, in terms of their size, their organisation, their financing and in the range of their objectives. As non-profit bodies, we might tend to assume that they operate outside conventional markets and that they are in some way insulated from competition. But in many instances they pursue objectives which place them in direct competition with private organisations and indeed, at least in potential, in competition with other CARTs. This raises several questions. Should such competition be avoided or does it stimulate cost-effective action and encourage survival of the fittest organisations? Where such competition does occur, are the fittest organisations in this sense the ones which we would want to survive from a public point of view? Is extinction of certain sorts of CART an acceptable outcome? Many CARTs also have very close relationships with other bodies, both public and private, and may depend upon these for their survival. Is this a sign of weakness, or of strength? If the field of 'countryside conservation' represents a complex and variable habitat, do the forms taken by CARTs reflect the different niches available to them within this habitat?

An ideal form?

Clearly in practice there is a considerable variation in the forms which CARTs adopt. By analogy with a biological taxonomy, we might define different classes (phyla) of organisation: private firms, government agencies and non-profit organisations. CARTs would then represent a family of 'species' within the non-profit class, alongside various other kinds of charity or club.

The appropriate form for a conservation trust will depend upon the type of benefits which are to be provided. In some circumstances there will be economies of size, so that a large organisation will be likely to be more cost-effective than a small one. For example, by virtue of its scale, the National Trust can develop expertise in conservation techniques for country houses. It can also develop a standard approach to merchandising through its chain of shops and sell its own branded items. These abilities give it an advantage over smaller organisations, enabling it to adopt a broad approach towards conservation and develop a wide range of specialist technical skills. At the other extreme, a body generating tangible benefits for a local population may gain advantages from being small, knowing local demands and being able to respond readily to them.

Of course, to be successful all CARTs need to respond positively to changes in their circumstances and adapt to a changing environment. While most of the organisations with which we are concerned have the long-term maintenance of valuable natural and human assets as a central objective, this does not mean that their approach to management, the form of ownership or the institutional arrangements of the organisation, can be static. On the contrary, survival generally depends upon adjustment. The development of charitable trusts to become the owners of country house estates, in place of individuals and families, represents such an evolution. In general, the private charitable trust arrangement is relatively new in this context, and many trusts have been formed in response to an increasingly difficult environment for large estates over the past sixty years or so. Significant shifts in capital and inheritance taxation and, more recently, declining agricultural incomes, have contributed to this.

We cannot assume that existing institutional arrangements necessarily represent the best of all possibilities. As the examples in this book illustrate, many organisations have characteristics which are largely due to quirks of history or to the actions and attitudes of particular individuals. For example, the differences among the Wildlife Trusts are not only due to differences in their local environments but also to differences in their origins which may be unrelated to their present objectives and actions. The critical roles played by a relatively small number of dominant individuals is a recurring theme in the histories of the organisations which we have examined.

Competition between CARTs

In theory, competition between CARTs for land could potentially be a mechanism whereby the preference of individuals for countryside benefits is translated into decisions influencing land use. Each organisation is under pressure to seek areas of land with the potential to provide benefits. In order to achieve control over these areas it needs to outbid other commercial and/or non-profit interests. Also, competition between CARTs for funds or for members could lead them to look for types of conservation benefit and styles of conservation management which will attract public interest and hence stimulate donations and membership. Where there is competition between trusts for a specific piece of land each will need to assess its willingness to pay on the basis of the contribution which the land will make to its ability to meet its wider objectives; balanced against its capacity to raise funds for this particular purchase.

In parallel, competition for membership funds might have stimulated trusts to seek out a range of particular niches which make each organisation attractive to different sections of the public, or perhaps more realistically, which attract the same individuals but in different ways (membership of more than one CART being very common). The niche might relate not only to the type of conservation practised but also to the form of institutional arrangement and organisational style adopted. This kind of behaviour gives CARTs an incentive to adapt to changes in public preferences and conservation priorities. But some niches might become overcrowded, perhaps because one or more trusts target a particular issue and devote resources to it, and then as public interest shifts towards other issues trusts must readjust or risk collapse. There is thus an incentive for trusts to seek out and colonise new niches as they develop. It must be accepted that not all trusts can be guaranteed existence in perpetuity. Some may outlive their usefulness or become relatively ineffective in the way in which they pursue their objectives; in which case it may be within the public interest that they should decline or cease, in favour of others. What is important is not that the organisations themselves should survive in the long term, but rather that the conservation and amenity assets which they control should be protected.

So, in practice, does competition act to ensure an efficient adaptation of trusts and the weeding out of less appropriate forms of organisation, in a way similar to that which is commonly expected in the commercial sector? This is a difficult question to answer for a number of reasons.

For CARTs, as voluntary organisations, there is no measure of success which equates to the role of profit in a commercial company. In a non-profit organisation a financial surplus may indicate the financial security of the organisation, but it does not necessarily measure the contribution which the organisation makes as a result of its day-to-day activities. There has recently been controversy over the large financial reserves which have been built up by some large and well-known charities, with suggestions that they fail to put the funds which they have at their disposal to good use.

Various measures of the social value of an organisation might be proposed, perhaps the value of funds raised or the expenditure on work completed. But these represent measures of *input* without taking account of the value of the *output* arising from the organisation's actions. In the commercial sector, profit represents the *difference* between the costs of the inputs and the revenue generated from sale of the output. The non-profit sector exists for the very reasons which mean that outputs are not sold on markets with the result that there is generally no revenue from sales and hence little basis for assessing the value of actions.

The ability of an organisation to raise funds for its stated objectives does offer one indication of the level of public support for those objectives. But that is far from the complete story. We have argued earlier that the amount which individuals will contribute on a voluntary basis is likely to understate total demand, given the free-rider incentive, and the importance of this effect will vary between organisations.

However, beyond this there will be differences between the effectiveness of organisations. It is clear that some organisations are more effective as fundraisers than others, achieving higher-profile campaigns, better advertising and so on. There will also be differences in the efficiency with which conservation efforts are undertaken, that is, in their ability to transform inputs into outputs. This might reflect the form of internal organisation which is adopted, the incentives facing the organisation's workers both employed and voluntary, or the method of production which is adopted.

In the commercial sector these factors are generally subject to competitive pressures. In theory, more efficient organisations will tend to achieve lower unit costs and higher profits than their competitors. This enables efficient firms to re-invest and to raise funds in capital markets, leading to growth. They then tend to displace the inefficient firms and ultimately lead to their demise. In the non-profit sector these forces may be similar, but financial difficulties will not necessarily mean that the particular niche occupied by that organisation is an unimportant one or one which society does not want to be occupied. It may simply mean that the external circumstances under which the non-profit organisation operates have become harsher, and because it cannot generate profits, it has a restricted ability to cope with these circumstances.

For example, there might be a trust dedicated to inner city redevelopment which has grown on the basis of private-sector funding from a large local employer with a longstanding association with the area. This firm could itself benefit from improved local conditions and so its funding of the trust might contain an element of self-interest. What would happen if this local company was then forced to close down? The source of the trust's funding would disappear, but the need for its work would surely become even more desperate because the firm's own employees would themselves now be joining the ranks of the unemployed. In this instance, the trust's financial status is clearly not an appropriate indicator of the social worth of its activities.

Notwithstanding these very severe limitations, in general, trusts which represent a popular cause and which are effective in the pursuit of that cause will tend to grow, while those pursuing less popular objectives and which are less effective in their organisation may stagnate and perhaps wither. These different trusts probably would not see themselves as being in direct competition, but it is implied by their evolutionary development.

CARTs compete in practice in various ways. For example, they must compete alongside other charitable organisations for donations, and people's budgets for donations may be particularly constrained in periods of recession or when there are strong appeals for funds for national or international disasters. Trusts may also be in competition for members. Some people who place a priority on access to nature reserves may be dissuaded from joining their local Wildlife Trust if there is another local organisation which offers them better opportunities for access to the countryside.

Generally speaking, we have found that there are more CARTs in areas with a high population density and a thriving economy, whereas in remote areas or in places of low economic activity, CARTs are relatively few and far between. The most significant exception to this pattern are trusts with strong public-sector support which often target areas of high unemployment and industrial decline, and the largest nationwide trusts which, because they are national groups with a relatively high profile, can actively reallocate funds from the more buoyant areas where they are raised to other, less thriving areas with higher conservation priority. This pattern implies that local support is a significant constraint upon CART activity, thus local competition might be inferred.

Competition for public-sector funds occurs at several levels among CARTs. Firstly, most public conservation and amenity agencies and government departments award funds to the voluntary sector on a discretionary basis, where grant-aid is awarded only to those who can demonstrate that they will use funds to further the objectives of the public agency. Because public funds are fixed year-by-year through the expenditure round, a grant to one CART in any one year means less grant will be available to others in that year. As this is frequently a significant source of CART income, these effects will be fairly substantial. Thus we observe competition in CARTs' attempts to present their cases to public bodies in the most favourable light, in order to secure funds.

Competition for public-sector support also occurs indirectly, through shifting government priorities in allocating funds to its different agencies. In some years, for instance, the relevant nature conservation agency may be undergoing a period of sustained growth in funding due to a number of initiatives that have found strong government support; while in other years this may be the case for a countryside or a heritage agency, or for some special initiative funded directly by a government department. These shifts in public-sector funding feed through into patterns of grant-aid available to CARTs, as mentioned in Chapter 13. Analysing the income of the Wildlife Trusts, for example, alongside their stated policy as laid out in annual reports, shows that while nature conservation agencies supplied the most funding, nature conservation remained the major preoccupation of the trusts. However, at the end of the 1980s, when countryside agencies were a more generous source of funds, many trusts began developing access policies and new means to promote the educational and enjoyment value of their sites and their local events, frequently with the help of funds from these agencies.

Trusts may find themselves in direct competition for land when attractive sites become available on the market. A well-publicised example occurred when Mar Lodge in Scotland was put onto the market. This estate was widely recognised as having significant conservation and amenity value and potential for more sensitive management for these ends. However, due to its large size and the value of its sporting rights, no single Scottish CART had sufficient funds to contemplate outright purchase and subsequent management of the estate. It was hoped that public funding, and perhaps assistance in lowering the asking price, for some kind of local trust purchase might be found, but then the RSPB showed an interest in purchase. This large trust was able to contemplate purchase much more easily than the smaller local trusts. However, the move caused some controversy – some organisations were concerned that the RSPB would not be an appropriate owner given its relatively narrow conservation focus, while others claimed that its record of relations with local communities in far-flung parts of the UK was a poor one, such that local interests would effectively be excluded from enjoying this important feature of the local heritage if RSPB were to purchase it. Eventually, as noted in Chapter 13, funds from the Heritage Lottery Fund have been allocated to enable the National Trust for Scotland to acquire the estate.

Contracting and consultancy are other more recent ways in which many CARTs can be in direct competition, not only among themselves but also with the commercial sector. In this, they often have a distinct advantage over private companies because of the significant extent to which their commercial operations can be subsidised by volunteer effort – both unskilled labour and, equally importantly, highly skilled management or professional input. This has obvious advantages to government when considering the least-cost ways to achieve countryside benefits. However, it may have less desirable economic side-effects, in undervaluing the skills employed – we return to this issue in Chapter 16.

If we accept the potential role of competition in deter-mining the pattern of growth of the conservation trusts movement, that is, which sorts of organisation are success-ful in gaining control over the nation's heritage assets, we should perhaps consider whether there is fair competition between them. One feature which is apparent from our description of conservation trusts is the vast range in their scale. The market is a clear oligopoly – with a small number of very large trusts on the one hand and a much larger number of generally small trusts on the other. This domination by the few could be a source of concern in a commercial or an industrial sector. But in respect of CARTs, there have been no calls for intervention by the Monopolies and Mergers Commission.

The vast scale of the National Trust has important implications for rural conservation. Without doubt there are economies of size in its operations. The National Trust is able to develop considerable expertise in the manage-ment of its assets; in conservation techniques, in fund-raising and in lobbying to protect its own position. Perhaps the same may also be claimed for the RSPB. As we have seen in Chapter 6, however, only the National Trust has succeeded in achieving special legal status as a landholder. This monopolistic position means that a substantial proportion of nationally valuable countryside and coast is managed in a more or less consistent way, to the potential exclusion of more radical alternative approaches or minority interests. There can be a balance in this, as long as the National Trust uses its scale and special status to strengthen the protection of our most valuable national conservation assets for future generations (a kind of long-term 'public' ownership) but does not prevent smaller, more varied local organisations from acquiring land in other areas beyond this national 'portfolio'.

Co-operation between CARTs

Perhaps one reason why competitive behaviour among trusts goes largely unremarked is because of the emphasis in the CART sector upon working in partnership, and co-operation between different trusts. There is certainly an equal body of evidence to suggest that co-operation is just as central a determinant of trust development and growth. Trusts themselves would probably rarely see themselves as competing.

Most obviously, CARTs generally have some specialist interest which sets them apart from others, hence they avoid competition from the start. Most originate in order to fill a specific gap in the provision for countryside conservation which was perceived when they were created. This pattern can be seen throughout trust history, from the origins of the Open Spaces Society and the National Trust in the last century, through to the establishment of the Countryside Restoration Trust in 1993 to rehabilitate intensive farmland. As land-use trends change and develop, new niches emerge. For example, the continuing decline of habitat and landscape features in the countryside suggests a growing range of niches for organisations concerned with habitat re-creation and environmental improvement, in contrast to the earlier predominance by organisations concerned with protection of existing assets. Of course over the years the specific objectives and methods adopted by many organisations have changed, but rarely in such a way as to bring them into direct conflict with one another. Each tends to define and occupy its own niche.

Beyond such apparent 'peaceful co-existence', it is often in the interests of trusts, like other groups, to co-operate directly in order to raise public awareness or public support for their most pressing campaigns. The existence of the 'Wildlife and Countryside Link' organisation is perhaps the most obvious evidence of this kind of behaviour. This forum brings together a wide range of conservation and amenity groups in order to work and campaign jointly on issues of national importance, such as the future of land-use policy or the government's response to international agreements on sustainability and biodiversity. But also at a local level, CARTs frequently co-operate in both formal and less formal ways, sharing some resources (offices, skills, etc.) and working together to devise joint strategies to pursue specific local aims (such as better management of a locally important kind of habitat, or a series of amenity facilities). In East Anglia, for example, there are several fora for different local areas, where CARTs and the public-sector agencies regularly meet to address issues of common interest. At local shows, CARTs may share stalls. But most often, CARTs report very close informal working relationships with other CARTs in their area, such that officers frequently discuss over the phone or meet at local events and thus keep abreast of each others' activities and can pinpoint possible areas for joint working fairly readily.

Formal co-operation in the management of land

One feature of interest is the way in which some trusts enter into arrangements to make use of the specialised skills which have been developed by others. It is not uncommon, for instance, for land managed by Wildlife Trusts to be owned by other CARTs. For example, as noted in Chapter 9, the Sussex Wildlife Trust manages land owned by the Edward James Foundation, and the Gloucestershire Trust manages a nature reserve on the Guiting Manor estate. The Landmark Trust leases the island of Lundy from the National Trust and takes responsibility for its finance, administration and maintenance. Some 10 per cent of the reserves' area of the Cornwall Wildlife Trust is owned by the National Trust. And as mentioned in Chapter 11, the Green Wood Trust offers educational and woodland management functions to the Severn Gorge Countryside Trust, which in return offers it a major woodland resource.

At the same time, some trusts lease out their property for management both by public-sector bodies, such as nature reserves owned by trusts and managed by English Nature, and by private individuals, such as when a landowning trust sets up or inherits agricultural tenancies for the management of its land.

Such arrangements often relate to the particular management needs of different sites and the balance of these in relation to a trust's other priorities. Where a site needs very specialised conservation management but the trust which owns it does not have this expertise, management by another more specialist trust, or an equally specialist public body, may be appropriate. On the other hand, when a trust wishes to devote its specialist expertise to the management of only some aspects of its landholdings, the remainder of its management responsibilities may most effectively be devolved to a more generalist group or to a commercial tenant, so long as these managers are adequately restrained from doing things which could damage the site's principal conservation or amenity interest.

These examples illustrate the potential for a complex, multi-layered system of landownership and management. Such arrangements can operate in both directions, where an essentially profit-driven organisation allows a non-profit organisation to operate on some of its land or, alternatively, where a non-profit CART might allow a purely private, profit-motivated organisation to pursue some venture on its land, such as commercial farming or a tourism enterprise. Such a commercial user might have the expertise necessary to undertake a commercial land use in the most effective way, maximising the rent paid to the non-profit organisation and hence the income available to it to pursue its own work.

Maintaining independence

However, not all conservation groups want to enmesh themselves in a formalised, wider hierarchy of CARTs, where it is perhaps inevitable that a few larger groups, or the public agencies, exert most influence. Some organisations are established for the very purpose of offering an alternative approach to land management, independent of those pursued elsewhere.

In Chapter 10, we discussed two landowning conservation groups who expressed their strong wish to remain relatively independent of 'established conservation', as far as possible: namely, the Scottish Tree Trust and Heritage Conserved. In one instance, the distance seemed emphasised by the choice not to seek charitable status for their activities, while in the other, a strong sense of serving a particular local community with a quite distinct social culture, in contrast with the broader and more comfortable ranks of membership of many other CARTs, had underpinned this approach. However, even these organisations, with their more opportunistic style of seeking funds and developing their landholdings, had seriously considered working more closely with other CARTs or public agencies at some time, mainly because of the obvious financial and operational strengths that such behaviour could potentially offer.

It seems reasonable that some conservation and amenity groups should remain as 'individuals' – the range of their styles and approaches should perhaps reflect the wide range of perspectives within the population, including the interests of minorities. Also, returning to our ecological analogy, it will be important to maintain 'genetic' variation amongst the organisations, enhancing the prospects of filling new niches as and when they emerge. It should not be forgotten that the National Trust has its origins in the iniative of only three or four individuals.

Conclusion

CARTs occupy an increasingly important area between the commercial sector and government agencies. Within this there is no single 'best' organisational model or indicator of performance. Indeed, variation between CARTs is a strength of the movement allowing the colonisation of new 'niches' of conservation opportunity. But we cannot assume that all possible organisations will survive. Some which are poorly managed or which fail to meet a demand effectively will not be successful. On the other hand, there is evidence that CARTs co-operate among themselves and with others, which can reduce the costs and increase the effectiveness of their operations. Many are small, and they can increase their medium-term stability by linking their actions both with other CARTs and with government and commercial bodies. There should, however, still remain room for more radically independent groups – a spawning ground for new approaches and organisational styles.

Sandwood Bay, Sandwood – Oldshoremoor Estate. Reproduced by permission of Dr T.E. Isles

15 The role of public policy

Introduction

CARTs are private organisations which provide public goods. We have discussed earlier in Chapter 3 the conceptual problems which this raises. The conclusion to that chapter was that while these organisations may provide the sorts of conservation goods which society wishes to have provided; in the absence of support from government they are unlikely to do so to the full extent or in exactly the way desired by society. But as we have seen in the succeeding chapters, in practice, government at all levels is closely involved with the CART movement, playing a critical role in both their establishment and operation. This chapter draws together some details of the way in which government takes action in support of CARTs and explores the role which government might play in the future.

Current forms of government support

Tax relief

Most CARTs are registered as charities and as such are eligible for tax exemptions. A charity is exempt from any tax on receipts from rents from land and property or trading profits, provided that they are used for the declared purposes of the charity. When donated under a covenant, gifts to charities may be made from income before tax. Also, as is particularly relevant in the context of private land trusts, such charities are exempt from inheritance tax.

The total cost to the exchequer – in the form of tax

revenue forgone through these exemptions and reliefs – is
unknown. We are not aware of any attempts to estimate
the magnitudes involved. It would be difficult to calculate,
given the varied and multiple activities of the many
charitable organisations concerned. Furthermore, it seems
likely that in the absence of these tax reliefs the pattern of
economic activity and land use in the UK would be quite
different. But bearing in mind the number of CARTs and
the size of their combined assets, the cost in terms of tax
forgone must be substantial.

Direct grants

As discussed in Chapter 13, grants are regularly given to
CARTs to assist them in acquiring land of conservation
value, in the ongoing management of land, in the support
of staff posts, and to buy equipment and other assets.

Land purchase

Grants for land purchase probably represent the most
direct and targeted assistance available to CARTs. The
'public interest' objectives of these organisations offer some
security to the grant-giving body that the land acquired
will be held and managed in the public interest.

Land management

As the owners and occupiers of rural land, CARTs are
eligible for a growing number and range of grants and
schemes to promote conservation objectives through land
management. The Forestry Commission has widened the
range of grants on offer for planting and maintaining
broadleaved woodlands. The Ministry of Agriculture,
Fisheries and Food gives capital grants for some
conservation work on farmland and additional revenue
payments for managing land by agreement in Environmentally Sensitive Areas. The Countryside Commission
offers both revenue and capital payments for targeted land
under the Countryside Stewardship Scheme, and English
Nature may offer payments through its management
agreements, and the Wildlife Enhancement Scheme, on

Sites of Special Scientific Interest (SSSIs). It also has a specific scheme for the Wildlife Trusts, as mentioned in Chapter 7: the Reserves Enhancement Scheme. At the local level, County and District Councils support a variety of trust work.

Support for personnel

Historically, government ministries and agencies, particularly the Nature Conservancy Councils and the Countryside Commission, have helped CARTs to fund the employment necessary to undertake specific types of work, for a limited period. In its most direct form such support is often given for a core member of staff – perhaps a local project officer, marketing director, footpaths officer or reserve warden. It may be a critical factor in the early days of a CART's development, as discussed in Chapter 10. In an equally significant but less direct form, a continuing support for various kinds of youth employment and training has provided trusts with sometimes very large, albeit sporadic, sources of relatively cheap labour. While in existence, the Manpower Services Commission represented an important source of funds for the employment of labour for conservation work.

Other support

CARTs may benefit from free advice from government agencies or from local authorities, often through relatively close and informal liaison between the relevant officers in each organisation. Small grants for equipment, publications and events are also frequently offered.

Further, although unique to the National Trust, it is important to note here those special legal privileges which were mentioned in Chapter 6. These do not entitle the National Trust to any extra source of government finance, but are of considerable importance in facilitating its activities and helping it to attract private donations both of property and finance.

Finally, as described in Chapter 11, public bodies have frequently been instrumental in setting up CARTs, and helping them through their early years; entailing a certain degree of managerial support as well as funding and advice.

In all these ways different facets of government, as expressed through its different departments and agencies at national and local levels, shape the scale and the activities of a wide range of CARTs. And it is even possible to detect the effect of shifts in government interpretations of 'the public interest' through this process of influence. We described earlier how, in the area of countryside conservation, shifts in the relative grant-aiding resources available from the Nature Conservancy Council (NCC) and subsequently English Nature (principally for nature conservation) and from the Countryside Commission (often for public enjoyment as well as more general landscape conservation) have been mirrored by shifts in the activities of CARTs. Some CARTs may have more strongly allied themselves with one or other of these aims, and thus when government funding priorities between the organisations change, their fortunes rise or fall in turn. However, more commonly, CARTs have a marked ability to 'change their spots' to match these changing priorities.

Another major example of this kind of behaviour has been trusts' responses to changing government-funded employment training initiatives. Undoubtedly many trusts were in a good position to capitalise upon the availability of the Community Programme in the early 1980s, whereby young people could become involved in local environmental improvement works as a form of training for future employment, with the help of government subsidy. As this programme was wound up, some trusts moved on to develop links with successor 'Employment Training' schemes, while others sought new ways to attract labour – either through increased volunteer resources, or sometimes through building professional contracts with now-skilled, former Community Programme trainees who then set themselves up in business.

The general case for government support for CARTs was provided in the theoretical analysis of Chapter 3. Indeed social scientists have had difficulty in explaining why individuals contribute towards the provision of countryside goods at all, in view of their public good characteristics. In practice such contributions clearly make an important contribution to countryside conservation. But given the difficulties inherent in raising contributions from the private sector, voluntary organisations cannot be expected to make the full provision which would be warranted by public demand: CARTs' activities generate benefits enjoyed by those who make no contribution towards their costs. Viewed as an instrument of government policy, the argument for state support of CARTs becomes still clearer. It is not generally disputed that government should fund other public goods such as the police, or some level of universal education (although the way in which such support is provided has been an issue of considerable dispute). Government support is warranted because the public at large is enjoying the specific benefits provided by these organisations. A decision by government not to support them would result in the benefit being lost. It is a case of identifying and supporting collective self-interest through the transfer of public funds.

It is clear that CARTs receive substantial assistance from the state through a variety of routes. From our investigations, the average level of subsidy for CARTs represented around 30 per cent of total income in 1990 (excluding capital grants for land purchase). But it is not true to say that the government has a unified policy towards CARTs; there is no coherent strategy. Rather, assistance tends to be piecemeal and incidental to other more general provisions, such as the laws relating to charities in general, and rural land-use policies and schemes. Initiatives and funds emerge through a number of independent government agencies with different policy objectives, and thus they are for rather different purposes.

Despite this, there are grounds for believing that CARTs play a special role in the conservation of the rural environment; one that may not be readily played by other forms of organisation and one with a particular potential for the future. The achievement of conservation goals through land management often requires detailed information both about the ecology of the habitats or features being managed, and about the management systems that have generated or sustained them. In some circumstances, general guidelines for management, such as those given to agreement holders within Environmentally Sensitive Areas, may provide sufficient management information without offering them a detailed understanding of the ecosystem involved or the environmental aims of the scheme.

In other circumstances, for instance where valuable habitat is being re-created or being protected against new external pressures, a more pro-active and innovative form of environmental management may be necessary, involving more regular monitoring and review of management responses. It may require a range of skills which are not commonly available and which are difficult to write into contractual agreements.

Towards a policy for CARTs

Policy by intermediary

As we have seen, CARTs' objectives may quite closely match those of the state, as representative of the public interest. While most policy mechanisms are directed towards existing owners or managers of land, an alternative mechanism for land management in the public interest is for the state to promote the actions of organisations which have objectives in common with this interest.

In theory, the approach adopted by the CART is likely to be different from that of a commercial landowner who is persuaded to undertake a particular type of land management in response to the financial incentives offered through an environmental contract. The commercial landowner will have an incentive to meet the terms of the contract, which generally specify what actions have to be taken, at minimum personal cost and it will be necessary for a government agency to monitor such contracts in some detail. The CART, by contrast, will have an incentive to seek out least cost but also most effective ways of generating and protecting the conservation or amenity goods in its stewardship. It will be prepared to trade off costs against conservation gains, where possible. We gave some examples of this in Chapter 12.

CARTs often specialise in particular types of conservation, such as the protection of birds, or may focus their efforts within a particular area. In this way, although they may be relatively small organisations, they can build up a level of expertise within their own particular speciality. This suggests that the conservation organisation may require less detailed monitoring than a conventional farmer and that in the longer term it might be likely to develop better approaches to conservation and more cost-effective methods of conservation management.

Because many CARTs are small or focused upon specific objectives, and without a need to demonstrate democratic accountability, they may also be more flexible and less bureaucratic than government agencies which manage land directly. Thus as landowners and managers they may be able to respond more rapidly to opportunities which arise, such as in purchasing conservation sites when they come onto the market. This certainly appears to be the experience in the United States.

As the many examples in this book show, creating and sustaining variety in the rural environment depends upon some level of innovation and entrepreneurship: to bring resources, ideas and information together, to organise them and to take risks. For CARTs, the risk either of an unsuccessful project or perhaps even of an unchanging portfolio of work will be the loss of membership or of public-sector support, which ultimately may undermine the survival of the organisation itself. In the language of Chapter 14, CARTs continually need to seek out and exploit new niches for conservation enhancement, to guard against this kind of risk. This type of behaviour is more often thought of as a characteristic of the profit-motivated market sector, which in conventional market theory represents the prime mechanism in economic growth. Being non-profit does not mean being non-risk. Thus the search for 'conservation growth' has much in common with the search for economic growth more widely. But, as we have stressed, the public good characteristics of conservation and amenity must limit the straightforward profitability of this type of action.

Once these aspects are recognised, it is clear that government and the public at large can benefit from a 'policy by intermediary' approach to pursuing conservation and amenity goals. Rather than government agencies taking actions to influence the way land is used directly, such a policy operates through the promotion of inter-mediate organisations which share the state's objectives but which can be largely left to determine the specific details of how these should be attained.

There are of course disadvantages to the indirect imple-mentation of policy in this way. As previously discussed, the objectives of intermediary organisations may not exactly match those of the state. They may respond first to the interests and priorities of members or directors, rather than to priorities as perceived by government. The degree of matching between the objectives of the organisation and those of the government will vary considerably between different sorts of organisation and it will often be appropriate for government incentives to be used to influence the way in which they operate as well as the scale of their operations.

Also, those small organisations with a largely inactive membership may be susceptible to capture by particular groups within the membership who try to modify the CART's action in order to pursue their own interests. Where this happens, CART activity may not live up to the stated goals of the organisation and thus may diverge further from the wider public interest. And even where both objectives and actions conform to the general wishes of government, such intermediary organisations may simply be inefficient. Those people responsible for CART administration may be experts in conservation, but less qualified for and/or less interested in effective administration or resource management. It is therefore important for government to monitor the activities of CARTs in order to check for these kinds of problem.

Beyond these concerns there may also be a difficulty inherent in this mode of policy implementation in that it implies a devolution of power away from existing public departments, ministries or agencies which they may sometimes find difficult to accept. Some degree of resistance to this approach could therefore be expected from those public sources which see it as threatening their *raison d'être*.

So, a policy towards CARTs clearly needs to do considerably more than just provide the relevant organisations with finance, although this will always remain an important element. It needs to promote a supportive environment for organisations with objectives which correspond to the aims of government policy, to assist them in pursuing these aims in a cost-effective way. It is also important to encourage a balance between different organisations which reflects the widest public interest and which encourages CARTs to seek out a variety of relevant opportunities.

A supportive environment

If it wishes to promote their activities in the wider public interest, it is important for the state to establish an environment within which CARTs can develop. This implies support for both CART establishment and for continuing operation.

Getting started

One of the key constraints to the development of voluntary-sector activity in land management seems to lie in the difficulties faced at the initial stages. It is perhaps notable that very few CARTs arise as a spontaneous reflection of public demand for environmental improvement. More often they arise either from organisations established with somewhat different objectives, or they have been founded through the public sector, or they have represented a response to a specific and urgent threat of environmental deterioration which has given the necessary incentive for public support.

There is perhaps a need to unlock the 'chicken and egg' conundrum: people will not donate to an organisation until it is in a position to demonstrate that it can make good use of the funds which it receives, but without these kinds of donation it cannot do very much. Donations may be encouraged when the CART has a specific project in view – often the acquisition of a particular site – but until the organisation has some security with respect to funding it cannot offer to buy land. In this kind of situation, a government organisation which felt that the CART's aims were consistent with the public interest could provide some bridging support. For example, the CART could be offered a cheap, long-term loan in a situation where government judges that it has a reasonable prospect of raising the necessary funds in the longer term, and of meeting a public demand through its use and management of the land thus acquired. In reality, this situation is often tackled by the simple grant-aiding of land purchase by a CART, but this is subject to strict rules regarding the valuation of the land and the proportion of that value that public funds can meet. Loans might not need to be so constrained, so long as reimbursement was reasonably assured in the medium term.

An important aspect of such an arrangement concerns the sharing of risk which would be implied. Financial transactions involve risks. If a contract is agreed to acquire some land and the finance cannot be raised, somebody must lose out. In making a loan government bears some risk that the funds to repay the loan cannot be raised. Against this there would be the land as security for the loan, so that the scale of any potential loss need not be excessive. But from the perspective of an emergent CART, passing a significant part of this risk on to government could represent a considerable gain, both for those who give up their free time to get the organisation off the ground, and to prospective donors who could have confidence that their donations will be used for the desired purpose.

There is, however, at least one drawback to this idea. If government is to guarantee that the land will be used in the way proposed, the urgency of the claim to potential private donors may be diminished. Why should people bother to contribute if the government has effectively made up any shortfall in funding? Such a potential disincentive to donors may be lessened by a deadline by which any government loan would have to be repaid. But there is an inevitable and unavoidable conflict between, on the one hand, the creation of a 'crisis' which is a powerful attraction to potential donors, without whose money the whole venture may collapse, and, on the other, a situation in which government support guarantees the venture but thus diminishes the urgency for donations. On balance it might be accepted that some possible lessening of the pressure for donations from the public is a price worth paying to be able to get the venture launched in the first place. This may explain the current tendency for government support to be limited to grant-aid of a fixed percentage, which automatically reduces the sum needed from donations but does not underwrite this sum and thus does not reduce the urgency of the call for funds.

Keeping going

Ideally when sites are acquired, the necessary funds will also be in place to provide for long-term management. As a large CART with a substantial existing portfolio of nationally important sites, the National Trust is able to operate this principle in its acquisition practice; refusing sites in cases where maintenance funds are inadequate. However, this strategy cannot be adopted by the majority of smaller trusts, to whom new sites are always an important means to increase or maintain membership or the local profile of the organisation. Adequate maintenance of the quality of a site will always depend upon ongoing sources of income. In some cases the CART may be able to develop innovative uses of land – sensitive developments which can raise either income or capital – or novel forms of raising independent finance to meet these maintenance requirements. It is a strength of such organisations that they have a real incentive to seek out such opportunities. But alongside this there can also be a role for government assistance. There will be situations where, by providing funds, the quality of environmental management can be improved or the range of people benefiting can be expanded. For example, better management of grazing, use of the site for research or the provision of public access and interpretation could all offer new benefits towards which government could contribute. The increasing ability of CARTs to tap agri-environment resources from the Common Agricultural Policy by joining environmental schemes is one way in which such a contribution can be made.

CARTs also have a frequent need for information and the relevant sources will often be within government, either central or local. And it will be important too to share information and experience amongst similar organisations and organisations with similar responsibilities. Staff will need training both in the technical aspects of managing land as well as in business and administrative skills. These requirements cannot be met by small organisations in isolation; co-operation is called for and government may be well placed to stimulate this. The kind of support called for here is similar to that which is offered for the development of small businesses and indeed many of the same skills are required: advice on technical issues, investigation of development options, training in management techniques, sharing of experience as to best practice and so on. Some government agencies (such as the Countryside Commission) have used this tactic in their support of a variety of voluntary organisations over the years.

Playing longstop

Some initiatives and some organisations will 'go wrong'.
Some will simply fail to raise the level of funds necessary
to keep the organisation in operation. Others will enter into
ambitious projects which fail to deliver, undermining the
finances of the whole organisation. A few may be brought
down by unscrupulous practice or deliberate fraud. All
these problems are equally those of small commercial
businesses. Nobody expects all small firms to be successful
and nobody questions the existence of many small firms in
business just because some become bankrupt or experience
fraud. It is however important to try to anticipate the
problems which will be faced by such small enterprises,
and to promote solutions to these problems where they
threaten the achievement of public goals through CART
activity. For instance, it might be appropriate to establish
some sort of CART watchdog which could promote good
practice, investigate problems and step in, should CARTs
fail. Given the public interest in the consequences of many
CART activities then the government will have an interest
in at least protecting the gains which have been achieved
by such organisations.

Promoting balance

As we have seen, the organisations which have been
discussed in this book embrace a very wide range of forms
and objectives. Some are close in form and spirit to
government agencies, others closely resemble purely
private estates. They are administered and governed in a
host of different ways. It would be inappropriate for
government policy to seek to constrain this variety
according to some standardised bureaucratic formula. The
different forms and arrangements can each fulfil different
purposes in the rural environment and variety is the
essence of this approach to policy.

By the same token, some organisations will justify higher
levels of public support and some will depend upon it,
while others will be largely self-financing and will make
marginal contributions to the public good. The differences
can be illustrated in terms of countryside examples. There
are organisations which provide for recreation which are

almost wholly private in orientation. A fishing club might own (or simply acquire access rights to) a lake in order to provide fishing for its members. It would have little claim for financial support from goverment. On the other hand an organisation might acquire an area of internationally rare and sensitive habitat. Public access to the site might risk damage to the site's fragile ecology, and so access might be barred and contributors would get no direct benefit from the protection of the site. The benefits of protection would be spread globally to all those who appreciate the contribution to biodiversity amongst both present and future generations. Clearly a very small proportion of benefits are enjoyed by members contributing to the cost and so some contribution from the public sector would be warranted.

This example suggests that government should be able to base its funding decisions upon some assessment of the extent and distribution of the public benefits and costs arising from a CART's activities. There is no clear and consistent way of doing this. The benefits and costs associated with many goods and services are indicated in their market prices – reflecting the balance between the supply and demand. This does not apply to public goods, because their benefits are not reflected in conventional markets. While we can observe how much people are willing to pay for cornflakes, they do not so directly reveal their demand for conserving wildflower meadows, or creating new areas for public enjoyment.

Conventional economists try to measure 'prices' for such goods indirectly, for example by surveys of people's opinions or by observing people's willingness to pay to travel to visit nature reserves. But the valuations derived from these methods are often neither complete nor very reliable.

One more concrete source of evidence of public benefits and costs is represented by the amount that people are willing to contribute towards the operation of CARTs. While we have argued that this does not represent a full measure of their willingness to pay for the benefits of CART activity, the allocation of donations between alternative CARTs which are soliciting money may offer some indication of the relative priority which the public attaches to the various benefits that they offer. An adjustment would need to be made for the different extents to which a donation gives direct access to personal benefits. If I join the National Trust I enjoy free access to Trust properties. If I contribute to the Save the Whale campaign I am unlikely to gain any direct personal benefit.

This could suggest that government support for CARTs should be linked to the level of donations which can be raised from the public; and indeed many government agencies are obliged to offer support in this way, requiring £1 raised from donations or private sources for every £1 of government grant. The appropriate ratio might perhaps deserve to be higher for organisations whose activities give a greater share of benefits to non-contributors or who espouse less publicly attractive but clearly equally worthy causes. Such shared funding deals can guarantee the CART a regular income from government whilst maintaining the incentive for the organisation to match its activities to the public interest, both in terms of what it does and in the way in which it goes about it, and actively to seek private donations. It may increase the incentive to potential donors who can see that a contribution to the organisation brings a greater total benefit.

Who should bear the costs of government finance for CARTs? The government operates at a variety of levels: should the cost be met from general taxation or should it be raised within local areas? To answer this we could again attempt to relate payments to the kind of benefits which are received, and by whom. Some organisations generate benefits which are enjoyed almost exclusively by people within a relatively small local area. For instance an area of open space without any habitat of particular rarity might be attractive to local people for walks, but not be a significant attraction to people from further afield. The implication then is that the funds to maintain the open space, and decisions about its management, should be raised locally. On the other hand a site of national conservation significance and/or which attracts visitors from across the country should be supported at a national level and national government should have some say in the way in which the area is controlled.

The principle here is that of subsidiarity. Decision-making should be taken at the level which relates most closely to the way in which people are affected. Of course most situations are more complex. The pattern of incidence is complicated; the beneficiaries are generally not evenly distributed across any particular administrative area (if such a single area can be identified); and local people tend to benefit most with some sort of 'distance-decay' across the rest of the country. This kind of issue is illustrated by the continuing debate as to how National Parks should be funded and steered. These are areas of nationally important countryside, but locals may experience a more than proportionate share of both the benefits and costs, so the balance of local versus national funds may be difficult to agree upon.

Widening options for the control of land

In Chapter 4, we described the means by which organisations can gain control of land. One method involved the use of covenants. These have the capacity to give local and particular interest groups sufficient control to achieve worthwhile conservation objectives in the long term for a lower financial outlay than is required for full landowner-ship. But there are a number of restrictions under present law which limit the CARTs' powers to take the benefit of covenants which are binding on land, and thus affect their willingness to do so. Particularly, covenantors have to own adjacent land and the covenant has to be 'negative' or restrictive. However, as we noted before, some organis-ations, notably the National Trust and local government, have special powers under statute to use covenants more widely.

It is also the case that current owners of property may be willing to donate covenants to such organisations in order to secure the long-term environmental quality of their land. The extent of these opportunities has not been investigated. Informal evidence from the National Trust suggests that they are regularly offered covenants over land (as well as gifts of land and property) which they are unable to accept, perhaps because the conservation values protected are not regarded as being of national significance, but which nevertheless would have the potential to secure future environmental values.

While local authorities have the powers to take the benefit of covenants, there is apparently some concern on the part of potential donors that they are not necessarily the appropriate bodies to take on this responsibility. Local authorities have broad and sometimes conflicting objectives and there is always the potential for shifts in the balance between priorities, sometimes in response to short-term pressures, which could threaten the continuity of covenants.

In the United States, most states have adopted legislation which provides for the use of 'conservation easements' which operate in the way in which a more flexible statutory conservation covenant could in England and Wales. The conservation easement is being increasingly widely used for conservation purposes.

In this country, a similar mechanism might offer potential as a tool for conservation. To implement this in practice, the first step would be to widen the range of conservation bodies with powers to take the benefit of statutory covenants. New legislation would be needed to allow government to maintain a schedule of those conservation trusts which could use these powers. It would be possible to devise a discrete statutory code specifically for conservation of or access to the countryside, under which an approved but regularly reviewed list of voluntary organisations could be given power to take the benefit of a covenant relating to land even though they owned no land nearby. These issues are discussed further in Hodge *et al.* (1993).

For example, a conservation covenant could be one which fulfilled one or more of these objectives:

- the maintenance or preservation of landscape features
- the provision or preservation of historic features
- the preservation of flora or fauna on the land
- the provision of public access to the land
- the prevention of various forms of development

To be of lasting benefit, covenants would have to be capable of binding the land even though ownership changes. Registration of a covenant would have to be possible, so that buyers of the land could obtain notice of it before they commit themselves. There would be no notional or actual requirement for the organisation benefiting from the covenant to own land nearby, and the covenants would be capable of being perpetual.

If the form of statutory power given is modelled on that currently held by local authorities, these covenants could be either positive or restrictive, and individual covenants could even include both positive and restrictive clauses; although it might be difficult to enforce the positive obligations of a covenant upon an unwilling landowner beyond the most basic kinds of management. Some body, perhaps a government agency, would need to take the responsibility for administering and advising on the system. There would have to be executive power to add to or subtract from the list of specified bodies and some fall-back provision would have to be made in case any specified body with the benefit of a conservation covenant is wound up, taken over or merged. The overseeing agency would promote compliance with good practice on the part of those benefiting from a covenant through the sanction of being able to remove organisations from the list.

Options for wider public recognition of the role of CARTs

To date the process of recognition by a public agency occurs not only on an organisation by organisation basis, but also in the context of individual events, such as an application for a grant for the purchase of a specific site. Local authorities could perhaps register organisations which met a certain standard in terms of their objectives and in terms of the effectiveness of their administration. Thus, for instance, organisations operating in England which pursue nature conservation objectives to a satisfactory standard might be registered by English Nature. Organisations offering recreational access to local people might be registered by the Countryside Commission or the local authority. Organisations with multiple activities could have the opportunity to seek registration with more than one agency.

Registration could give the organisation a certain cachet which might be of assistance in its pursuit of funding from private-sector sources, acting as a form of guarantee that certain standards will be met in the use of any funds donated. It might be linked with the potential covenanting powers that we have just discussed. It would still be open to organisations to continue to operate without registration, under the existing arrangements for charitable status and grants for land management. Conversely, registration still allows agencies to operate more pro-actively in seeking to establish organisations where they identify niches which have not been filled by those currently in existence. Registration could thus be viewed as facilitating rather than as constraining CART activity.

We might also see registered CARTs taking up a more formal role in respect of government schemes. For example, they might act as agents for targeting and/or implementing habitat creation on long-term set-aside land. This could offer a means by which European agricultural support finance could enable CARTs to extend their activities further beyond land which they own. They could be pro-active, seeking long-term agreements with farmers in target areas adjacent to their own reserves or in places where a new site could play a critical role in realising their own objectives. Such a mechanism might encourage CARTs to shift their land management policy further from an emphasis upon isolated site-based conservation towards a broader landscape approach.

As indicated in Chapter 13, the new Heritage Lottery Fund offers an opportunity for the development of some sort of broader strategy or recognition for CARTs. It is not clear at this stage to what extent funds will be directed towards the protection of existing features of high value as opposed to major restoration projects or the creation of new value. Newbould (1994) indicates general support for habitat creation, but at the same time comments that land of national scientific importance will normally carry a Site of Special Scientific Interest designation. This would seem at least potentially to limit scientific projects to those that protect SSSIs or their surrounds. The historic park category may similarly be limited to English-Heritage-graded park-lands.

We suggest that the critical issue should be whether projects can generate high levels of benefit in relation to the costs incurred. Where the level of public demand is high, projects of lower scientific or historic importance could generate considerable benefits, such as may be illustrated by restoration and rehabilitation initiatives in the urban fringe. It is possible to contemplate some sort of assessment system that would score the range of individual values (landscape, wildlife, history, amenity, resource protection) anticipated from individual projects, and relate this to the level of grant offered.

The Fund's emphasis on capital grants is understandable because it must be seen to be making an impact. However, there is the risk that projects will be set up without the capacity for effective and continued management. As mentioned in previous chapters, it is often easier for CARTs to raise funds for an initial land purchase than it is to raise funds for continuing management. While one can argue on value-for-public-money grounds that managing organisations should be kept under pressure to raise whatever funds they can from private sources, capital grants will be wasted if the assets thus acquired are subsequently allowed to deteriorate. It may well be that quite modest initial endowments could ensure the continuing management of land to a sufficient standard. Further, in considering the justification for endowments, it will be appropriate to recognise not only situations where management costs are likely to be high, such as in maintaining buildings, but also situations where there are particular difficulties faced in generating revenue.

The requirement for some sort of strategic view is important. As we have seen, certain sorts of organisation can be much more effective in gaining public support and funding than others. And countryside projects, supplying near-public goods, may find it relatively difficult to generate their own sources of funding. It will be important that flexibility is retained in respect of matching funding so as to recognise the different types of benefit arising from different types of project.

Conclusions

It might be argued that the existence of a well-developed array of CARTs removes the need for government action for the environment at all (e.g. Anderson and Leal, 1991). In a free market, such organisations would operate as clubs, acquiring property rights on behalf of their members, funded by member contributions. We have emphasised that, in practice, CARTs are not like this. The conservation goods provided often have significant public good characteristics and complete exclusion is rarely possible, nor indeed desired by CARTs themselves. In these circumstances, CARTs cannot be expected to provide an optimal level of conservation goods in the absence of government support. Rather they offer useful means for an ongoing partnership with government, within which they pursue the provision of countryside goods together, to the benefit of the public at large. We have examined this relationship, noting its current diversity and highlighting new approaches that could offer potential for the future.

Flying a kite on Magog Down, Magog Trust

Implications and the future

16

There are many novel aspects to our study of CARTs, but the novelty of this type of organisation is not one of them. We have found several which have already been in existence for over a hundred years. Some, of course, have developed more than others. But there are a number of reasons for believing that they have the potential to play a more extensive role in the management of the countryside than they do today. The evidence of their recent rapid growth points towards this.

Partnership with government

The conventional distinction between the public and private sectors is breaking down. It has perhaps always been something of a convenience with many marginal cases, but recent years have seen a steady blurring of the division to the point where we must at least recognise a continuum rather than a dichotomy. The erosion of the distinction is a consequence of a recognition of the limits of government on the one hand and of the limits of the 'free' market on the other. We outlined this point in Chapter 1. While our focus here has been exclusively on the management of the countryside, it is a change taking place throughout the economy, both in the UK and beyond. Private firms now contract to undertake tasks which have previously been regarded as the exclusive role of the public sector: managing prisons, collecting rubbish or cleaning hospitals. The limits are no longer clear. At the same time, private voluntary bodies act as agents for government policy, such as in the areas of social services and housing. CARTs fit into this pattern in respect of countryside management.

CARTs are heavily dependent upon government agencies

and finance. Many have been set up by government, especially at the local level, in order to pursue government objectives, and continue to be guided by government-appointed trustees. We have seen that both land purchase and continuing land management are often only possible through government support. But there are ways in which we may see the relationship between government and CARTs developing further in the future. CARTs are becoming involved in the development of planning for the wider countryside, in collecting data on habitats and species, in advising on initiatives and in commenting on policies and plans. We raised the possibility in Chapter 15 that some CARTs might develop a role as agents for government programmes, perhaps in the identification and implementation of habitat restoration of farmers' land which is entered into long-term set-aside or similar schemes. This opportunity would allow them to influence directly the management of countryside beyond their own reserves and to operate more pro-actively and entrepreneurially than can most government departments and agencies.

In the United States, there is also a close partnership. Endicott (1993) comments that 'it is almost the exception if significant land acquisition is accomplished without a partner from the private sector and one from the public sector, if not more than one from each side.' We might say the same for the position in the UK. But the nature of the relationship in the United States is often rather different. The smaller-scale and more limited land-use planning powers of much local government, particularly in rural USA, places a greater emphasis on contributions from the private sector.

Government agencies and local governments in the USA often depend more upon the purchase of land in the pursuit of planning objectives and co-operate in this with private organisations. The private, non-profit bodies can generally act more quickly than is possible in the public sector. While private organisations may be able to apply financial reserves almost immediately in response to an opportunity to purchase land, in the public sector it may be necessary to hold a referendum to determine whether funds can be used for this purchase. There are also limits to the way in which deals may be arranged in the public sector which do not constrain private organisations. For instance, some governments are not able to bid at auction or to pay for land by instalments. Landowners and potential donors would also often rather deal with a private-sector organisation. This means that a private organisation may be able to come to an agreement with a landowner to acquire a property in such a way as to maximise the tax advantage or to buy property under conditions which are acceptable to the owner, perhaps allowing him or her to remain in occupation of the property. As a result, it is quite common for private organisations to undertake land purchase and for them then to resell property to government. Private organisations may also be more successful in attracting donations from individual and corporate donors for land purchase and management.

While circumstances differ in the UK, it seems quite likely that under continuing budgetary pressures on the one hand and under pressures from local people to make provision for countryside amenity and recreation, local authorities could work more with CARTs in order to lever control over larger areas of land with the limited funds available, so that we could see some movement towards the US example.

CARTs and the private sector

We must not neglect the important relations which CARTs have with other elements of the private sector. The CART model offers a means whereby private individuals can ensure the survival beyond their own lifetimes of countryside assets which they may have created, accumulated or inherited. Provided that there are benefits for the community, the charitable status of CARTs offers significant relief from the taxes which make the survival of countryside estates particularly difficult. While there have been no detailed appraisals of this as a mechanism for providing countryside benefits, it seems likely that it could be relatively cost-effective.

The commercial sector is also an increasingly important source of finance, although one that has clearly suffered somewhat from the recent recession. Corporate donors can gain recognition and status by donating funds for environmental projects. They seek to reflect current public concern for environmental issues, which means that as a source of

funds such donations will tend to ebb and flow in line with
the public consciousness. But it is clearly a source to be
capitalised on whenever possible. Corporate sponsors want
some recognition of their generosity and there may be
innovative ways in which funds can be attracted.

But there is a flip-side to the particular relationship with
private donors, relating to the degree to which CARTs will
consistently act to pursue the public interest. Firstly, the
ability of any private company or individual suddenly or
regularly to offer substantial funds to a CART in order to
influence its actions is bound to create a certain tension in
the relationship between the CART and the wider public
interest. For those CARTs registered as charities, registration exerts a measure of discipline over the use of such
support because it must serve to further the CART's
charitable objectives. However, the balance of objectives
may well shift to favour certain actions and tactics over
others, and this may alter the relationship of the CART
with public funders. For example, as mentioned in Chapter
6 it has variously been argued that, by concentrating upon
the preservation of the great estates, certain CARTs may
have served one sector of society at the expense of other,
less-well-endowed sectors, and that this has not been in the
wider public interest. The recent moves by the National
Trust to stress its commitment to preserving small buildings and industrial architecture is, in part, a response to
this kind of criticism.

The other potentially negative aspect of the relations
between CARTs and the private sector is quite different,
and relates to the competitive advantage which CARTs
enjoy as a result of their charitable status and the support
of numerous volunteers. Viewed from the stance of a
public body seeking to stimulate environmental management, the ability of CART activities to 'undercut' the costs
of commercial land managers is clearly an advantage
because it allows them to do more with limited funds. But
in the longer term, in a period where government is keen
to revitalise the rural economy, CARTs could be accused of
'selling themselves short' – working for a price which
effectively prevents others from making a commercial
business out of such activity. This may arise most clearly in
the case of activities such as hedge-laying and other labour-
intensive management works, but given that CARTs enjoy
a broad level of fiscal subsidy it could theoretically apply to

other areas of activity. In this situation, we may question which tactic will be ultimately more in the public interest – to stimulate fully commercial countryside management, or to rely upon the voluntary sector to provide?

In practice, however, government rarely has the ability or the necessity to make such a clear choice. CARTs themselves are relatively limited in their use of low-cost labour, and the small size of environmental management budgets, as compared to those for other agricultural support, continues to mean that governments have good reasons to look to CARTs to provide, alongside limited public resources. There are also ways to recognise the cost differences between CARTs and private individuals as land managers – such as having separate schemes for each category of manager, as English Nature does with its Wildlife Enhancement and Reserves Enhancement Schemes. We need perhaps only to note that this issue could become more contentious if fundamental reform of the Common Agricultural Policy were to shift the balance of funds towards environmental management, to a significant extent.

Countryside entrepreneur

We have emphasised the importance of entrepreneurship in the development of countryside values. While some private individuals will undertake this role in pursuit of their own interests, and we have seen that several CARTs have been established on this basis, and while governments may wish to act more entrepreneurially, the identification and implementation of novel projects for the enhancement of the countryside still depends to a significant extent upon the activities of CARTs. It appears that the agricultural circumstances will be favourable for this in the medium term at least. The past two decades have seen a long-term decline in the prices of agricultural land,[1] making it easier for those not wishing to maximise farm profitability to enter the land market. There is also an increasing number of schemes in place which offer financial subsidies for those wishing to pursue 'CART'-

1. Notwithstanding the current, temporary buoyancy caused by the effects of the UK leaving the European Union's Exchange Rate Mechanism.

type objectives. Such schemes ease the burden of land management costs subsequent to land purchase.

It is hazardous to attempt to predict the way in which public policies will develop in the future. Environmental schemes will undoubtedly be available for some while, but in the longer term it is less certain that taxpayers will continue to support highly visible, annual payments through the exchequer for providing environmental benefits. If at the same time farming evolves to compete more or less freely in world markets, the provision of environmental and amenity benefits could increasingly be seen as an unaffordable luxury for many commercial landholders. Under such circumstances the protective purpose of CART landholdings and the innovative role of these organisations in conservation management could prove even more valuable.

Steward for countryside values

Who shall be the guardian of conservation values for the future? The problem of conservation is often portrayed in terms of a failure of the market to create the appropriate incentives for resource conservation. It is then placed in the hands of government to take action so as to alter incentives in an appropriate way. But governments, too, have short-term priorities and pressures. There are many examples of policy failure and 'U-turns'. It is difficult for governments to find the resources needed to fund sufficient positive management of even the most 'precious' sites, let alone the wider countryside. The political pressure to find funds for health, education or defence may be more strongly felt. Governments may not be able to withstand the calls from developers for new sites and from rural people for new jobs, in order to protect areas of valuable habitat. There are many other examples. There is an important role for voluntary organisations, where they have the ability, to act for longer-term resource conservation.[2]

---

2. The notable exception here is of course development which is subject to compulsory purchase. As mentioned in Chapter 6, even in the unique case of the National Trust with its powers to accept land inalienably, government retains the final say over these kinds of development.

CARTs can and do play an important role in support of conservation values for the future. We have seen that the National Trust and other national CARTs are a powerful force in protecting assets and campaigning more generally on conservation issues. Lobbying central and local government to influence policies and plans is important, but for some landowning CARTs, especially when a close relationship with government is critical to their land management activities, there will be limits to the extent to which they can lobby actively for causes which the government does not support.

Clearly, the most immediate contribution of many CARTs is the way in which they manage their own land, but it is possible for them to extend their influence in various ways. Through more direct influence over land owned by others, by experimentation and by demonstration, they can advance the practice of sustainability. For example, they may establish good conservation practices and serve as an example to other farmers. The National Trust has been active in developing and implementing various approaches through the use of conservation clauses on its tenanted farms. It has been under pressure from its membership to push its tenants towards organic farming. Whatever approaches are established, they will offer an important source of information for other farmers considering alternative farming methods, and its farms will generate a potentially valuable source of data for analysis. Similarly the RSPB has developed considerable experience in various types of conservation management and habitat restoration which is of value to other organisations and to government. Thus the variety of experience which CARTs accumulate from their diverse approaches to land management is in itself an important contribution to the continuing search for alternative forms of sustainable management for the countryside.

What sorts of organisation?

We have emphasised the idea that there is no single ideal type of organisation for a CART, but this does not mean that there are no guidelines as to what approach towards organisation is to be preferred under certain circumstances.

This is an issue which deserves further investigation. We may however anticipate the nature of some of the diversity to be found amongst CARTs.

An increase in the scale of CART activity in general will not necessarily mean an increase in the size of all individual CARTs. Clearly it may be expected that there will be a tendency towards larger organisations but there will still be a role for small groups which meet local demands. Given the range of ways in which CARTs may develop specialisms, a diversity of sizes is to be welcomed. But it will be important for small organisations to participate in networks which can give them effective economies of size. Small organisations may find it difficult to achieve high standards in such areas as financial management or fundraising and they will need to draw upon skills and experience from outside of their own organisations.

Much of what we have discussed so far implies an increasingly close partnership between CARTs and various levels of government. This will not be surprising given the similarites between their objectives. Many CARTs will be and indeed often are integrated into a conservation establishment which pursues an agreed conservation agenda. Closeness with government will give them influence in determining the way in which the agenda develops through time and they can expect government to be an important supporter of their activities. But this closeness may also constrain the sorts of options which CARTs feel that they can pursue. Some may want to distance themselves from this and retain their independence. These CARTs will be free to be more radical in their missions, pursuing novel and experimental approaches. They may adopt more extreme forms of land management or link their activities to spiritual beliefs, not readily accepted by the majority. They may however offer a spawning ground for new ideas which may subsequently be incorporated into the mainstream of CART activity.

CARTs in perspective

Perhaps as a final note, we should also consider the practical limits to future aspirations for CARTs. Most importantly, they cannot be expected to replace the private commercial landowners and occupiers who will continue to manage the bulk of rural land. The profit motive is an essential incentive for the maintenance of a productive agricultural sector. Current problems of surplus food do not mean that the productive capacity of agriculture is of no concern to the public any more. Agriculture is a valuable and in many ways fundamental sector of the economy, and it continues to play a central role in the economies of many rural areas. If UK farmers fail to meet market demands at a competitive price, purchasers will switch to imported products. Within the European Union and increasingly in wider international markets, farmers have to compete in order to maintain their market shares. We are therefore not advocating a whole alternative system of landownership and management, although like many others we support a broad shift in the balance between food production and environmental conservation in rural land management. Rather, we see CARTs as working alongside a dynamic and essentially commercial agricultural sector jointly to achieve the variety of purposes for which we value the countryside.

Neither do we see CARTs as becoming incorporated into the government system. We have suggested some ways in which the relationship could develop, but the difference between the non-profit sector and government is an important one. There are dangers in an excessively close relationship in which individual CARTs become too closely linked with, and dependent upon, one single local authority or one single government agency. Their scope for independent and longer-term decision-making and action may thereby be lost.

Rather we see CARTs as offering an alternative approach within a system which includes the whole range of forms of landownership. Within this, CARTs act to meet the interests of a variety of different groups, some centred upon a particular locality, others with a common concern for some particular facet of countryside value. They should be dynamic and entrepreneurial, seeking new ways of meeting the demands of a collective interest and yet constrained to take full account of the costs which their actions involve. But they should also give weight to the interests of future generations in determining how to take action in the present. We expect the range and characteristics of CARTs

to change through time in response to differing patterns of
public interest and conservation priorities. There is thus no
single ultimate goal, rather a framework which can be
responsive to changing demands.

References

Abecassis, J. (1989) Types of land trusts and their uses, Chapter 3, pp. 6–15, in M.A.B. Boddington, C.W.N. Miles and R.V.N. Surtees (eds) *Charitable Land Trusts: Their History, Nature and Uses*, Land Trusts Association.

Anderson, T.L. and Leal, D.R. (1991) *Free Market Environmentalism*, Westview Press, Boulder, Colorado.

Boddington, M.A.B., Miles, C.W.N. and Surtees, R.V.N. (eds) (1989) *Charitable Land Trusts: Their History, Nature and Uses*, Land Trusts Association.

Bromley, D.W. (1989) *Economic Interests and Institutions*, Basil Blackwell, Oxford.

Bromley, D.W. and Hodge, I.D. (1990) Private property rights and presumptive policy entitlements: reconsidering the premises of rural policy, *European Review of Agricultural Economics* 17(2), 197–214.

Bull, C. (1986) Popular support for wildlife conservation, PhD thesis, University College London.

Butlin, R.A. (1982) *The Transformation of Rural England c. 1580–1800: A Study in Historical Geography*, Oxford University Press, Oxford.

Civic Trust (1989) *Regeneration: New Forms of Community Partnership*. CT Regeneration Campaign, London.

Clarke, T. and Ruddock, J. (1994) Case study of the Grimsthorpe and Drummond Castle Trust, pp. 18–21, *Land Trusts Association Occasional Papers* No. 3, Greensmiths, Henley-on-Thames.

Collins, E.J.T., Giles, A.K. and Malleson, J.G.K. (eds) (1989) *Innovation and Conservation: Ernest Cook and His Country Estates*, Department of Agricultural Economics and Institute of Agricultural History, University of Reading.

Country Landowners' Association (1989) *Enterprise in the Rural Environment*, Country Landowners' Association, London.

CPRE (1985) Memorandum to the House of Commons Environment Committee, *Operation and Effectiveness of Part II of the 1981 Wildlife and Countryside Act*, First Report, HMSO, London.

CPRE (1992) *The Lost Land – Land Use Change in England 1945–1990*, Council for the Protection of Rural England, London.

Dahlman, C.J. (1980) *The Open Field System and Beyond*, Cambridge University Press, Cambridge.

Davies, G.H. (1992) The taxman comes to the rescue, *Countryside* 54, 4–5.

Drury, M. (1987) The early years of the country houses scheme, *The National Trust Magazine* No. 52, 31–34.

Endicott, E. (1993) *Land Conservation through Public/Private Partnerships*, Lincoln Institute of Land Policy, Island Press, Washington, DC, and Covello, California.

Expenditure Committee (1978) *The National Land Fund*, Third report from the Expenditure Committee, Session 1977–78, HMSO, London.

Gaze, J. (1988) *Figures in a Landscape: A History of the National Trust*, Barrie & Jenkins in association with the National Trust, London.

Griffith, J.J. and Knoeber, C.R. (1986) Why do corporations contribute to the Nature Conservancy? *Public Choice* 49, 69–77.

Hardin, R. (1982) *Collective Action*, Johns Hopkins University Press, Baltimore.

Hearn, K. (1992) talk given to the Glebes Conference, Arthur Rank Church and Conservation Centre, Stoneleigh.

Hearn, K. (1994) The 'natural aspect' of the National Trust, *British Wildlife* 5 (6), 367–378.

Hodge, I. (1992) Supply control and the environment: the case for separate policies, *Farm Management* 8(2), 65–72.

Hodge, I. (1995) *Environmental Economics: Private Incentives and Public Choices*, Macmillan, London.

Hodge, I., Castle, R. and Dwyer, J. (1993) *Covenants as a Conservation Mechanism*, Monograph 26, Department of Land Economy, University of Cambridge.

Jenkins, J. and James, P. (1994) *From Acorn to Oak Tree; The Growth of the National Trust 1895–1994*, Macmillan, London.

Jones, A. (1985) *Britain's Heritage: The Creation of the National Heritage Memorial Fund*, Weidenfeld & Nicolson, London.

Kernan, M. (1994) One man's fantasy stands tall in a jungle in Mexico, *Smithsonian* 25(1), 61–70.

Land Trusts Association (1994) *Occasional Papers No. 3*, Greensmiths, Henley-on-Thames.

Lees-Milne, J. (1992) *People and Places: Country House Donors and the National Trust*, John Murray, London.

Legg, R. (1990–91) *Common Roots*, The Open Spaces Society, Henley-on-Thames, mimeo.

Le Vay, C. (1983) Co-operative theory: a review. *Journal of Agricultural Economics* 34(1), 1–44.

Le Vay, C. (1988) Agricultural co-operation, PhD thesis, University College of Wales, Aberystwyth.

Lowe, P. (1983) Values and institutions in the history of British nature conservation, pp. 329–352 in A. Warren and F.B. Goldsmith (eds) *Conservation in Perspective*, Wiley, Chichester.

Lowe, P.D. and Goyder, J.M. (1983) *Environmental Groups in Politics*, Resource Management No. 6, George Allen & Unwin, London.

Marquand, D. (1988) *The Unprincipled Society: New Demands and Old Policies*, Fontana Press, London.

Micklewright, S. (1986) *Who are the new conservationists? An analysis of the views and attitudes of the membership of two new urban trusts.* UCL Discussion Paper in Conservation No. 46, University College London.

Micklewright, S. (1993) The voluntary movement, Chapter 18, pp. 321–334, in F.B. Goldsmith and A. Warren (eds) *Conservation in Progress*, Wiley, Chichester.

Murdoch, J. and Marsden, T. (1994) *Reconstituting Rurality; Class, Community and Power in the Development Process*, Restructuring Rural Areas 2, UCL Press, London.

National Audit Office (1992) *Inheritance Tax*, No. 336, HMSO, London.

National Audit Office (1994) *Protecting and Managing Sites of Special Scientific Interest in England*, No. 379, HMSO, London.

National Trust (1983) *The Arkell Report; The National Trust: Its Members and the Public*, The National Trust, London.

Newbould, P. (1994) Nature conservation and the National Lottery, *Ecos* 15(3/4), 63–65.

Northfield (1979) *Committee of Inquiry into the Ownership and Occupation of Agricultural Land*, Cmnd 7599, HMSO, London.

Nuttall, V.A. (n.d.) The role of the Charity Commissioners, Charity Commission, London, unpublished mimeo.

Oliver (1993) *The Oliver Report on the Constitution*, The National Trust, London.

Orwin, C.S. (1949) *A History of English Farming*, Thomas Nelson & Sons Ltd, London.

Orwin, C.S. and Whetham, E.H. (1964) *History of British Agriculture 1846–1914*, Longmans, London.

Ostrom, E. (1990) *Governing the Commons: The Evolution of Institutions for Collective Action*, Cambridge University Press, Cambridge.

Pearce, D.W. and Turner, R.K. (1990) *Economics of the Environment and Natural Resources*, Harvester Wheatsheaf, London.

Potter, C.A. with Burnham, C.P., Edwards, A.E., Gasson, R. and Green, B.H. (1991) *Diversion of Land: Conservation in a Period of Farming Contraction*, Routledge, London.

Rackham, O. (1986) *The History of the Countryside*, J.M. Dent & Sons Ltd, London.

Rubinstein, W.D. (1986) *Wealth and Inequality in Britain*, Faber & Faber, London.

Sayer, M. (1993) *The Disintegration of a Heritage: Country Houses and their Collections*, Michael Russell, Norwich.

Scott Committee (1942) *Report on Land Utilisation in Rural Areas*, Cmnd 6378, HMSO, London.

Sheail, J. (1976) *Nature in Trust, The History of Nature Conservation in Britain*, Blackie, Glasgow and London.

Sheail, J. (1982) *Nature in Trust*, Oxford University Press, London.

Sheail, J. (1993) The management of wildlife and amenity – A UK post-war perspective, *Contemporary Record* 7(1), 44–65.

Shirley, P. and Knightbridge, R. (1992) Consultancy and county trusts – unhappy bedfellows? *Ecos* 13(1), 27–31.

Shoard, M. (1988) *This Land is Our Land: The Struggle for Britain's Countryside*, Paladin Grafton Books, London.

Smith, A.E. (1990) The county trusts 40 years on, *Ecos* 11(2), 12–16.

Society for the Promotion of Nature Conservation (1978) *A Study of the Nature Reserves Policies and Programmes of the Conservation Trusts associated with the SPNC*, RSNC, Lincoln.

Soltner, D. (1985) *L'Arbre et la Haie pour la production agricole, pour l'équilibre écologique et la cadre de rie rurale*. Feme édition, Collection Sciences et Techniques Agricoles, Angers.

Sterling, A. (1994) Spare the axe, *The National Trust Magazine* 72, 3.

Strong, R. (1988) A museum in love with itself, *Guardian*, 8 June.

Sturmey, S.G. (1955) Owner-farming in England and Wales, 1900–50, *Manchester School of Economic and Social Studies* 23, 245–268.

Thompson, F.M.L. (1963) *English Landed Society in the Nineteenth Century*, Routledge & Kegan Paul, London.

Thompson, F. (1986) Land in community ownership: sixty years of the Stornoway Trust, pp. 50–54, in J. Hulbert (ed.) *Land Ownership and Use*, Andrew Fletcher Society, Dundee.

Weideger, P. (1994) *Gilding the Acorn: Behind the Façade of the National Trust*, Simon and Schuster, London.

Whitby, M. (1993) The UK system for the delivery of conservation goods, paper presented at the Association Descartes Conference, Paris.

Wibberley, G.P. (1987) The effects of an implementation of stricter legislation: the reaction of the consumer, pp. 111–117, in B. Duesenberg and B. Girling (eds) *The Impact of Environmental Legislation upon Agriculture*, Seminar Paper no. 16, Centre for European Agricultural Studies, Wye College, Kent.

Wigan, M. (1995) High minded in the Highlands, *The Field* 284(7089), March, 60–63.

Williams, H. (1992) Banking on the future, *Nature Conservancy* 42(3), 23–27.

Wilson, I. (1994) Round the bends, *The National Trust Magazine* 71, 26–27.

Worth, J. (1984) What we think of the countryside, *Ecos* 5(1), 35–37.

Index